Software Architecture with ASP.NET 8 MVC
Fourth Edition

Lynn Smith

ISBN-13: **979-8-8690-0707-0**

ACKNOWLEDGMENT

We thank Dr. Youlong Zhuang for reviewing this edition and providing valuable suggestions

CONTENTS

Chapter 1: Introduction to Software Architecture

Chapter Learning Objectives

1.1 Recall and outline the key features of client/server architecture.
1.2 Demonstrate comprehension of HTTP GET and HTTP POST distinct functionalities.
1.3 Articulate the advantages of ASP.NET MVC, showcasing a deeper comprehension of its benefits.
1.4 Showcase a foundational understanding of the concept of software architecture.
1.5 Compare and contrast the three programming paradigms.

1.1 World Wide Web

The Web is based on client/server architecture. A client, usually a browser, sends a request to the web server for a webpage. A server, such as an IIS server, is always waiting to respond to a request from a client, responding with the webpage that the browser requested if found. We put all the files on the server. When a browser requests a page, the server sends it. The browser then displays it on the computer screen. Figure 1.1 illustrates the process.

Figure 1.1 A simple client/server architecture.

For simple business problems, the above process works fine. However, many business problems are not that simple. For example, a webpage can calculate a customer's total purchase. This requires the browser (a bad choice in this case but technically possible) or the server to be able to do the calculation. Another example, data is stored in a database server. If the page the browser requests includes dynamic data, the server has to retrieve relevant data from the database before sending the page to the browser. Many times, a page should display dynamic data.

Browsers can only understand instructions written in HTML, CSS, and JavaScript. It won't understand any instructions written in C# unless WebAssembly is used. On the other hand, web servers, such as IIS, can understand instructions written in C#. Web servers can follow instructions written in C# and generate code in HTML, CSS, and JavaScript for the client to process. Figure 1.2 shows a slightly different architecture with a database component.

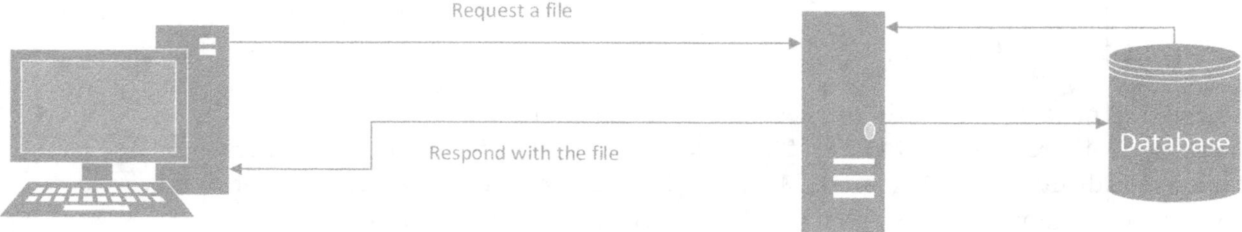

Figure 1.2 Client/server architecture with a database.

Web applications require more than just adding static pages on the server. This book teaches you how to develop a web application so that more complex business problems can be solved.

Test Your Understanding 1.1
The World Wide Web uses __________ architecture.
a. peer-to-peer
b. software
c. client/server
d. one-to-one

Test Your Understanding 1.2
In client/server architecture, ________.
a. client usually works alone
b. server usually works alone
c. client usually sends requests to the server
d. server usually sends requests to the client

Test Your Understanding 1.3
In World Wide Web, an example of client is _____________.
a. browser
b. IIS
c. Apache

d. Personal Computer(PC)

Test Your Understanding 1.4
In World Wide Web, an example of server is _________________.
a. browser
b. IIS
c. cellphone
d. Workstation

Test Your Understanding 1.5
In World Wide Web, browsers usually cannot understand instructions written in _______________.
a. HTML
b. CSS
c. JavaScript
d. C#

1.2 Hyper Text Transfer Protocol (HTTP)

HTTP or HTTPS is a standard that rules the communications between clients and servers in the World Wide Web. When a browser requests a page, it may send an HTTP GET message to the server. A GET message contains the content that appears in the browser's URL, something like: www.somewebsite.com/ViewCourse?Id=3. This way, the browser can request more than just a page. It can also pass data to the server. In the above example, the Id=3 is sent to the server in the GET message. There is a limited amount of data that can be sent from a browser to a server in this way. Also, the data shown in the URL is viewable to anyone, which can be a security concern.

Another popular request is the HTTP POST message which is used when a large size content of a Web form is sent to the server. For example, if you fill out a job application with all information about you and click on the submit button, an HTTP POST message with all the data is sent to the server.
Even though a web form content can be sent from client to the server by either GET or POST, we will use the POST method most of the time so that we don't need to worry about the content data size and also be more private.

As an analogy, HTTP GET is like the postcard used in the postal service where anyone can read the message on the card. HTTP POST is like using the letter in an envelope. You will learn to program the server to respond to HTTP GET and HTTP POST message in this book.

Test Your Understanding 1.6
A message sent from client to server by using HTTP can be either GET or POST.

a. GET
b. POST
c. GET or POST
d. Neither GET nor POST

Test Your Understanding 1.7
___________ is a standard that rules the communications between the clients and servers in the World Wide Web.
a. Client/Server
b. IP
c. TCP
d. HTTP

Test Your Understanding 1.8
When a client sends an HTTP ____________ message to the server, the data is shown in the URL.
a. GET
b. POST
c. SECURE
d. UNSAFE

Test Your Understanding 1.9
When a large size web form content is sent from a client to the server, it often uses HTTP _______ method.
a. GET
b. POST
c. SECURE
d. PRIVATE

Test Your Understanding 1.10
As an analogy, when a browser sends HTTP GET request to the server is like using ________ in the postal service.
a. package
b. envelope
c. postcard
d. express mail

1.3 ASP.NET MVC

ASP.NET is a framework for building web applications. MVC is a software architectural design pattern that employs three components (Model-View-Controller) for web applications. It is a way to organize all files in an application.

The model component includes files that represent data. A model defines the data structure, but is not data themselves. For example, if the application includes products, inventory, and warehouses, then the model component will include classes that define product, inventory, and warehouse. Model shapes the data like a mold used to give shape to hot liquid materials such as wax or metal. A model is often used in both the controllers and views described next. In the MVC architecture, you define the class structure and specify which class a View or a method requires. The data encapsulated within this structure can then be transferred automatically.

The view component is responsible for the presentation of the application. This component contains files that are sent to the clients. Each file may include HTML, CSS, JavaScript, and C# code. Some code (such as C#) will be processed by the server before being sent out to the clients. In the MVC architecture, files in the View often contain dynamic data that is passed from the Controller in the form of a Model. This allows the View to render data based on what the Controller sends it. The final presentation is then sent to the Controller, which delivers the data to the user output. This pattern helps to achieve separation of concerns4.

The Controller component in the MVC architecture is responsible for managing interactions between the Model and View components. Specifically, it processes client requests, retrieves data from the database according to the data structure defined in the Model, passes this data to the appropriate View, and then sends the rendered View back to the client.

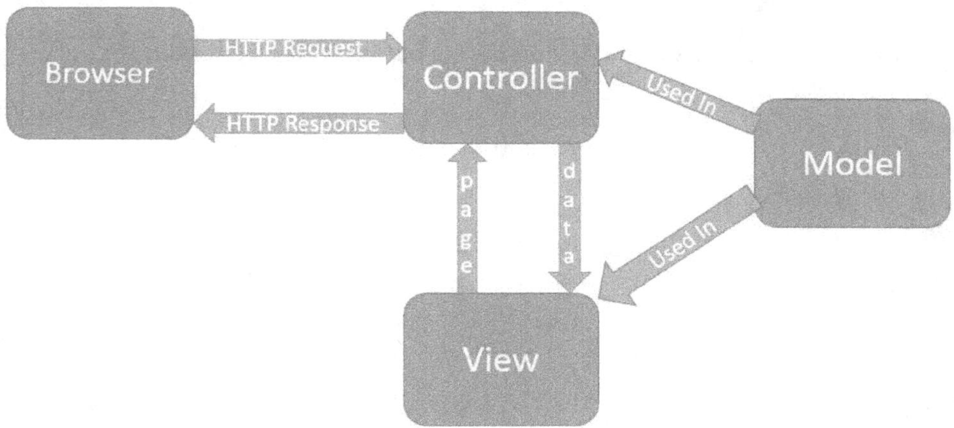

Figure 1.3 MVC architectural software pattern overview.

Summary of MVC Steps:

Initiation - The browser sends an HTTP request to the controller.
Data Retrieval - The controller fetches any required data from the database or other sources. It passes relevant data to the view through a model object.
Presentation - The view uses the model data to generate the content and UI presentation as HTML/CSS. The view matches the structure of the model object.
Back to Controller - The view passes the rendered content back to the controller for further processing or to send it to the browser.
Response to Browser - The controller packages the full response including the view content and sends the HTTP response back to the client browser.

Test Your Understanding 1.11
______________ is software architectural pattern that uses three components (Model-View-Controller) for a web application.
a. ASP.NET
b. ASP.NET Core
c. Controller
d. MVC

Test Your Understanding 1.12
In ASP.NET MVC, the model component includes files that represents __________ and is often used in the controllers and views.
a. mold
b. URL
c. data
d. HTTP request

Test Your Understanding 1.13
In ASP.NET Core MVC, the _____ component is responsible for the presentation of the application.
a. model
b. view
c. controller
d. MVC

Test Your Understanding 1.14
In ASP.NET MVC, the ______ component is responsible for interactions between different components.
a. model
b. view
c. controller
d. MVC

Test Your Understanding 1.15
What is MVC in the context of ASP.NET?
a. A programming language
b. A design pattern
c. A database management system
d. A server configuration tool

Test Your Understanding 1.16
What does the Model component in MVC represent?
a. HTML and CSS files
b. Data structure
c. Server-side code
d. User interface

Test Your Understanding 1.17
In MVC, what is responsible for the presentation of the application?
a. Controller
b. View
c. Model
d. Database

Test Your Understanding 1.18
Which component in MVC manages interactions between the Model and View?
a. View
b. Controller
c. Model
d. Database

Test Your Understanding 1.19
What does the Controller do in MVC?
a. Defines the data structure
b. Sends HTML files to clients
c. Manages interactions between Model and View
d. Shapes data like a mold

Test Your Understanding 1.20
What is the purpose of the View in MVC?
a. Manage data retrieval
b. Shape data structure
c. Handle client requests
d. Present the application to clients

1.4 Benefits of MVC

MVC presents several advantages, the first being the principle of separation of concerns. This architectural approach allows for the creation and modification of view files independent of backend database considerations. For instance, alterations to the structure or attributes of a product, such as adding a new column to a database table, don't necessitate modifications to existing view files that remain unaffected by the change.

The second notable advantage of MVC is its facilitation of easy unit testing. Unit testing involves evaluating individual components of an application in isolation from the rest. In the context of MVC, testing controller logic becomes straightforward, as typically, only one method of the controller is examined during unit tests. This focused testing approach streamlines the creation of test code.

Furthermore, MVC champions the concept of 'convention over configuration' as its third benefit. By ensuring that identifier names align correctly, the need for extensive configuration is minimized. For instance, when a method calls a view file, the system intuitively navigates to a folder with the same name as the controller, where the method is located, and locates a file with the same name as the method itself. This convention simplifies the development process, eliminating the need for explicit configuration for routine operations within the framework.

Test Your Understanding 1.21
Which of the following is NOT a benefit of MVC?
a. separation of concerns
b. easy unit testing
c. convention over configuration
d. use very few files

Test Your Understanding 1.22
When a method calls a view file, it will automatically go to a folder with the same name as the controller name (where the method is located) and find a file with the same name as the method name. This is an example of ______________.
a. separation of concerns
b. easy unit testing
c. convention over configuration
d. use very few files

Test Your Understanding 1.23
Which of the following is NOT an advantage presented by MVC architecture?
a. Easy unit testing
b. Separation of concerns
c. Convention over configuration
d. Database modification

Test Your Understanding 1.24
How does MVC allow for the creation and modification of view files?
a. Independently of backend database considerations
b. Only after modifying the backend database
c. Through direct manipulation of the database
d. By altering the entire MVC architecture

Test Your Understanding 1.25
What does 'convention over configuration' mean in the context of MVC?
a. Complex configurations are preferred over simple conventions
b. Explicit configuration is always required
c. Correct identifier names eliminate the need for extensive configuration
d. Configuration should override established conventions

Test Your Understanding 1.26
How does MVC simplify the development process according to the 'convention over configuration' benefit?
a. By enforcing strict configuration guidelines
b. By minimizing identifier names
c. By allowing extensive customization
d. By eliminating the need for explicit configuration in routine operations

Test Your Understanding 1.27
In unit testing within MVC, what is typically examined?
a. Entire application
b. Multiple controllers
c. One method of the controller
d. Backend database structure

1.5 Your First ASP.NET 8 MVC application

Step 1: Ensure that your Visual Studio is up to date and that you have downloaded and installed ASP.NET 8 before proceeding. Launch Visual Studio and navigate to the 'Create a new project' option, as depicted in Figure 1.4. Choose the project type 'ASP.NET Core Web App (Model-View-Controller)'; you may need to search for 'asp c# model' to locate it. Once selected, click the 'Next' button to continue.

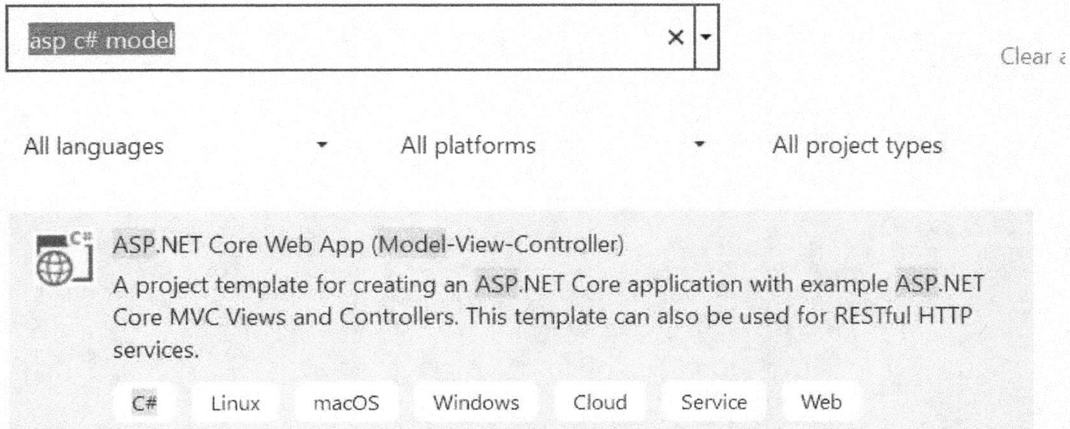

Figure 1.4: Starting a new project in Visual Studio.

Note: If you cannot find 'ASP.NET Core Web App (Model-View-Controller),' click on the 'Install more tools and features' link at the bottom of the type list (scroll down in Figure 1.4). In the installer window (Figure 1.5), ensure that 'ASP.NET and web development' and 'Data storage and processing' are selected, as shown in Figure 1.5. Then, click on the 'Modify' button at the bottom right to install. For first-time installation, the button is labeled 'Install.'

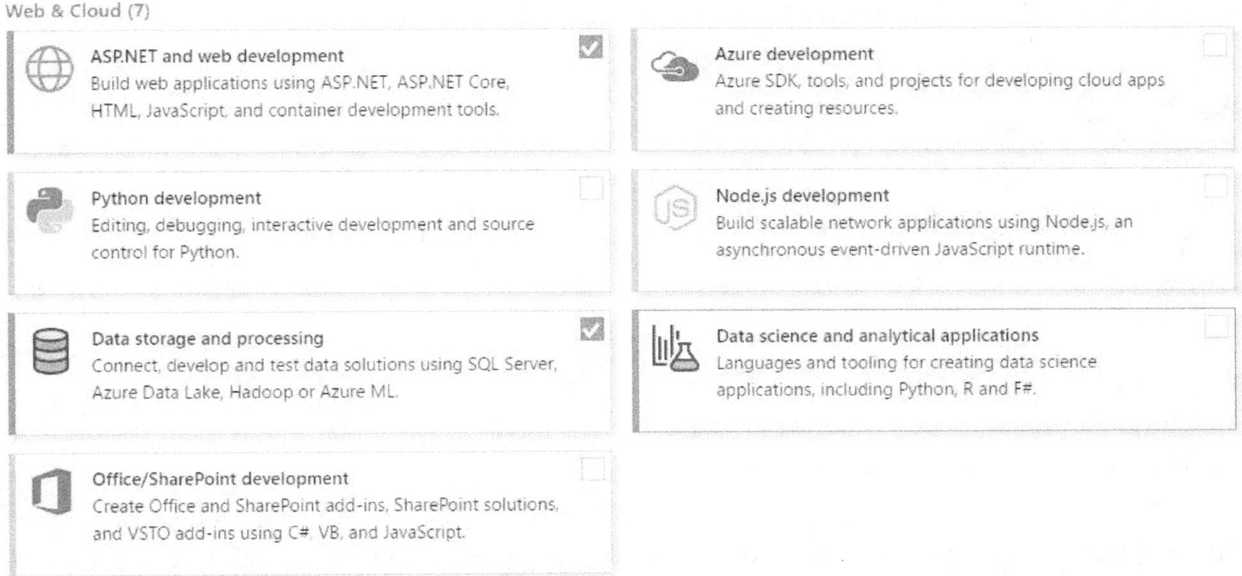

Figure 1.5: Visual Studio Installer (Layout may be different in your case).

Step 2: In the 'Configure your new project' window, enter 'Chapter1Example1' in the 'Project name' field. Create a new folder named 'ASP' on your desktop, and select the 'ASP' folder as the location. Ensure that 'Place solution and project in the same directory' is checked (see Figure 1.6). Click 'Next' to proceed.

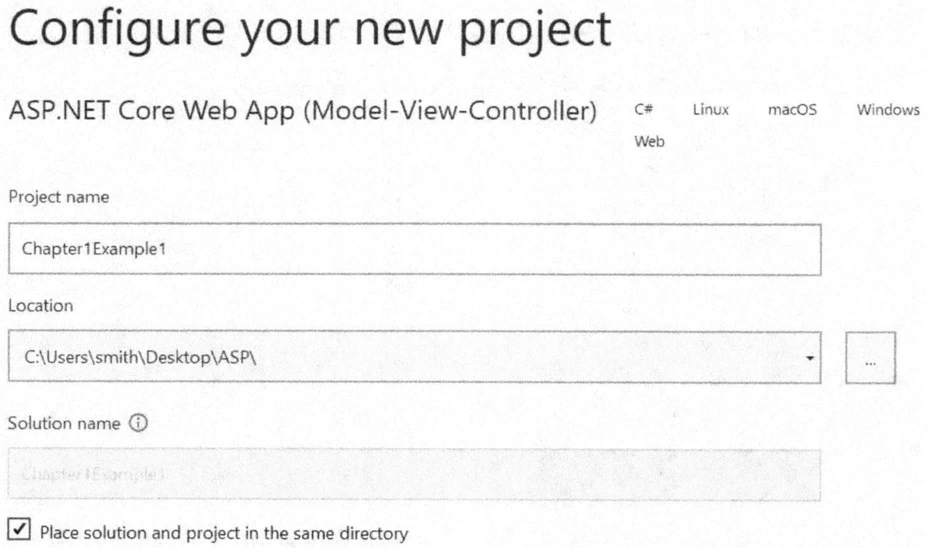

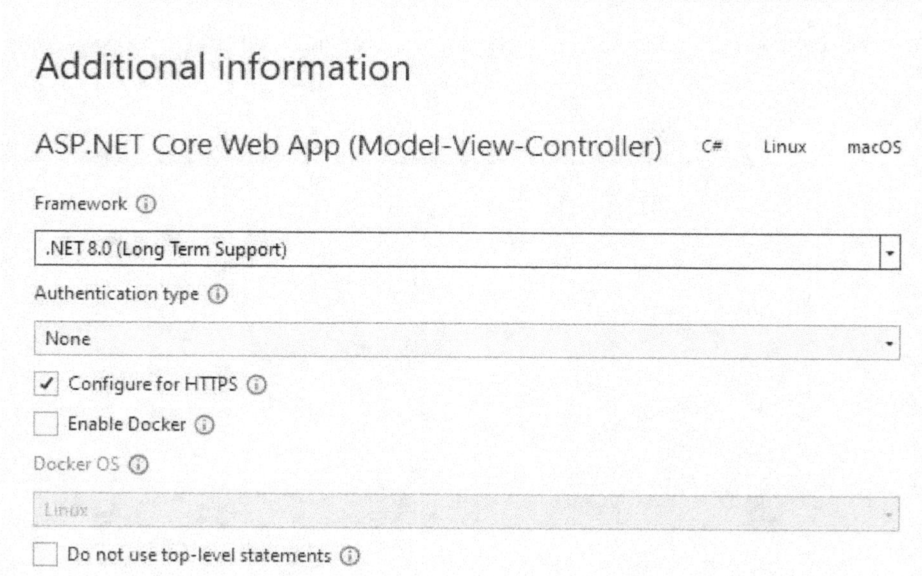

Figure 1.6: The New Project window for saving the project to a specific folder.

Step 3: In the 'Additional Information' window (refer to Figure 1.7), confirm that the framework is set to '.NET 8.0 (Long-term support).' This enables the use of ASP.NET 8.0. Click the 'Create' button at the bottom right to continue (not shown in Figure 1.7).

Figure 1.7: Additional Information window.

If ASP.NET 8 is not in the dropdown, follow these steps: 1) Update Visual Studio to the latest version; 2) Download and install .NET 8 SDK. Restart Visual Studio and retry.

Step 4: Run the Web Application

The project is created without typing a single line of code. To run the application, 'Debug' then 'Start without debugging' or press Control + F5 on your keyboard. Your default browser will open the home page, as illustrated in Figure 1.8.

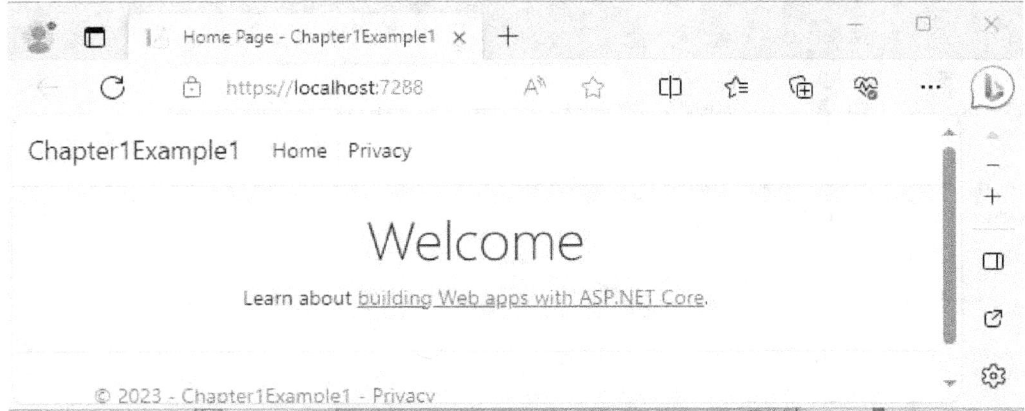

Figure 1.8: Chapter1Example1 displayed in a browser.

Step 5: Play with Chapter1Example1

Locate the 'Solution Explorer' window. Expand the 'Views' folder, then expand the 'Home' folder within it. Select 'Index.cshtml' to open it. Figure 1.9 shows the selected file in the Solution Explorer window.

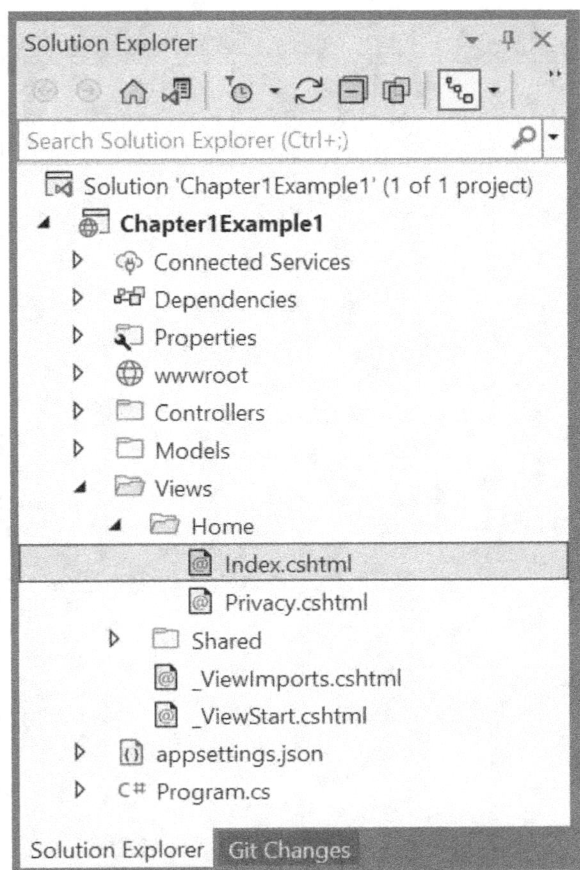

Figure 1.9: Solution Explorer window with Index.cshtml selected.

In the code window, customize the code with your information. A sample is displayed in Figure 1.10.

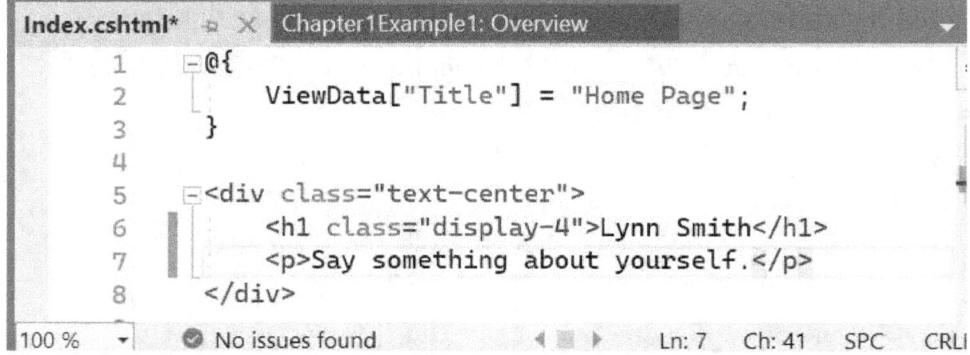

Figure 1.10: Index.cshtml opened in the code window.

You can use any HTML tags to write this page. Save all and press Control + F5 or 'Debug', then 'Start without debugging' on the menu to view the page in your browser. You should see a page like Figure 1.11.

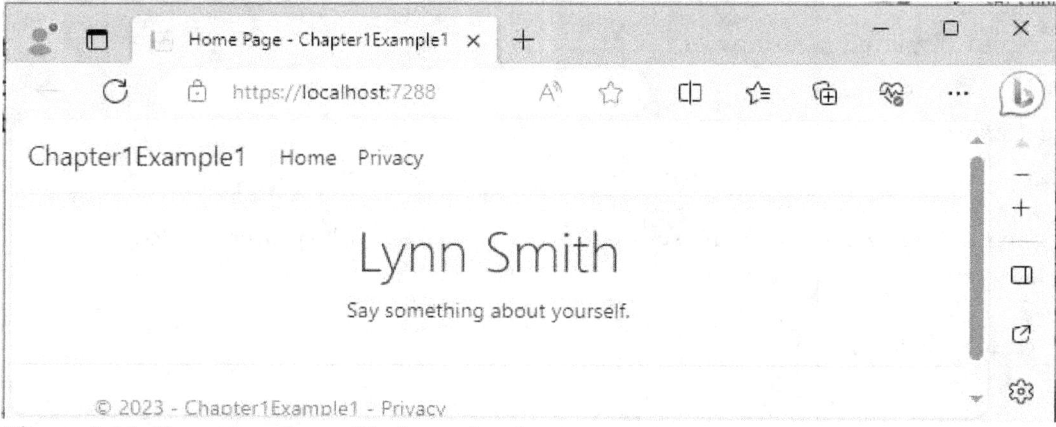

Figure 1.11: Browser view of Index.cshtml.

Test Your Understanding 1.28
What is the first step in creating an ASP.NET 8 MVC application?
a. Run the Web Application
b. Play with Chapter1Example1
c. Update Visual Studio and install ASP.NET 8
d. Configure your new project

Test Your Understanding 1.29
How do you run the web application?
a. Press Control + F5 on your keyboard
b. Click on the 'Create' button
c. Select 'Index.cshtml' to open it
d. Customize the code with your information

Test Your Understanding 1.30
How do you run the web application?
a. On the menu, click on "Debug", then "Start without debugging"
b. Click on the 'Create' button

c. Select 'Index.cshtml' to open it
d. Customize the code with your information

Test Your Understanding 1.31
Where can you find 'Index.cshtml' in Chapter1Example1?
a. In the 'Configure your new project' window
b. In the 'Additional Information' window
c. In the 'Solution Explorer' window
d. In the 'Visual Studio Installer' window

Test Your Understanding 1.32
What can you use to write the page in 'Index.cshtml'?
a. Any HTML tags
b. Only ASP.NET tags
c. Only C# code
d. Only JavaScript code

1.6 Explanation of Chapter1Example1

The views folder contains all cshtml files. A cshtml file contains both HTML and C# code. If you are familiar with PHP, you know a PHP file contains both HTML and PHP code. This is a server side script file that will be processed first by the server, and then sent to the browser to process and display to the user.

On an MVC View (or Razor View, or a cshtml file), the C# Code is included in the @{} block while HTML tags can be freely added anywhere.

You may wonder why the cshtml page (such as Index.cshtml in Figure 1.10) does not contain something like <!DOCTYPE html> and many other tags that are required on an HTML file. To find all those missing HTML tags, expand the other folder called "Shared" inside the Views folder. Select _Layout.cshtml to view the code. You should see all necessary HTML tags, including all code for the navigation menu. You should find the following line right after the navigation section.

```
@RenderBody()
```

This is where the cshtml file such as Index.cshtml will be inserted. You may also wonder if you rename the Home folder inside the Views folder as something like HomePage, will the application still work?

The answer is "No". Remember "convention over configuration". If you go to the "Controllers" folder in the "Solution Explorer" window and expand it, you should see a file called HomeController.cs. The "Home" in the HomeController.cs should match the Home folder inside the Views folder. Also, find the

"Index" method in the HomeController.cs file that should match the "Index.cshtml" name inside the Home folder.

In short, every controller in the Controllers folder should have a matching folder inside the Views folder. Almost every method in the controller class should have a matching cshtml file inside the View/ControllerName folder. If the above sounds confusing. Don't worry. You will learn more about the MVC applications in future chapters.

Test Your Understanding 1.33
Which of the following statements about MVC Razor View is correct?
a. An MVC Razor View can include any mix of C# and HTML tags.
b. An MVC Razor View can include any mix of C# and HTML tags with C# code inside @{} block.
c. An MVC C# page will include all C# code while an MVC HTML page will have all HTML tags.
d. An MVC Razor View can include any mix of C# and HTML tags with HTML tags inside @{} block.

Test Your Understanding 1.34
Under ASP.NET MVC convention, if there is a controller called StudentController.cs, there must be a folder called ____________.
a. Student
b. StudentController
c. Student inside the Views folder
d. StudentController inside the Views folder

Test Your Understanding 1.35
Under ASP.NET MVC convention, if there is a controller called StudentController.cs and a method called About(), there must be a folder called ____________ inside the Views folder and an MVC View file called __________ inside this folder.
a. Student, About
b. About, Student
c. StudentController, Student
d. StudentController, About

Test Your Understanding 1.36
What type of content can be found in a cshtml file?
a. Only HTML code
b. Only C# code
c. Both HTML and C# code
d. JavaScript code

Test Your Understanding 1.37
Where is C# code typically included within an MVC View?
a. Within HTML comments
b. Inside a @{} block
c. Within script tags
d. At the end of the file

Test Your Understanding 1.38
Where can one find the necessary HTML tags such <html> for a cshtml file like Index.cshtml?
a. Inside the Views folder
b. In the Controllers folder
c. Within the Shared folder
d. In the Models folder

Test Your Understanding 1.39
What happens if the folder name inside the Views folder does not match the controller name in MVC?
a. It doesn't affect the application
b. The application throws an error
c. It changes the URL structure
d. The browser displays an empty page

Test Your Understanding 1.40
Which folder structure should be maintained for every controller in MVC?
a. Controllers should match Models
b. Controllers should have matching Views
c. Views should match Shared folders
d. Views should match Models

Test Your Understanding 1.41
What should match between a controller's method and the cshtml file inside the corresponding folder?
a. The file extension
b. The method name
c. The folder name
d. The server name

1.7 What Is Software Architecture?

Software comprises instructions for computers to follow, with two primary types: system software and application software. For the sake of simplicity in this book, when referring to software, we specifically mean application software.

Architecture involves structure and design. In smaller applications with only a few lines of code, architecture may not be necessary. However, in larger applications composed of smaller components with interconnected relationships, architecture becomes crucial to manage complexity and accommodate changes in software.

We define software architecture as the structure of software components, the relationships among these components, and the properties and behaviors exhibited by both components and relationships.

To grasp this concept better, it is beneficial to explore related ideas. System architecture encompasses both software architecture and hardware architecture. The software architecture covered in this book is just one facet of system architecture. System architecture extends to servers, networks, operating systems, security, storage, database infrastructure, and other technical infrastructures.

Enterprise architecture comprises business architecture and system architecture (Lankhorst, 2017). Business architecture involves elements like vision/mission, strategy, and business capabilities (Versteeg and Bouwman, 2006). System architecture supports the broader goals of business architecture.

Conversely, software architecture encompasses application architecture and data/information architecture. This book elucidates software architecture through ASP.NET Core MVC, which incorporates both application and data components.

Application architecture encompasses aspects such as application development, service definitions, and process alignments. On the other hand, data architecture includes facets like data integration and delivery, as well as data analytics and reporting.

Software architecture often operates at a higher level, offering an abstract view to facilitate communication among stakeholders. It is documented with drawings and text, ensuring comprehension by both business managers and software developers.

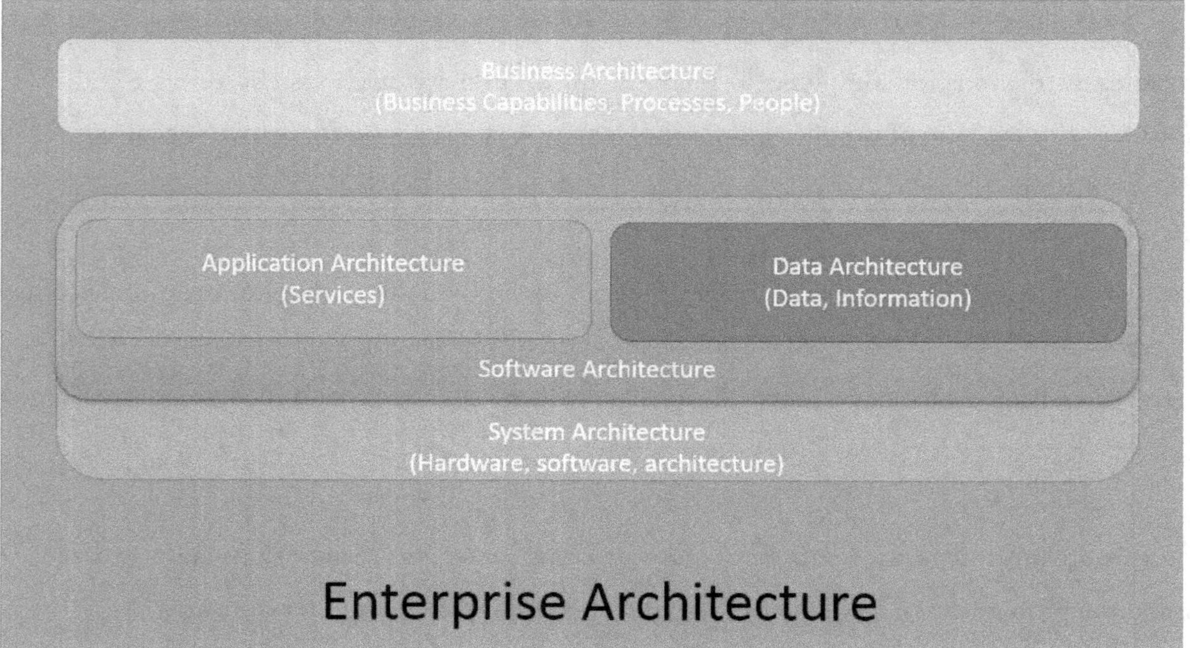

Figure 1.12: Relationships of Different Types of Architecture

Test Your Understanding 1.42
Business architecture and System Architecture are parts of _______________ architecture.
a. application
b. data
c. software
d. enterprise

Test Your Understanding 1.43
____________ architecture includes vision/mission, strategy, and business capabilities.
a. Application
b. Business
c. Software
d. Data

Test Your Understanding 1.44
Software architecture includes ____________ architecture and ____________ architecture.
a. application, data
b. business, application
c. enterprise, business
d. business, system

Test Your Understanding 1.45
Structure of software components, relationships among these components, and properties and behaviors of these components and relationships defines _________.
a. software
b. software architecture
c. business
d. enterprise

Test Your Understanding 1.46
When is architecture considered unnecessary in applications?
a. In applications with interconnected relationships
b. In applications with only a few lines of code
c. In large applications with complex structures
d. In applications involving system software

Test Your Understanding 1.47
How is software architecture defined?
a. Only as the structure of software components
b. As the structure of software components and relationships among them
c. Only as the behaviors of software components
d. As the structure of hardware components

Test Your Understanding 1.48
What does system architecture encompass?
a. Only software architecture
b. Hardware architecture only
c. Both software and hardware architecture
d. Application architecture

Test Your Understanding 1.49
What does enterprise architecture include?
a. Only system architecture
b. Business architecture and system architecture
c. Application architecture and data architecture
d. Only data/information architecture

Test Your Understanding 1.50
How does software architecture facilitate communication among stakeholders?
a. By operating at a lower level
b. By focusing on hardware components
c. By offering an abstract view
d. By detailing system infrastructure

1.8 Three Types of Software Structure

Software architecture revolves around the organization of software elements. This section, based on Bass et al. (2013), delves into three distinct types of structures, each tailored to specific purposes.

1.8.1. Module Structure

Definition: This structure provides a static view of the software, focusing on individual modules and their functionality.

Application: Ideal for understanding and extending the functionality of modules. It involves breaking down modules into smaller, more manageable components.

Layered Approach: Often, software is organized into layers, each concentrating on specific services. This facilitates the study of portability. For instance, a data layer can offer services compatible with various Database Management Systems (DBMS) like SQL Server, Oracle, or DB2. Changes in database services within a layer do not impact modules in other layers.

Examples: Class diagrams, as covered in previous books, and Entity Relationship Diagrams (ERD) from relational database development courses.

1.8.2. Component-and-Connector Structure

Definition: This architecture emphasizes the run-time behaviors of the software, illustrating how different components interact.

Application: Useful for understanding how components share resources, such as databases, and for identifying potential deadlocks in the run-time behavior.

Service Identification: Allows a clear view of services provided by each component, facilitating an understanding of communication protocols, like SOAP (Simple Object Access Protocol), which enables cross-platform communication.

1.8.3. Allocation Structure

Definition: This structure focuses on how software relates to its environment, including considerations like CPU usage and network bandwidth requirements.

Application: Valuable for deployment planning, offering insights into software-machine relationships and the potential impact on performance and security when adding or redistributing software.

Development Efficiency: Enables tracking of development tasks associated with each software component, enhancing overall development efficiency.

Management Insights: Provides valuable information for management purposes, identifying responsibilities for specific components or teams within the software.

Understanding these three structures equips software architects with versatile tools tailored to different aspects of software development, runtime behavior analysis, and deployment considerations.

Test Your Understanding 1.51
Which of the following is NOT a type of structure in software architecture?
a. Module
b. Procedural
c. Component-and-connector
d. Allocation

Test Your Understanding 1.52
Which type of architectural structure emphasizes run-time behaviors of the software?
a. Module
b. Class
c. Component-and-connector
d. Allocation

Test Your Understanding 1.53
Which type of architectural structure provides a static view of the software?
a. Module
b. Class
c. Component-and-connector
d. Allocation

Test Your Understanding 1.54
Which type of architectural structure focuses on how the software related to its environment, such as CPU usage, network bandwidth requirements?
a. Module
b. Class
c. Component-and-connector

d. Allocation

1.9 The Three Programming Paradigms

Software architecture serves as a guiding framework for programmers in their coding endeavors. However, it does not instruct them on the specifics of individual programming languages, such as C#. Since there are numerous programming languages in use, it is more practical to discuss programming paradigms when addressing languages (Martin, 2018).

A programming paradigm pertains to the approach or structure adopted in programming. The first paradigm is structured programming. It employs logical structures, such as if...else statements, to enhance program efficiency, readability, and maintainability. Structured programming replaces hard-coded GoTo statements, which were prevalent before the advent of structured programming.

The second paradigm is object-oriented programming (OOP). In a previous book, I expounded on the three foundational principles encapsulated in C#: encapsulation, inheritance, and polymorphism. From an architectural standpoint, OOP facilitates the easy assembly or disassembly of a program, particularly when employing MVC for the "separation of concerns."

The third paradigm is functional programming, characterized by code written using functions. In contrast to OOP, where application state is often shared among various methods in the same object, functional programming eschews state sharing. Those familiar with JavaScript programming may already be acquainted with functional programming concepts.

By exploring these three paradigms, programmers gain insights into diverse approaches to programming, each offering unique benefits and considerations.

Test Your Understanding 1.55
Which of the following is NOT a programming paradigm?
a. Loop
b. structured
c. OOP
d. functional

Test Your Understanding 1.56
The ______________ programming uses logical structure such as if ... else statement to make the program more efficient and easier to understand and maintain.

a. conditional
b. structured
c. OOP
d. functional

Test Your Understanding 1.57
Encapsulation, inheritance, and polymorphism describes _________.
a. conditional
b. structured
c. OOP
d. functional

Test Your Understanding 1.58
Different from OOP in which application state is often shared with several methods in the same object, _____________ programming avoids state sharing.
a. conditional
b. structured
c. OOP
d. functional

Test Your Understanding 1.59
What is the primary role of software architecture in programming?
a. Instructing programmers on specific languages
b. Guiding programmers in coding endeavors
c. Coding in various programming languages
d. Enhancing individual programming skills

Test Your Understanding 1.60
What characterizes structured programming?
a. Encapsulation, inheritance, and polymorphism
b. Logical structures like if...else statements
c. State sharing among methods
d. Hard-coded GoTo statements

1.10 Chapter Summary

This chapter introduced ASP.NET Core MVC through a simple web application that displays personal information using minimal HTML. It aimed to familiarize you with MVC components. The next chapter will guide you in building your own MVC web application from scratch. You also learned about software architecture, its relationship with system, enterprise, application, and data architectures. You were introduced to three architectural structures and programming paradigms, highlighting their connection to software structure.

1.11 Review Questions

Question 1.1
The World Wide Web is an information system that utilizes client/server architecture. Explain how this architecture works.

Question 1.2
Hyper Text Transfer Protocol (HTTP) is the standard that guides the communications between a browser and the web server. Explain the two major types of HTTP request discussed in this chapter, focusing on the differences between them.

Question 1.3
MVC is a software architecture pattern that is used in many software frameworks. Explain each letter of MVC and how they work together to accomplish a response to a browser request.

Question 1.4
In ASP.NET MVC, you have to name a controller in certain ways and then when you name the corresponding view, you have to name it accordingly and save the view file in a certain location. Use an example to explain how these naming rules work.

Question 1.5
There are several architectures related to software architecture. Explain the relationships among the following architectures: Software architecture, system architecture, enterprise architecture, application architecture, and data architecture.

1.12 References

Bass, L., Clements, P., and Kazman, R., (2013). Software Architecture in Practice, 3rd Edition, Addison-Wesley, Upper Saddle River, NJ.
Lankhorst, M. (2017), Enterprise Architecture at Work: Modeling, Communication and Analysis, 4th Edition. Springer, Berlin, Germany.
Martin, R. C. (2018), Clean Architecture, A Craftsman's Guide to Software Structure and Design, Prentice Hall, Boston, MA.
Versteeg, G., & Bouwman, H. (2006). Business architecture: A new paradigm to relate business strategy to ICT. *Information systems frontiers, 8*(2), 91-102.

1.13 Answers to Test Your Understanding

1.1 C; 1.2 C; 1.3 A; 1.4 B; 1.5 D; 1.6 C; 1.7 D; 1.8 A; 1.9 B; 1.10 C; 1.11 D; 1.12 C; 1.13 B; 1.14 C; 1.15 B; 1.16 B; 1.17 B; 1.18 B; 1.19 C; 1.20 D; 1.21 D; 1.22 C; 1.23 D; 1.24 A; 1.25 C; 1.26 D; 1.27 C; 1.28 C; 1.29 A; 1.30 A; 1.31 C; 1.32 A; 1.33 B; 1.34 C; 1.35 A; 1.36 C; 1.37 B; 1.38 C; 1.39 B; 1.40 B; 1.41 B; 1.42 D; 1.43 B; 1.44 A; 1.45 B; 1.46 B; 1.47 B; 1.48 C; 1.49 B; 1.50 C; 1.51 B; 1.52 C; 1.53 A; 1.54 D; 1.55 A; 1.56 B; 1.57 C; 1.58 D; 1.59 B; 1.60 B;

Chapter 2: Routing and Controllers

Chapter Learning Objectives

2.1 Demonstrate the ability to match a URL to an action method of a controller.
2.2 Implement the creation of controllers and action methods.
2.3 Analyze the role and significance of middleware in a web application.
2.4 Assess the benefits and drawbacks of dependency injection in a given software development context.

2.1 Routing Basic

In Chapter One, you gained a swift introduction to creating a web application without the need to input a single line of code. However, the journey takes a deeper turn in this chapter as you embark on constructing a web application from the ground up, providing you with a hands-on understanding of the underlying processes.

When a user enters a URL into the browser and presses "enter," a series of actions is triggered. The browser initiates an HTTP request to the server, marking the commencement of the communication flow. At this crucial juncture, the routing engine, a vital component residing on the server, takes the reins to handle the incoming request. The routing engine, with its logic, scrutinizes the request URL to determine the appropriate "controller" and "method" that should be invoked. This strategic decision-making process is pivotal for orchestrating the subsequent steps, ensuring an effective response is generated and sent back to the browser.

To delve deeper into the intricacies, let's break down the sequence of events:

User Input: A user enters a URL into the browser.

HTTP Request: The browser sends an HTTP request to the server, initiating the communication.

Routing Engine Activation: The routing engine, a crucial component on the server, is activated to handle the incoming request.

URL Analysis: The routing engine analyzes the request URL, deciphering the destination controller and method based on predetermined rules and configurations.

Controller Invocation: The determined controller and method are invoked, initiating the execution of the corresponding code logic.

Response Generation: The invoked controller and method work in tandem to generate an appropriate response, which is then sent back to the browser.

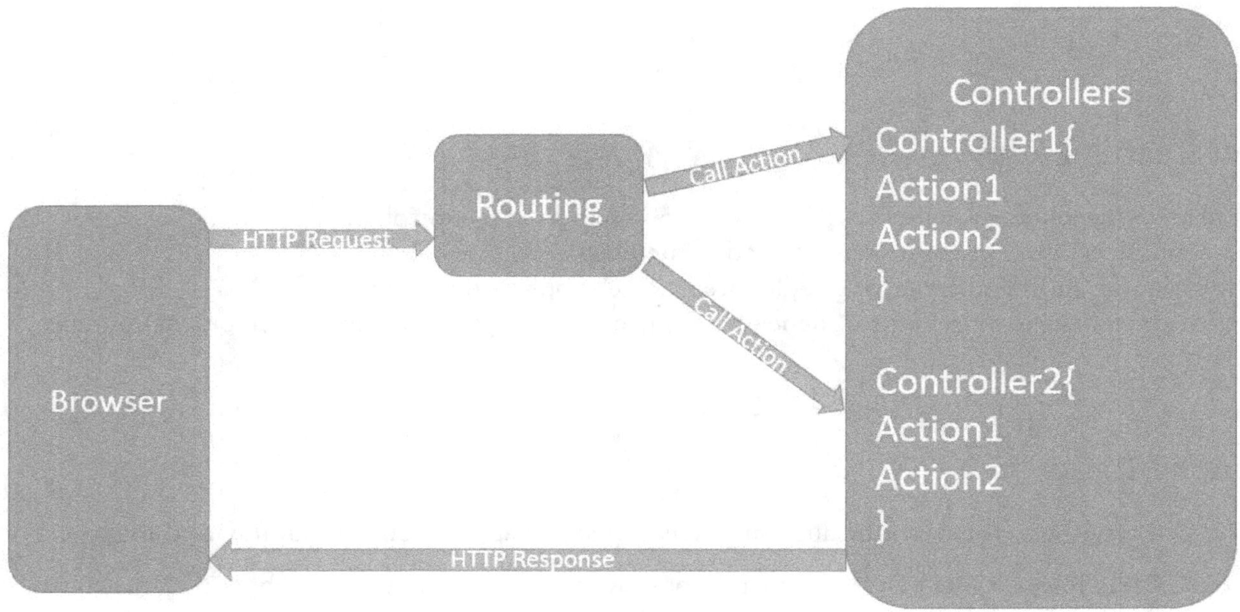

Figure 2.1: Request and Response with Routing and Controllers

The illustration in Figure 2.1 visually encapsulates this dynamic process, offering a conceptual roadmap for understanding the seamless flow of requests and responses orchestrated by the routing engine and controllers. As we proceed, you will not only grasp the theoretical underpinnings but also actively engage in the construction of a web application, solidifying your comprehension through practical application.

Test Your Understanding 2.1
In ASP.NET MVC, the routing engine of the server decides which method of which controller to call based on the browser _________.
a. user
b. URL
c. brand name
d. connection speed

Test Your Understanding 2.2
The naming of _______ and _______ in an MVC app determines what URL you can have for a page.
a. routing engine, controller
b. routing engine, method
c. controller, method
d. controller, project name

Test Your Understanding 2.3

What triggers the series of actions when a user enters a URL into the browser and presses "enter"?
a. HTML rendering
b. Browser initialization
c. An HTTP request to the server
d. JavaScript execution

Test Your Understanding 2.4
What is the role of the routing engine in the communication flow?
a. Generating HTML responses
b. Initiating the browser's response
c. Handling the incoming request
d. Analyzing user input

Test Your Understanding 2.5
What does the routing engine analyze to determine the appropriate "controller" and "method"?
a. User's preferences
b. Request URL
c. Server logs
d. Browser settings

Test Your Understanding 2.6
When are the determined controller and method invoked in the sequence of events?
a. After HTTP request initiation
b. After URL analysis
c. Before routing engine activation
d. After response generation

2.2 Controller Basics

A controller, in the context of ASP.NET MVC, is a C# class responsible for handling browser requests and orchestrating the generation of the necessary responses for users. Central to a controller are its actions, encapsulated within methods. The statements residing in these methods essentially dictate the server's course of action in generating the desired response.

Let's delve into the core components that constitute a controller:
C# Class: At its essence, a controller is a C# class, embodying the principles of object-oriented programming. This class is tasked with managing and responding to incoming browser requests.
Actions: Within a controller, you find one or more actions, which are essentially methods encapsulated in the class. These actions represent distinct functionalities or responses that the controller can perform.

Consider the following example to concretize the controller concept:

Suppose a user inputs "localhost:12345/Student/CheckGrade" into the browser URL. In this URL, "localhost:12345" denotes the network part, serving network management purposes and not directly impacting the website. For simplicity in future examples within this book, we'll use "localhost" without the port number.

When the routing engine encounters "Student/CheckGrade" in the URL path, it undertakes a series of actions:

Controller Identification: It searches for a controller named "StudentController" within the designated Controllers folder.

Method Invocation: Inside the identified controller, the routing engine calls a method named "CheckGrade."

Assuming the "StudentController" class has the following method:

```
public string CheckGrade()
{
    return "Your grade is A";
}
```

The server, in response to the user's request, produces the string "Your grade is A," which is then returned to the browser for display.

To enhance your understanding of controllers, it's advantageous to examine different action types, comprehend parameter passing, and investigate the use of action results, such as ViewResult for view rendering or RedirectResult for redirecting users to alternate URLs. These additional aspects contribute to a comprehensive grasp of controller functionality within the ASP.NET MVC framework. As we move forward, you'll delve deeper into these concepts, strengthening your capability to build dynamic and responsive web applications.

Test Your Understanding 2.7
A controller in MVC is a C# _______ that accepts user requests and generates necessary response to the user.
a. method
b. class
c. server
d. namespace

Test Your Understanding 2.8
An MVC controller includes one or more _______ which are methods in a class.
a. actions
b. URLs
c. web addresses
d. sub controllers

Test Your Understanding 2.9
If the URL of the browser is localhost/Student/CheckGrade, the __________ method of ________
controller will be called to generate the return message.
a. Student, CheckGrade
b. CheckGrade, Student
c. localhost, Student
d. localhost, CheckGrade

Test Your Understanding 2.10
What is a controller in the context of ASP.NET MVC?
a. A JavaScript module
b. A C# class
c. An HTML document
d. A CSS styling file

Test Your Understanding 2.11
What is central to a controller's functionality?
a. HTML elements
b. Actions
c. CSS styles
d. JavaScript functions

Test Your Understanding 2.12
What does the C# class, representing a controller, embody?
a. Object-oriented principles
b. Database queries
c. Browser styles
d. Network protocols

Test Your Understanding 2.13
In the given example, what does "localhost:12345" denote in the URL?
localhost:12345/Student/CheckGrade
a. A network protocol
b. The port number
c. The network part
d. The domain name

Test Your Understanding 2.14
What does the routing engine do when encountering "Student/CheckGrade" in the URL path?
localhost:12345/Student/CheckGrade
a. Performs a database query
b. Searches for a controller
c. Executes JavaScript code
d. Renders a view

Chapter 2 Example 1

Problem:

Create a web application where entering "localhost/Student/CheckGrade" in the browser URL displays

"Your grade is A".

Solution:

Step 1:Launch Visual Studio.

Click on "Create a new project" to open the "Create a new project" window.

Step 2: Select "ASP.NET Core Empty" as the project type.

In the "Configure your new project" window:

Enter "Chapter2Example1" in the "Project name" field. Maintain the ASP folder used in the previous project. Ensure "Place solution and project in the same directory" is checked. Click "Next" to proceed.

Step 3: Keep default settings.

Ensure ".NET 8.0 (Long-term support)" is selected as the framework. Click "Create" to initiate the new project.

Step 4: Add a Controller

Create a folder named "Controllers":

Right-click on the Chapter2Example1 project in the Solution Explorer.

Select "Add" > "New Folder," then name it "Controllers."

Step 4.1 Add a new controller named "StudentController":

Right-click on the "Controllers" folder in Solution Explorer.

Select "Add" > "New Item..."

In the "Add New Item..." window, choose "MVC Controller - Empty" and name it "StudentController."
Click "Add."

The new StudentController.cs class appears in the code window. Remove the default method inside the class and add a new method called CheckGrade as shown below:

```csharp
using Microsoft.AspNetCore.Mvc;

namespace Chapter2Example1.Controllers
{
    public class StudentController : Controller
    {
        public string CheckGrade()
        {
            return "Your grade is A.";
        }
    }
}
```

Explanation:

The CheckGrade method within StudentController.cs returns the string "Your Grade is A." An ASP.NET Core MVC controller is a C# class inheriting from the Controller class, containing fields, constructors, and methods like other C# classes.

Step 5: Add Routing Middleware

ASP.NET MVC utilizes routing middleware to match incoming URLs to a controller and its action method. To integrate routing middleware into Chapter2Example1: Locate the Program.cs file in the Solution Explorer window and open it in the code window.

With the Program.cs file open, remove or comment out the following lines:

```
app.MapGet("/", () => "Hello World!");
```

Instead, add the following code:

```
app.MapControllerRoute(
    name: "default",
    pattern: "{controller=Home}/{action=Index}/{id?}");
```

This code establishes a route named default and incorporates routing middleware into the application. This middleware maps a URL to an appropriate controller method.

Step 6: Register MVC Services to the Project

While still in the Program.cs file's code window, add the following statement as the second line in the code file:

```
builder.Services.AddControllersWithViews();
```

This statement registers the MVC service, enabling your project to follow the MVC mechanism provided. This registration is also known as dependency injection, a concept you'll delve deeper into later in the chapter. The completed Program.cs file after Steps 5 and 6 should resemble the following:

```
var builder = WebApplication.CreateBuilder(args);
builder.Services.AddControllersWithViews();
var app = builder.Build();
app.MapControllerRoute(
    name: "default",
    pattern: "{controller=Home}/{action=Index}/{id?}");
app.Run();
```

Explanation:

The MapControllerRoute() method utilizes default values: 'Home' for the controller if none is provided in the URL and 'Index' for the action method if not specified in the URL. The 'id' value is optional (indicated by the question mark). This template will be used consistently throughout the book.

Hence, the following three URLs are identical:

```
localhost
localhost/Home
localhost/Home/Index
```

They all request the 'Index' action method of the 'Home' controller. Note that if you change the values in the arguments of the MapControllerRoute() method, the above three URL will not be identical.

Step 7: Run the Application

Save the project. Click on "Debug" > "Start Without Debugging" to initiate the program. Once the default browser opens, add (do not replace) /Student/CheckGrade/ to the URL. You should observe the following output in your browser:

Your grade is A.

Test Your Understanding 2.15
If you start an ASP.NET Empty project and want to use MVC, you must add a folder called ______.
a. Project
b. Projects
c. Controller
d. Controllers

Test Your Understanding 2.16
An ASP.NET Core MVC controller is a C# _________ that inherits from the ___________ class.
a. object, object
b. method, object
c. class, Controller
d. class, Controllers

Test Your Understanding 2.17
If you start an ASP.NET MVC project using an empty template, you must add the following line of code to ________ file: `builder.Services.AddControllersWithViews();`
a. project.cs
b. service.cs
c. program.cs
d. main.cs

Test Your Understanding 2.18
If you start an ASP.NET Core MVC project using empty template, you should add the following statement inside the _________ file.
`app.MapControllerRoute(`

```
    name: "default",
    pattern: "{controller=Home}/{action=Index}/{id?}");
```
a. project.cs
b. service.cs
c. program.cs
d. main.cs

Test Your Understanding 2.19
If the following `MapControllerRoute` is used,
```
pattern: "{controller=Home}/{action=Index}/{id?}");
```
Which of the following URLs is different from the other three?
a. localhost
b. localhost/Home
c. localhost/Home/Index
d. localhost/Index/Home

Test Your Understanding 2.20
In Chapter2Example1 project of the book, when you complete the project and start without debugging, what is on your browser?
The following `MapControllerRoute` is used,
```
pattern: "{controller=Home}/{action=Index}/{id?}");
public string CheckGrade()
{
return "Your grade is A.";
}
```
a. blank page.
b. page can't be found.
c. Your grade is A.
d. default home page.

Test Your Understanding 2.21
In Chapter2Example1 project of the book, If the following `MapControllerRoute` is used,
```
pattern: "{controller=Student}/{action=CheckGrade}/{id?}");
public class StudentController : Controller
{
    public string CheckGrade()
    {
        return "Your grade is A.";
    }
}
```
what is on your browser?
a. blank page.
b. page can't be found.
c. Your grade is A.
d. default home page.

Programming Challenge 2.1

Create a web application with ASP.NET MVC Empty project template. When the user enters URL:

localhost/Employee/PayRate, the following content will be displayed on the browser screen.

"Your pay rate is $25.00."

2.2 Passing Parameters via URL in HTTP Requests

When a browser sends an HTTP request to the server, the URL serves as a means to transmit parameters to the server. A notable example is observed during a Google search, where the search query forms a part of the URL sent to the server. At google.com, upon entering a search string and pressing enter, the search string becomes evident in the URL.

This mechanism leverages the GET method of HTTP requests, which is one among various ways to transfer data from a browser to the server.

Chapter 2 Example 2

Problem:

In continuation with Chapter2Example1, upon entering the URL:

localhost/Student/CheckRealGrade?name=Lynn&score=75, the following content should be displayed on the browser screen:

"Lynn's grade is C." Users should be able to input different names and scores in the URL to view similar results.

Solution:

Launch Chapter2Example1. Inside the StudentController.cs controller, add a new action method called CheckRealGrade(). This method accepts a student name and a numeric score, returning the student's name and a letter grade formatted as follows: "Lynn's grade is C".

```csharp
public string CheckRealGrade(string name, int score)
{
    char letterGrade;
    if (score >= 90)
        letterGrade = 'A';
    else if (score >= 80)
        letterGrade = 'B';
    else if (score >= 70)
        letterGrade = 'C';
    else if (score >= 60)
        letterGrade = 'D';
    else
        letterGrade = 'F';
    return $"{name}'s grade is {letterGrade}";
}
```

Save your changes and start without debugging.

Enter the URL: localhost/Student/CheckRealGrade?name=Lynn&score=75.

The browser will display "Lynn's grade is C". Modify the name value and score value in the URL to view different results on the browser.

Test Your Understanding 2.22
The HTTP _______ method allows the browser to send data to the server through URL.
a. GET
b. SEND
c. EXPRESS
d. DELIVERY

Test Your Understanding 2.23
To make the following URL work, what do you need in the StudentController?
localhost/Student/CheckRealGrade?name=Lynn&score=75
a. A method called CheckRealGrade.
b. A method called CheckRealGrade with two parameters: name and score.
c. A method called CheckRealGrade with two parameters: Lynn and 75.
d. Such URL is not allowed.

Test Your Understanding 2.24
What is a notable example of passing parameters through a URL in HTTP requests?
a. Sending emails
b. Google search queries
c. File downloads
d. Social media sharing

Test Your Understanding 2.25
Which HTTP method is primarily involved in passing parameters via URLs?
a. POST
b. GET
c. DELETE
d. PUT

Test Your Understanding 2.26
To make the following URL work, what do you need in the EmployeeController?
localhost/Employee/PayAmount?name=Lynn&rate=25&hours=12
a. A method called PayAmount.
b. A method called PayAmount with two parameters: rate and hours.
c. A method called PayAmount with three parameters: name, rate, and hours.
d. A method called PayAmount with four parameters: name, Lynn, rate, and hours.

Programming Challenge 2.2

Build upon Programming Challenge 2.1. Upon entering the URL

localhost/Employee/PayAmount?name=Lynn&rate=25&hours=12, the browser should display "Lynn's

pay amount is $300.00." The specific amount varies based on the rate and hours values included in the URL.

2.3 Passing Parameters via HTML Form

In addition to passing values through URLs from the browser to the server, HTML forms offer an alternative method. The URL-based method has limitations on data size and exposes values to users. In contrast, using HTML forms with the POST method of HTTP requests overcomes these limitations, sending form data as part of the message to the server without the restrictions of the HTTP GET method.

Chapter 2 Example 3

Problem:

Extend the work from Examples 1 and 2. This time, incorporate an HTML form to facilitate data transmission from the browser to the server using the HTTP POST method. Upon accessing the URL localhost/index.html, a form displaying two fields—one for student name and another for the score—will appear, enabling users to input corresponding data. Additionally, the form will include a "Submit" button. Upon clicking this button, the entered data will be transmitted to the server. Subsequently, the screen will exhibit a resulting string such as "Lynn's grade is B." depending the student name and score submitted.

Solution:

Open the Chapter2Example1 project to continue working.

Step 1: Add an HTML Form to the wwwroot Folder

In the Solution Explorer window, right-click on the "Chapter2Example1" project and create a folder named "wwwroot.". Inside the "wwwroot" folder, add a new item by selecting "HTML Page" from the "Add New Item" window. Name the new HTML page as "Index.html". Enter the form code in the "Index.html" file to create a form structure:

```html
<!DOCTYPE html>
<html>
<head>
    <meta charset="utf-8" />
    <title></title>
</head>
<body>
    <form method="post" action="./Student/CheckRealGrade">
        Enter student name:
        <input type="text" name="name" />
        <br />
        Enter student score:
        <input type="text" name="score" />
        <br />
        <input type="submit" value="Submit" />
    </form>
</body>
</html>
```

Step 2: Update the Program.cs File

Update the Program.cs file to enable the server to locate the new "Index.html" file created in Step 1 by incorporating static file middleware. Add the line `app.UseStaticFiles();` to the Program.cs file right before the following line:

```
app.MapControllerRoute(
```

Execution:

Save your changes and start without debugging. Enter the URL localhost/Index.html. Input data into the displayed form and submit it. The application should function as expected, sending the form data to the server.

Test Your Understanding 2.27
The HTTP _______ method allows the browser to send data to the server through HTML form.
a. Form
b. SEND
c. POST
d. DELIVERY

Test Your Understanding 2.28
In order to allow browsers to access a file stored at wwwroot folder of the server, __________ should be added to the Program.cs file.
a. HTML form
b. form engine
c. static file middleware
d. dynamic file middleware

Test Your Understanding 2.29
You can use just one action method to handle data passed from either browser ______ or browser ______.
a. URL, HTML title
b. URL, HTML form
c. default setting, HTML title
d. default setting, HTML form

Test Your Understanding 2.30
An action method that can handle data from a browser must have _______.
a. a return type that is not void
b. a name that matched the HTML form name
c. a name that matched the HTML file name
d. a parameter list

Programming Challenge 2.3

Continue working on Programming Challenges 2.1 and 2.2. For this task, you'll need to create an HTML form to send the employee's name, pay rate, and hours worked to the server using an HTTP POST request.

After the user submits the form, a message should be displayed, such as: "Lynn Smith, your total pay amount is $325.34." Please note that the actual amount will vary based on the data entered in the form. Here's the form you'll need to fill out:

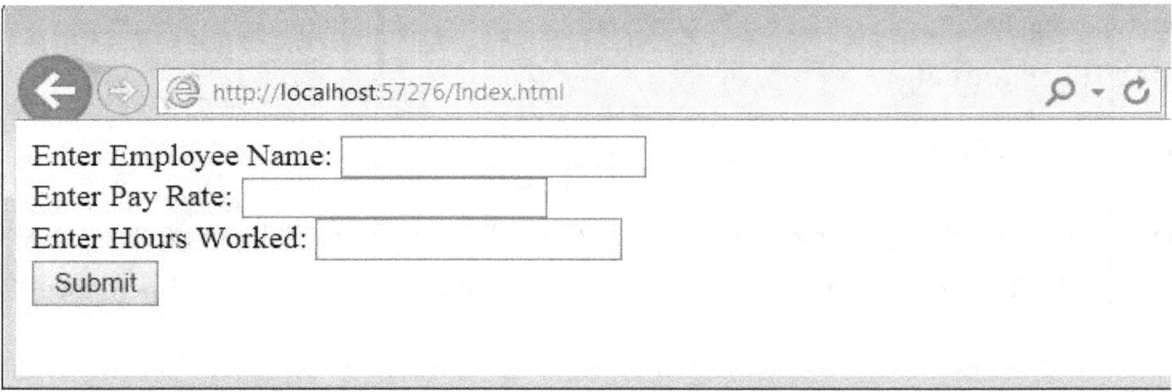

2.4 Middleware Basics

Middleware is a software component that acts as a bridge between an application and other applications or platforms (Al-Jaroodi and Mohamed, 2012). It provides tools that simplify the development of complex applications. Without middleware, building a complex application would be akin to developing an application without using operating systems. Middleware abstracts the details of the underlying environments and provides a common architecture for adding services and functionalities without having to modify the application. This includes adding features such as authentication, security, and quality of service as needed. Middleware facilitates the easy transfer of data between 'pipes' (Anonymous, 2017).

In ASP.NET MVC, middleware is typically added to the IApplicationBuilder in the Program.cs file using extension methods. This chapter provides examples of adding middleware through two such extension methods: AddControllersWithViews() and UseStaticFiles().

The AddControllersWithViews() method adds a routing middleware component to configure the routing engine, enabling requests to be forwarded to the appropriate controller and action method.

The UseStaticFiles() method adds static file middleware, allowing direct access to static files such as HTML, CSS, JavaScript, and image files stored in the wwwroot folder.

In future chapters, you will see the use of UseAuthentication() to add authentication middleware for user authentication.

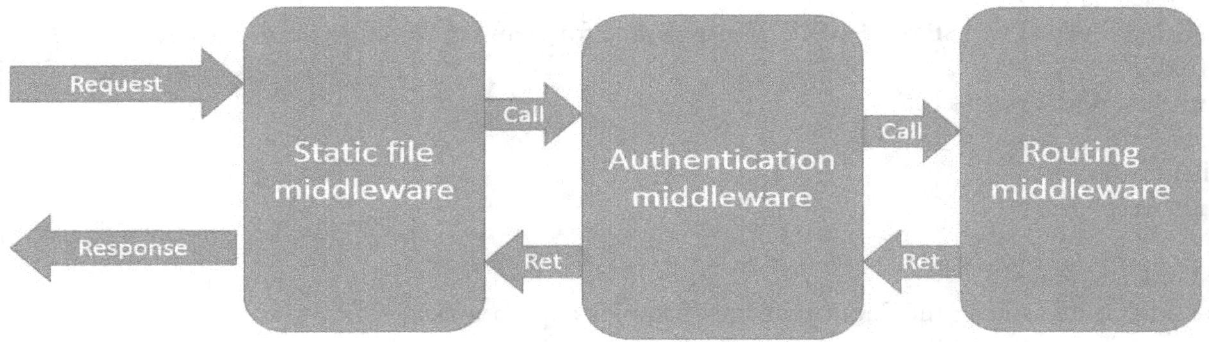

Figure 2.25 provides an example of a middleware pipeline.

Test Your Understanding 2.31
_______ is a software component that works like a connector between an application and other applications or platforms
a. MVC
b. ASP.NET Core MVC
c. Namespace
d. Middleware

Test Your Understanding 2.32
Which of the following is NOT a benefit of using middleware?
a. It allows the hiding of details in the underlying environments.
b. It provides a common architecture for adding services and functionalities without having to change the application.
c. It allows beginners to build complex applications.
d. It makes data easily passed between the "pipes"

Test Your Understanding 2.33
Which extension method adds routing middleware components to configure the routing engine so that a request can be forwarded to the appropriate controller and action method?
a. AddControllersWithViews()
b. UseStaticFile()
c. UseAuthentication()
d. UseDeveloperExceptionPage()

Test Your Understanding 2.34
What purpose does middleware serve in software architecture?
a. Simplifies complex application development
b. Bridges hardware components
c. Manages operating system functionalities
d. Enhances user interface design

Test Your Understanding 2.35
What role does middleware play in ASP.NET MVC applications?
a. Modifying underlying environments
b. Simplifying routing configurations
c. Enforcing security protocols
d. Creating user interfaces

Test Your Understanding 2.36
Which extension method in ASP.NET MVC is responsible for enabling direct access to files in the wwwroot folder?
a. AddControllersWithViews()
b. UseStaticFiles()
c. UseAuthentication()
d. AddMiddlewareFiles()

Test Your Understanding 2.37
How does middleware assist in the development of complex applications?
a. By directly modifying application code
b. By abstracting underlying environment details
c. By isolating operating system functionalities
d. By providing user interface design templates

Test Your Understanding 2.38
What is the primary function of the AddControllersWithViews() method in ASP.NET MVC?
a. Handling user authentication
b. Configuring routing for requests
c. Enabling access to static files
d. Managing quality of service

Test Your Understanding 2.39
Which middleware method is typically used for incorporating user authentication in ASP.NET MVC applications?
a. AddControllersWithViews()
b. UseStaticFiles()
c. UseAuthentication()
d. AddAuthentication()

2.5 Dependency Injection

Before delving into what Dependency Injection (DI) entails, let's explore a scenario that illustrates a potential issue without the use of DI. Consider a class named "Course" encompassing attributes like a course number, title, and an instructor. In this context, an instructor in the "Course" class is an object derived from the "Instructor" class. This establishes a "has a" relationship between the "Course" and "Instructor" classes, creating a dependency.

While it may seem unproblematic to instantiate an instructor class to utilize its methods, the complexity arises when a course can also be taught by a teaching assistant, inherently a student, with different available methods. One apparent solution might involve adding a teaching assistant object to the "Course" class. However, a challenge surfaces as only one of the two objects—either an instructor or a teaching assistant—will be used. Introducing both simultaneously is disallowed (although this may not be a universal constraint across all universities).

This design flaw violates the Dependency Inversion Principle (Dooley, 2017), which stipulates that high-level modules should not depend directly on low-level modules. Instead, they should depend on abstractions. The "Course" and "Instructor" design violates this principle because a course depends directly on an instructor. Consequently, when changes occur, the high-level module must undergo modifications.

The Dependency Injection pattern (Johnson, 2018) emerges as the remedy to this predicament. Initially, an abstraction class—often implemented as an interface in C#—is created, named "ICourseLeader," containing all the necessary methods. Subsequently, the "Course" class no longer depends on specific instructor or teaching assistant classes but relies on the "ICourseLeader" interface, adhering to the inversion of control pattern.

The lower-level classes, such as "Instructor" and "Teaching Assistant," should then implement the "ICourseLeader" interface.

However, a lingering issue persists. When a method from the "ICourseLeader" interface is needed in the "Course" class, an instance of a specific concrete class—a choice between the instructor class, teaching assistant class, or even a new type of "ICourseLeader"—is still required.

The ultimate solution lies in dependency injection. Instead of instantiating a concrete implementation within the "Course" class, an instance is created externally. The object is then passed into the "Course" class through any of the three possible means: constructor, method, or property (Bui, 2017; Freeman, 2017).

In transitioning to ASP.NET Core MVC 8, the responsibility of defining the services the application will use, such as ASP.NET Core MVC, lies with the AddControllersWithViews() method. However, this method is typically called in the ConfigureServices method of the Program class, not the Startup class as in previous versions. Throughout the examples in this chapter, the ASP.NET MVC service is incorporated using the AddControllersWithViews() extension method. This method registers the services needed for web app development using Controllers and Views, including everything that AddController installs plus the support for Views, such as the View Engine and related infrastructure, HTMLHelper, View Components, TempData, AntiForgery, Component rendering, and more.

Test Your Understanding 2.40

The statement, "high level modules should not depend on low level modules", describes _________ design principle.
a. "Is-a"
b. "Has-a"
c. dependency
d. dependency inversion

Test Your Understanding 2.41
Instead of instantiating a concrete implementation inside a class, you can create an instance outside the class. Then passing the object into the class describes __________.
a. dependency
b. dependency injection
c. outside-in
d. inside-out

Test Your Understanding 2.42
Consider a class named "Course" encompassing attributes like a course number, title, and an instructor. In this context, an instructor in the "Course" class is an object derived from the "Instructor" class. What design flaw does the "Course" and "Instructor" relationship exhibit?
a. Violation of the Inversion of Control Principle
b. Violation of the Dependency Inversion Principle
c. Violation of the Dependency Injection Pattern
d. Violation of the Open/Closed Principle

Test Your Understanding 2.43
An interface named "ICourseLeader," containing all the necessary methods is created. The lower-level classes, such as "Instructor" and "Teaching Assistant," then implement the "ICourseLeader" interface. What is the primary purpose of introducing the "ICourseLeader" interface?
a. To create a dependency between the "Course" and "Instructor" classes
b. To violate the Dependency Inversion Principle
c. To establish a "has a" relationship between classes
d. To allow the "Course" class to depend on an abstraction rather than specific classes

Test Your Understanding 2.44
What does the Dependency Injection pattern aim to resolve in the book example?
a. Violation of the Open/Closed Principle
b. Violation of the Inversion of Control Principle
c. Design flaws in the "Course" and "Instructor" relationship
d. Violation of the Dependency Inversion Principle

Test Your Understanding 2.45
How are lower-level classes, such as "Instructor" and "Teaching Assistant," expected to relate to the "ICourseLeader" interface?
a. Violate the Dependency Inversion Principle
b. Implement the "ICourseLeader" interface
c. Establish a direct dependency on the "Course" class
d. Violate the Single Responsibility Principle

Test Your Understanding 2.46
In the Dependency Injection pattern, how is an instance of a specific concrete class, such as Instructor

passed into the "Course" class?
a. Through the "AddControllersWithViews()" method
b. Via the "AddControllersWithViews()" extension method
c. Using the "ICourseLeader" interface
d. Through constructor, method, or property

Test Your Understanding 2.47
In ASP.NET MVC, what method is responsible for defining the services the application will use?
a. "AddControllersWithViews()" method
b. "Program.cs" method
c. "TransitionToMVC()" method
d. "DefineServices()" method

Test Your Understanding 2.48
What services are registered by the AddControllersWithViews() method in ASP.NET Core MVC?
a. Only controllers
b. Views and View Components
c. Support for static files
d. Database services

Test Your Understanding 2.49
What differentiates the AddControllersWithViews() method in ASP.NET Core MVC 8 from its usage in previous versions?
a. It's called in the Configure method of the Program class
b. It's not required in ASP.NET Core MVC 8
c. It's called in the ConfigureServices method of the Program class
d. It's integrated within the Controller class

2.6 Chapter Summary

In this chapter, you have gained an understanding of how controllers operate. A controller class receives data from the browser, forwards it to the relevant component (which we haven't covered yet), and ultimately returning the result for display in the browser. Additionally, you've been introduced to two crucial concepts essential for comprehending the inner workings of ASP.NET Core MVC: middleware and dependency injection. Middleware facilitates the seamless utilization of services from other applications, enhancing the overall functionality. On the other hand, dependency injection contributes to reducing interdependence among components within an application, thereby simplifying maintenance processes.

2.7 Review Questions

Question 2.1
Controllers are one part of the whole MVC framework. Explain the major responsibilities of a controller in ASP.NET Core MVC.

Question 2.2

In ASP.NET Core MVC, how does a URL match a controller and its action method?

Question 2.3
Data can be passed from a browser to a server by either URL or HTML form. What's the differences between the two ways of passing data?

Question 2.4
In this chapter, you learned that the following three URLs return the same result:
localhost
localhost/Home
localhost/Home/Index
Is it always true that these URLs return the same result? Why or why not?

Question 2.5
Middleware is an important concepts for understanding the ASP.NET MVC. Define middleware and the benefits of using it.

Question 2.6
Dependency injection is an important concept for understanding ASP.NET MVC. Explain why dependency injection is a good software architecture design pattern.

2.8 References

Al-Jaroodi, J., & Mohamed, N. (2012). Middleware is STILL everywhere!!!. *Concurrency and Computation: Practice and Experience*, *24*(16), 1919-1926.

Anonymous, (2017), What is middleware? Microsoft Azure, https://azure.microsoft.com/en-us/overview/what-is-middleware/ Visited December 27, 2017.

Bui, D. (2017). Reactive Programming and Clean Architecture in Android Development.

Dooley, J. F. (2017). Object-Oriented Design Principles. In *Software Development, Design and Coding* (pp. 121-140). Apress, Berkeley, CA.

Freeman A. (2017) Dependency Injection. In: Pro ASP.NET Core MVC 2. Apress, Berkeley, CA.

Johnson, P. (2018). Inversion of Control (IoC) & Messaging. In *Using MVVM Light with your Xamarin Apps* (pp. 49-65). Apress, Berkeley, CA.

2.9 Answers to Test Your Understanding

2.1 B; 2.2 C; 2.3 C; 2.4 C; 2.5 B; 2.6 B; 2.7 B; 2.8 A; 2.9 B; 2.10 B; 2.11 B; 2.12 A; 2.13 C; 2.14 B; 2.15 D; 2.16 C; 2.17 C; 2.18 C; 2.19 D; 2.20 B; 2.21 C; 2.22 A; 2.23 B; 2.24 B; 2.25 B; 2.26 C; 2.27 C; 2.28 C; 2.29 B; 2.30 D; 2.31 D; 2.32 C; 2.33 A; 2.34 A; 2.35 B; 2.36 B; 2.37 B; 2.38 B; 2.39 C; 2.40 D; 2.41 B; 2.42 B; 2.43 D; 2.44 C; 2.45 B; 2.46 D; 2.47 A; 2.48 B; 2.49 C;

Chapter 3: Views

Chapter Learning Objectives

3.1 Demonstrate the skill of generating MVC View pages within the ASP.NET MVC framework.
3.2 Match action method of a controller to an MVC View page.
3.3 Use ASP.NET MVC tag helper in MVC View pages.
3.4 Create _Layout.cshtml to minimize code duplication.
3.5 Comprehend software design and development principles.

3.1 Introduction to Views

In Chapter Two, you gained insight into returning a string to the browser via an action method of a controller. However, in real-world scenarios, the objective is not merely to return a string but to deliver an entire web page to the browser. This desired outcome is achieved through an action result known as ViewResult. Throughout the majority of this book, an action method will typically return an instance of IActionResult (or Task<IActionResult> for asynchronous methods).

"IActionResult" serves as an interface in MVC, representing the result of an action method. A specific implementation of this interface is the "ViewResult" class, designed to handle the rendering of views. Leveraging IActionResult empowers the method to extend its functionality beyond the simple delivery of a webpage—features such as using ModelState for validation become accessible.

In the terminology of ASP.NET MVC, a webpage is referred to as a view, specifically an MVC Razor View. Recognizable by its "cshtml" file extension, an MVC View seamlessly integrates both C# code and HTML elements. Typically, HTML elements are employed for defining the page structure, while C# code facilitates the incorporation of dynamic content. The coordination between a controller's action and a view is essential, where the former sends data to the latter for formatting, ultimately resulting in the generation of a webpage.

Figure 3.1 visually depicts the integral relationship between views and action methods, emphasizing the need for distinct view pages corresponding to each action of a controller in the MVC architecture.

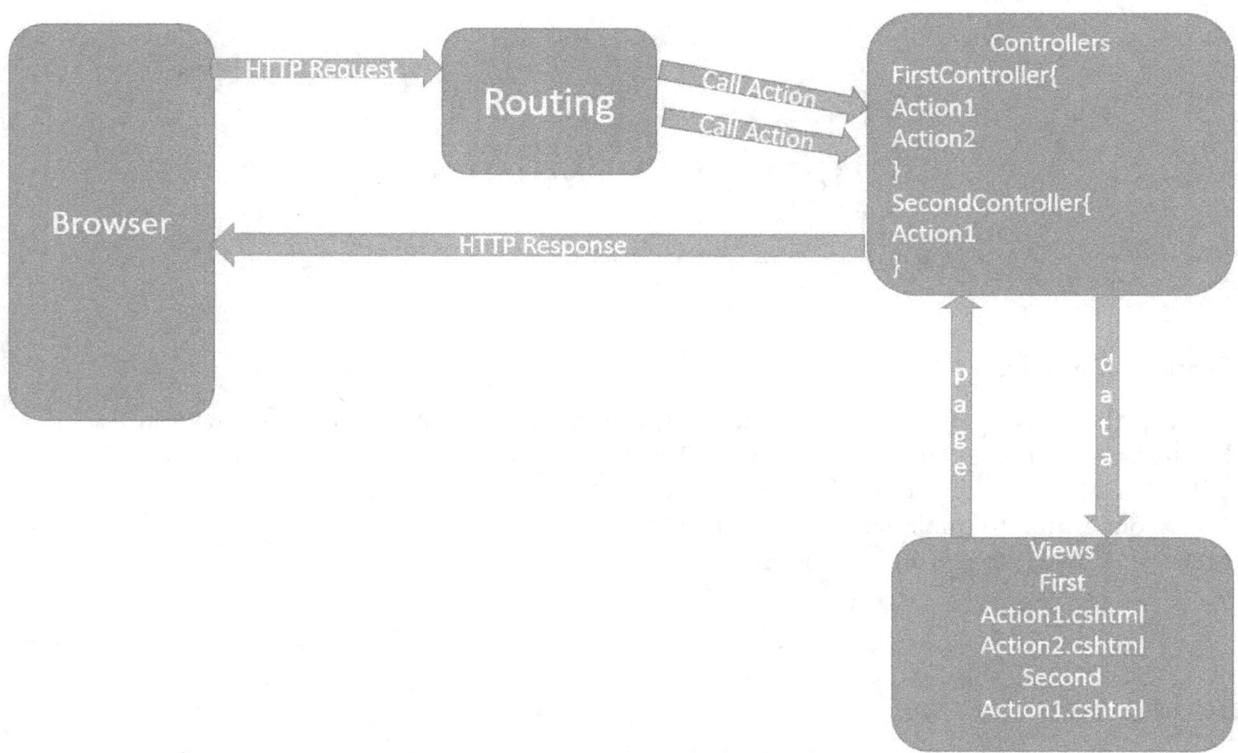

Figure 3.1 Views contains MVC Razor View that correspond to action methods.

Test Your Understanding 3.1
If the URL is localhost/Student/Home, by convention there must be a folder called ___________ inside the Views folder.
a. Student
b. Home
c. Default
d. Index

Test Your Understanding 3.2
If the URL is localhost/Student/Home, by convention there must be an MVC View file called _________.
a. Student.cshtml
b. Home.cshtml
c. Student.Home
d. Home.Student

Test Your Understanding 3.3
An MVC Razor View file can contain __________.
a. C# code only
b. HTML elements only
c. both C# code and/or HTML elements
d. neither C# code nor HTML elements

Test Your Understanding 3.4
An HTML file inside wwwroot folder of ASP.NET MVC project can contain __________.
a. C# code only
b. HTML elements only

c. both C# code and/or HTML elements
d. neither C# code nor HTML elements

Test Your Understanding 3.5
For most of the book, a(n) _______ will return an instance of IActionResult (or Task<IActionResult> for async methods).
a. class
b. object
c. action method
d. controller

Test Your Understanding 3.6
An action of a controller sends ________ to a view for formatting. The latter puts the ________ into a webpage.
a. data, data
b. webpage, data
c. URL, URL
d. URL, data

Test Your Understanding 3.7
What is the primary purpose of the "ViewResult" class in ASP.NET MVC?
a. To represent the result of an action method
b. To handle validation using ModelState
c. To deliver a string to the browser
d. To serve as an interface for MVC Razor Views

Test Your Understanding 3.8
In ASP.NET MVC, what file extension is associated with MVC Razor Views?
a. .html
b. .cs
c. .aspx
d. .cshtml

Test Your Understanding 3.9
Which feature becomes accessible when leveraging IActionResult in an action method?
a. Action binding
b. Static content incorporation
c. Validation using ModelState
d. Delivery of a picture to the View

Test Your Understanding 3.10
What is the coordination process between a controller's action and a view in ASP.NET MVC?
a. The controller sends HTML elements to the view for formatting.
b. The view sends data to the controller for validation.
c. The controller sends data to the view for formatting.
d. The view sends C# code to the controller for execution.

Test Your Understanding 3.11
In real-world scenarios, what is the typical return type of an action method in ASP.NET MVC?
a. Task<ActionResult>

b. string
c. void
d. IActionResult

3.2 ASP.NET MVC Tag Helpers

HTML elements, often referred to as client-side elements, are instructions for browsers. In a similar vein, ASP.NET tag helpers function like HTML elements but operate on the server side.

Tag helpers enhance the development experience when creating MVC Razor Views by providing a rich IntelliSense environment. This not only boosts productivity but also aids in producing more reliable and maintainable code.

To enable the functionality of tag helpers, a Razor View named _ViewImports.cshtml must be added to the Views folder of the project. The process of adding _ViewImports.cshtml will be explained in the following sections.

Chapter 3 Example 1

Create an ASP.NET MVC application called Chapter3Example1, using the empty template to showcase a list of courses along with a link for adding a new course. The URL for this page should be localhost/Student/Course. The browser display should resemble:

<u>Add a new course</u>

Available Course List
1. Java
2. C#
3. Agile

Upon clicking the "Add a new course" link, the URL should transition to localhost/Student/AddCourse. The browser should present an HTML form with a single text field for user input of the course title and a submission button. If a user enters a new course title, such as "Advanced C#", and clicks on Submit, the URL will revert to localhost/Student/Course. The page will exhibit all the courses, including the recently added one.

Solution:

Step 1: Set Up the Project

Start a new Empty ASP.NET MVC Project (.NET 8.0) and follow the routing middleware addition (Step 5) and registration of Mvc services (Step 6) detailed in Chapter 2 Example 1.

Step 2: Add a Controller

Create a "Controllers" folder within the project.

Inside the "Controllers" folder, add a new controller named StudentController.cs (Refer to Step 4 of Chapter 2 Example 1 for details).

Remove the default Index() method.

Inside the StudentController class, create a List field named "allCourses":

```
static List<string> allCourses = new List<string> { "Java", "C#", "Agile" };
```

Add an action method named "Course" inside the StudentController class:

```
public IActionResult Course()
{
    // Assign allCourses to ViewData dictionary to pass to the view.
    ViewData["Courses"] = allCourses;
    return View();
}
```

Step 3: Add a View

Create a "Views" folder within the project.

Inside the "Views" folder, add a subfolder named "Student" (matching the controller name).

Within the "Student" folder, create a new Razor View named "Course.cshtml" (right-click on the Student folder, add new item, using the Razor View – Empty template, name it Course.cshtml).

Replace the default code in Course.cshtml with the following:

```
<!DOCTYPE html>
<html>
<head>
    <meta charset="utf-8" />
    <title>Chapter3 Example 2</title>
</head>
<body>
    <p>
        <a asp-controller="Student" asp-action="AddCourse">
            Add a new course
        </a>
    </p>
    <h3>Available Course List</h3>
```

```
    <ol>
        @{
            foreach (string course in ViewData["Courses"] as List<string>)
            {
                <li>@course</li>
            }
        }
    </ol>
</body>
</html>
```

Explanation:

The anchor tag `<a asp-controller="Student" asp-action="AddCourse">` utilizes ASP.NET Core MVC tag helpers, converting them into appropriate HTML element attributes. The asp-controller and asp-action helpers specify which controller's action method to invoke when the link is clicked. The code `ViewData["Courses"] as List<string>` converts the dictionary collection into a List of string generic type.

Step 4: Add _ViewImports.cshtml

To enable ASP.NET Core MVC Tag Helpers:

Right-click on the "Views" folder in the Solution Explorer.

Select "Add New Item" and choose "Razor View Imports" in the window.

Use the default name, _ViewImports.cshtml (with an underscore as the first character).

Add the following lines in the _ViewImports.cshtml file:

```
@using Chapter3Example1
@addTagHelper *, Microsoft.AspNetCore.Mvc.TagHelpers
```

Step 5: Test the Code So Far

Save the progress and start without debugging. Enter localhost/Student/Course into the browser URL. You should see a hyperlink at the top followed by a list of courses.

Step 6: Make the "Add a new course" hyperlink work.

To activate a link, you'll need an action method and a corresponding view. First, add an action method to the controller. Examine the code for the "Add a new course" link:

```
<a asp-controller="Student" asp-action="AddCourse">Add a new course</a>
```

This code requests a "Student" controller (already in place) and an action method called "AddCourse". Add the following action method inside the StudentController:

```
public IActionResult AddCourse()
{
    return View();
}
```

Next, create a corresponding view. For the AddCourse() action method to function, you need a view named "AddCourse.cshtml" inside the Student subfolder of the Views folder.

Right-click on the Student subfolder in the Views folder and add a new "Razor View - Empty" named AddCourse.cshtml with the content below:

```html
<!DOCTYPE html>
<html>
<head>
    <meta charset="utf-8" />
    <title>Add a new course</title>
</head>
<body>
    <form asp-controller="Student" asp-action="AddCourse"
        method="post">
        Enter course title:
        <input type="text" name="courseTitle" />
        <button type="submit">Submit</button>
    </form>
</body>
</html>
```

Step 7: Test the Link

Save the changes and start without debugging. Type localhost/Student/Course into the URL. Click on the "Add a new course" link. You should see an HTML form with one text field and a button labeled 'Submit'.

Step 8: Make the Step 7 Form "Submit" Button Work

Upon clicking the button, the form data is sent to an action method. You want to add the course data to the allCoures list you added in Step 2

The following line in the "AddCourse.cshtml" file shows what occurs when the user clicks the "Submit" button:

```html
<form asp-controller="Student" asp-action="AddCourse" method="post">
```

The form content will be submitted to the Student controller, needing the "AddCourse" action method for handling the "Post" method. The Student controller already has a method called "AddCourse" for HTTP GET requests. You'll need to add another action method called "AddCourse" explicitly stated for HTTP POST. Add the following method inside the StudentController.cs file:

```
[HttpPost]
public IActionResult AddCourse(string courseTitle)
{
    allCourses.Add(courseTitle);
    return RedirectToAction("Course", "Student");
}
```

Note the [HttpPost] action verb selector above the new AddCourse() method. This differentiates this method from another method of the same name. This book will only use [HttpPost] action verb when necessary. Other action verbs exist but won't be covered in this chapter.

The [HttpPost] AddCourse() method will accept a string as the course title and then add it to the allCourses List. Afterwards, it will redirect to the Course action method of the Student Controller. The Course action already has a corresponding Course.cshtml View, so you don't need a Razor View for this method.

Step 9: Test the Button

Save the changes and start without debugging. Everything should work as expected.

Test Your Understanding 3.12
_________ is a C# dictionary that can pass values from a controller to corresponding views.
a. Student<TKey, TValue>
b. ViewData
c. ViewBag
d. ViewModel

Test Your Understanding 3.13
What is the major benefit of using tag helpers in ASP.NET MVC?
a. Intelligent
b. IntelliSense
c. Intellectual
d. shorter code

Test Your Understanding 3.14
ASP.NET MVC tag helpers run on ______.
a. server side
b. client side
c. both server side and client side
d. neither server side nor client side

Test Your Understanding 3.15
To make the tag helpers work, you must add a Razor View called _________ inside the Views folder of the project.
a. _ViewImports.cshtml
b. _Layout.cshtml
c. _ViewStart.cshtml
d. Program.cs

Test Your Understanding 3.16
Suppose there is an action method like this:
```
public IActionResult Course()
{
    ViewData["Courses"] = allCourses;
    return View();
}
```

You will need a Razor View called __________.
a. IActionResult.cshtml
b. Course.cshtml
c. ViewData.cshtml
d. View.cshtml

Test Your Understanding 3.17
Suppose the following code is in an MVC Razor View:
```
<p><a asp-controller="Student" asp-action="AddCourse">Add a new course</a></p>
```
You will need a controller called _______ and an action method called _______ inside that controller.
a. Controllers, Actions
b. Student.cs, AddCourse
c. StudentController.cs, AddCourse
d. StudentController, AddCourseAction

Test Your Understanding 3.18
Can you have two action methods with the same name in the same controller?
a. Yes, as long as their signatures are different.
b. Yes, as long as they have different action verbs.
c. Yes, as long as they have different content.
d. No.

Test Your Understanding 3.19
Suppose the following code is in an MVC View page:
```
<p><a asp-controller="MyLibrary" asp-action="AddBook"> Add a new course</a></p>
```
You will need a controller called _______ and a method called _______ inside that controller to handle the data submitted from the form.
a. Controllers, Actions
b. MyLibrary.cs, AddBook
c. MyLibraryController.cs, AddBook
d. MyLibraryController, AddBookAction

Test Your Understanding 3.20
What is the purpose of _ViewImports.cshtml in an ASP.NET MVC application?
a. To store view-specific data

b. To enable ASP.NET Core MVC Tag Helpers
c. To define the default controller
d. To manage client-side HTML elements

Test Your Understanding 3.21
Which file type allows the use of ASP.NET Core MVC Tag Helpers in Razor Views?
a. .html
b. .cs
c. .css
d. .cshtml

Test Your Understanding 3.22
In the Chapter3Example1 application, what should happen when a user clicks on the "Add a new course" link? `<p><a asp-controller="Student" asp-action="AddCourse">Add a new course</a></p>`
a. The user is directed to the Index page
b. The URL changes to localhost/Student/AddCourse
c. The browser displays a list of all available courses
d. The server generates a new course automatically

Test Your Understanding 3.23
What is the primary role of the [HttpPost] attribute in the AddCourse method of the StudentController?
a. To enable the form submission
b. To restrict access to the form
c. To render the form in HTML
d. To define the course title

Test Your Understanding 3.24
Which element in the AddCourse.cshtml file captures the course title input from the user?

```
<form asp-controller="Student" asp-action="AddCourse" method="post">
Enter course title:
<input type="text" name="courseTitle" />
<button type="submit">Submit</button>
</form>
```

a. <form>
b. <input>
c. <button>
d. <a>

Test Your Understanding 3.25
What does the [HttpPost] AddCourse method do after adding the new course title to the allCourses list?

```
public IActionResult AddCourse(string courseTitle)
{
    allCourses.Add(courseTitle);
    return RedirectToAction("Course", "Student");
}
```

a. Renders a new view
b. Redirects to the AddCourse action method
c. Redirects to the Course action method
d. Deletes allCourses list

Programming Challenge 3.1

Create an ASP.NET MVC application. This application will display a list of books, along with a link to add a new book. The URL for this page will be localhost/MyLibrary/Book (as depicted in Figure 3.2).

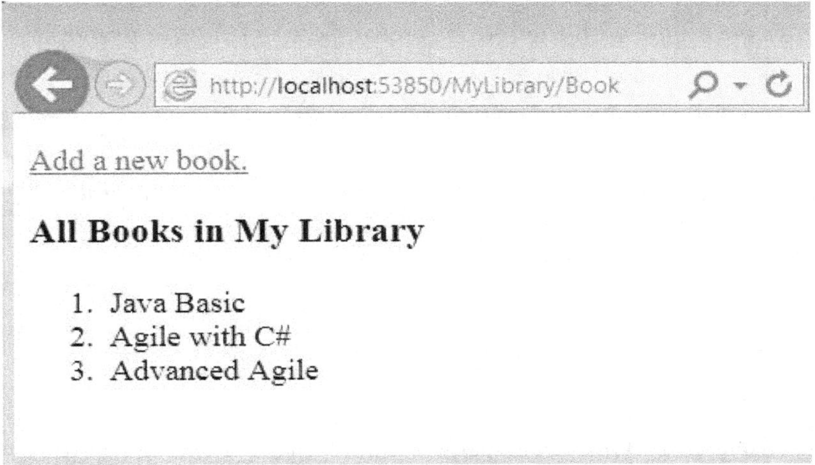

Figure 3.2: The browser display of localhost/MyLibrary/Book.

Upon clicking the "Add a new book" link (shown in Figure 3.2), the URL will change to localhost/MyLibrary/AddBook (as illustrated in Figure 3.3).

Figure 3.3: The browser display of localhost/MyLibrary/AddBook.

When you enter a book title and click the "Add Book" button, the new title will be added to the book list. Subsequently, the page will redirect to localhost/MyLibrary/Book with the newly added book visible in the list (as shown in Figure 3.4).

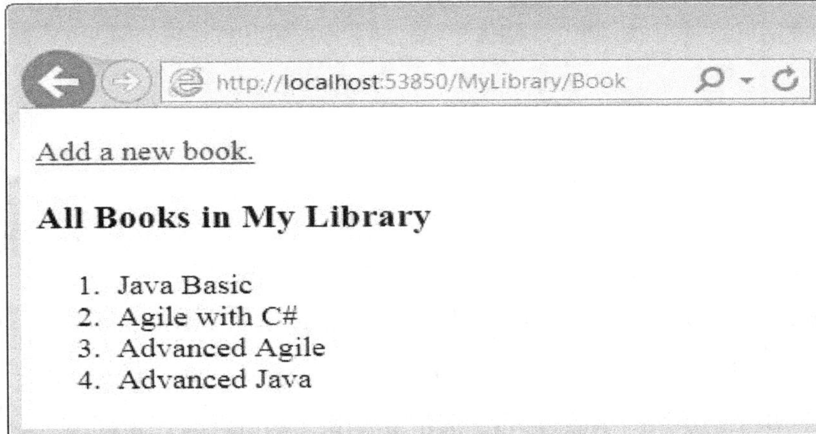

Figure 3.4 The browser display with a new book added to the list.

3.3 The _Layout.cshtml Razor View

In every Razor View file, you're likely duplicating basic HTML elements. To avoid this redundancy, we use a _Layout.cshtml file that contains common code shared across all Razor Views. Each individual file then retains only its unique code. This helps keep views in line with the Don't Repeat Yourself (DRY) principle by reducing duplicate content.

This book will work with a single _Layout.cshtml file, but you can employ multiple _Layout.cshtml files, each applying to a set of Razor Views.

Chapter 3 Example 2

Problem:

In Chapter 3 Example 1, there are two Razor View files: AddCourse.cshtml and Course.cshtml. We'll utilize a _Layout.cshtml for common code between these views, allowing each file to hold its unique content.

Solution:

Open Chapter3Example1.

Add a subfolder named "Shared" inside the Views folder.

Within the Shared subfolder, add a new item and choose "Razor Layout" type. Use the default file name _Layout.cshtml and keep the default code (if empty, use the following):

```html
<!DOCTYPE html>

<html>
<head>
    <meta name="viewport" content="width=device-width" />
    <title>@ViewBag.Title</title>
</head>
<body>
    <div>
        @RenderBody()
    </div>
</body>
</html>
```

The `@RenderBody()` tag is where each view will be inserted when called. ViewBag in is a dynamic property that provides a convenient way to pass data from a controller action to its corresponding view. It's similar to ViewData dictionary you learned earlier. Add the following line inside the Course() method of the Student controller (Add a similar line to AddCourse()): `ViewBag.Title = "Display courses";`

Open AddCourse.cshtml and Course.cshtml. Remove code above and below the <body> tags.

Next, within the Views folder, add a new item of "Razor View Start" type. Use the default file name _ViewStart.cshtml. Keep the default code:

```
@{
    Layout = "_Layout";
}
```

This _ViewStart.cshtml file runs before any Razor View file and specifies that all view files will utilize the _Layout.cshtml file.

Save the changes and start without debugging. The functionality should be similar to Chapter 3 Example 1.

Check the Solution Explorer window; it should display all files in a structure resembling Figure 3.5. Pay attention to the nesting levels of each folder/file.

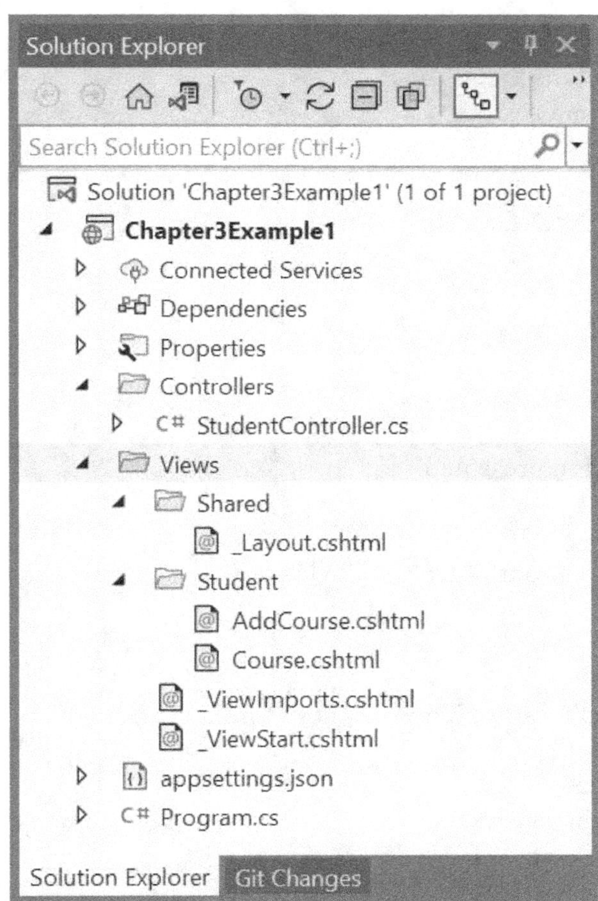

Figure 3.5 Solution Explorer window showing all project files.

Test Your Understanding 3.26
Common code on all Razor View files can be removed and put in one ___________ file.
a. _ViewStart.cshtml

b. _ViewImports.cshtml
c. _Layout.cshtml
d. Program.cs
Test Your Understanding 3.27
Which method in _Layout.cshtml file is used to insert individual view file?
a. RenderBody()
b. InsertBody()
c. AddBody()
d. PartialView()

Test Your Understanding 3.28
Which file is called before any file in the Views folder is called?
a. _ViewStart.cshtml
b. _ViewImports.cshtml
c. _Layout.cshtml
d. _FirstView.cshtml

Test Your Understanding 3.29
What purpose does the _Layout.cshtml file serve in ASP.NET Razor Views?
a. It contains unique code for each Razor View.
b. It centralizes common HTML elements shared among multiple Razor Views.
c. It only works with a single Razor View.
d. It duplicates HTML elements in each Razor View file.

Test Your Understanding 3.30
How does the @RenderBody() tag function in the _Layout.cshtml file?
a. It specifies the viewport width for the HTML content.
b. It renders the entire content of the Razor Views.
c. It defines the title for each Razor View.
d. It sets the default layout for the Razor Views.

Test Your Understanding 3.31
What is the purpose of the _ViewStart.cshtml file in the solution presented?
a. It defines the rendering order of the Razor Views.
b. It specifies the structure of the _Layout.cshtml file.
c. It runs before any Razor View file and designates the _Layout.cshtml file for all views.
d. It initializes the content within each Razor View.

Test Your Understanding 3.32
How does employing a _Layout.cshtml file align with the Don't Repeat Yourself (DRY) principle?
a. It separates HTML elements into multiple files for each view.
b. It duplicates code across multiple Razor Views for consistency.
c. It centralizes common code to reduce duplication in individual views.
d. It applies unique code to each Razor View for better organization.

Test Your Understanding 3.33
What is the primary purpose of creating a "Shared" subfolder within the Views folder?
a. To segregate different types of Razor Views.
b. To store layouts for specific Razor Views.
c. To organize common resources shared among multiple views.

d. To establish unique settings for each Razor View.

Test Your Understanding 3.34
What role does the @ViewBag.Title serve within the _Layout.cshtml file?
a. It specifies the title for each Razor View.
b. It defines the layout structure for the entire project.
c. It determines the viewport size for the HTML content.
d. It sets the default HTML meta tag for the views.

Test Your Understanding 3.35
To make @ViewBag.Title in the _Layout.cshtml file work, which code should you add to the action?
a. `@ViewBag.Title;`.
b. `ViewBag.Title;`.
c. `@ViewBag.Title = "Display courses";`.
d. `ViewBag.Title = "Display courses";`.

Programming Challenge 3.2

In Programming Challenge 3.1, you worked with two Razor View files: Book.cshtml and AddBook.cshtml. These files contain some duplicated code. To eliminate this redundancy, create a new Razor View file named _Layout.cshtml. Then, refactor the code in Book.cshtml and AddBook.cshtml by removing the duplicated sections and incorporating them into _Layout.cshtml. Additionally, don't forget to add the _ViewStart.cshtml file.

3.4 Software Design and Development Principles

Throughout the years, numerous software design and development principles have been proposed by software architects. In this section, we will delve into three key principles. The following chapter will explore the widely acclaimed SOLID principles, particularly popular in the realm of Object-Oriented Programming (OOP).

3.4.1 Don't Repeat Yourself (DRY) Principle

The Don't Repeat Yourself (DRY) principle, articulated by Hunt in 1999, addresses the challenges associated with code redundancy. When a block of code is copied and pasted into another module, it introduces a potential maintenance nightmare. Modifications necessitate updates in multiple locations, increasing the likelihood of errors and inconsistencies in the software.

DRY extends beyond code to encompass data as well (Wilson et al., 2014). At the code level, modularization is key to avoiding code clones. This practice offers several advantages, as elucidated by Sarkar in 2009.

Firstly, modularization aids in fault localization. When troubleshooting, developers can focus on the code within a specific module rather than the entire application. Secondly, modular code is inherently more comprehensible. Each module revolves around a significant functionality, fostering clarity and understanding. Lastly, modularization promotes enhanced ownership among developers. Developers only need to grasp the intricacies of a specific domain module rather than the entire product (Kelly and Pohjonen, 2009).

In the broader context, programmers are encouraged to maximize code reuse whenever feasible. Utilizing code libraries and packages not only enhances reliability but also bolsters security, given their extensive usage and testing across various programs.

On the data level, the quality of raw data is paramount. Collecting data with a focus on quality assurance is crucial to prevent the introduction of erroneous information. In the context of relational databases, adhering to at least the third normal form is advisable to minimize data duplications. This ensures that the stored data remains robust and reliable, adhering to established best practices.

Test Your Understanding 3.36
When coding, if you need to copy and paste a block of code, you may violate the _______ principle.
a. DRY
b. KISS
c. YAGNI
d. WET

Test Your Understanding 3.37
Which of the following is NOT a benefit of modularization?
a. fault localization
b. global code
c. code is easier to understand
d. enhanced code ownership among the developers

Test Your Understanding 3.38
When something goes wrong, you just need to examine the code in the module instead of the whole application describes ___________.
a. fault localization
b. global code
c. code is easier to understand
d. enhanced code ownership among the developers

Test Your Understanding 3.39
What is the primary focus of the Don't Repeat Yourself (DRY) principle in software development?
a. Maximizing code reuse
b. Introducing code backup

c. Emphasizing code complexity
d. Encouraging code duplication

Test Your Understanding 3.40
Why is modularization important at the code level according to the DRY principle?
a. To keep code running longer
b. To foster clarity and understanding
c. To complicate fault localization
d. To discourage code reuse

Test Your Understanding 3.41
In the broader context, what is the encouraged practice for programmers, as mentioned in the book?
a. Minimizing code reuse to encourage creativity
b. Maximizing code redundancy to backup programs
c. Utilizing code libraries and packages
d. Avoiding modularization to simplify the applications

Test Your Understanding 3.42
What is emphasized at the data level to ensure data quality according to the book?
a. Encouraging data duplication for data availability
b. Focusing on code complexity for data integrity
c. Adhering to the third normal form in databases
d. Minimizing the use of relational databases

Test Your Understanding 3.43
How does the DRY principle contribute to reducing maintenance challenges in software development?
a. By encouraging code redundancy
b. By promoting extensive code duplication
c. By emphasizing modularization and code reuse
d. By complicating fault localization

3.4.2 Keep It Simple, Stupid (KISS) Principle

The KISS principle, originating from the US Navy in 1960 (Rich, 1995), emphasizes the efficacy of simplicity in design. According to this principle, a simple system performs optimally, whereas a complex system is prone to inducing errors (Walker, 2017). Therefore, simplicity should be the overarching goal in architecture design, and unnecessary complexity should be avoided. In extensive software development, system complexity can be concealed within well-tested interfaces, allowing developers to utilize them without delving into the intricate details. This, in turn, enables developers to allocate more time to creating applications that align with customer requirements.

Complexity in design often stems from a lack of understanding of the business problem (Walker, 2017). Business managers unfamiliar with information technology and developers with limited business knowledge may contribute to this complexity. Treating user stories as definitive requirement documentation can exacerbate the issue, particularly when modifications are required as the business evolves. The solution lies in effective communication between managers and developers to ensure a comprehensive understanding of both the problem and its solution. When faced with a complex software design, developers are advised to explore alternative options that prioritize simplicity, ease of understanding, and cost-effective maintenance.

The KISS principle aligns seamlessly with agile software development practices (Abrahamsson, 2017). Agile teams strive to continuously deliver well-tested working software to customers in short increments or sprints. This approach compels developers to maintain simple and understandable code, minimizing technical debt and facilitating easy maintenance.

Architects often prioritize reusability and generality in software development, aiming for software that accommodates expansion as the business grows. While this may seem advantageous, it can conflict with the KISS principle (Turk et al., 2014). The inherent adaptability in such software tends to introduce complexity. Additionally, future needs are challenging to predict, rendering pre-built adaptability unnecessary. This does not imply that developers should disregard reusability; instead, it suggests focusing on current requirements while considering potential reusability for future applications.

Test Your Understanding 3.44
According to the ____________ principle, a simple system works the best while a complex system induces errors.
a. DRY
b. KISS
c. YAGNI
d. WET

Test Your Understanding 3.45
The architects who focus too much on reusability and generality in software development may violate the ________ principle.
a. DRY
b. KISS
c. YAGNI
d. WET

Test Your Understanding 3.46
What is the primary emphasis of the KISS principle in design and software development?
a. Complexity is necessary for optimal performance
b. Simplicity leads to errors in the system
c. Well-tested interfaces are indispensable
d. Simplicity should be the overarching goal

Test Your Understanding 3.47
According to the KISS principle, why is a simple system preferable to a complex one?

a. Simplicity facilitates easy maintenance
b. Complexity leads to well-tested interfaces
c. Complexity is essential for optimal performance
d. Simplicity introduces technical debt

Test Your Understanding 3.48
What can well-tested interfaces in extensive software development help achieve?
a. Increased complexity in the system
b. Simplicity and ease of understanding
c. Delving into intricate details
d. Business managers' unfamiliarity with technology

Test Your Understanding 3.49
What is identified as a source of complexity in software design, according to the book?
a. Lack of adaptability in software
b. Business managers' familiarity with technology
c. Treating user stories as definitive requirements
d. Well-tested interfaces in agile development

Test Your Understanding 3.50
How does the KISS principle align with agile software development practices?
a. By encouraging complex code for adaptability
b. By prioritizing extensive documentation
c. By promoting simple and understandable code
d. By minimizing customer involvement

Test Your Understanding 3.51
What is the potential conflict between the KISS principle and architects' priorities in software development?
a. The focus on current requirements
b. The emphasis on simplicity
c. The prioritization of reusability and generality
d. The adaptability of well-tested interfaces

3.4.3 You Aren't Gonna Need It (YAGNI) Principle

The YAGNI principle, an integral aspect of agile software development, strongly discourages the inclusion of unnecessary functionality in applications based on currently known requirements (Wäyrynen, 2004). Illustrating this concept is the 80/20 rule, suggesting that 80 percent of business requirements can often be fulfilled with just 20 percent of the features in the software. Consider Microsoft Word as an example—how many features are genuinely necessary for your daily work requirements?

Developing features that won't be utilized constitutes a significant waste (Sedano et al., 2017). This waste extends beyond the investment of developers' time and effort to the expenditure of customers' money. Moreover, it can impact team morale, code ownership, and customer satisfaction. The concept of "not used" is critical; sometimes, a feature desired by the business may not align with users' actual needs, resulting in an unused feature in the application.

In project management terminology, the inclusion of unnecessary functionality is termed over-requirement. Emotional involvement of software developers, as noted by Shmueli et al. (2015), contributes to over-requirement. Developers, having invested effort in understanding a particular feature, may become emotionally attached to it, considering it crucial even when it may be deemed unnecessary by the client or the team.

The DRY (Don't Repeat Yourself) and YAGNI principles share a connection. While complex applications may demand additional time for the development of extra features, these features could prove unnecessary. The DRY principle addresses complexity by enhancing problem understanding and code organization, while the YAGNI principle focuses on waste reduction by eliminating unnecessary code altogether. Both principles contribute to efficient and effective software development practices.

Test Your Understanding 3.52
__________ is an agile software development principle that discourages adding any unnecessary functionality to applications based on currently known requirements
a. DRY
b. KISS
c. YAGNI
d. WET

Test Your Understanding 3.53
Developing features that are not in the software requirements is NOT related to _______.
a. lower team morale
b. code ownership
c. team extra income
d. lower customer satisfaction

Test Your Understanding 3.54
We learn three software design and development principles. Which two are more likely share a connection?
a. DRY and KISS
b. KISS and YAGNI
c. DRY and WET
d. DRY and YAGNI

Test Your Understanding 3.55
What does the YAGNI principle discourage in agile software development?
a. In-depth problem understanding
b. Inclusion of unnecessary functionality
c. Extensive code organization
d. Frequent feature updates

Test Your Understanding 3.56
How is the concept of the 80/20 rule related to the YAGNI principle?
a. It encourages the inclusion of unnecessary features.
b. It suggests that 20 percent of features are often unnecessary.
c. It prioritizes comprehensive code organization.
d. It discourages problem understanding.

Test Your Understanding 3.57
According to the book, what is the impact of developing features that won't be utilized?
a. Enhanced team morale
b. Reduced customer satisfaction
c. Efficient code ownership
d. Cost-effective development

Test Your Understanding 3.58
What does the term "over-requirement" refer to in project management terminology?
a. Efficient code organization
b. Emotional attachment of developers
c. Inclusion of unnecessary functionality
d. Customer satisfaction improvement

Test Your Understanding 3.59
How does emotional involvement of developers contribute to over-requirement, as mentioned in the book?
a. By reducing the need for understanding features
b. By prioritizing cost-effective development
c. By making developers reluctant to exclude certain features
d. By promoting team morale

Test Your Understanding 3.60
What is the primary focus of the YAGNI principle in terms of code development?
a. Comprehensive code organization
b. Maximizing feature updates
c. Eliminating unnecessary code
d. Enhancing problem understanding

3.5 Chapter Summary

In this chapter, you learned about MVC Razor views, represented by cshtml files called from controller action methods. For instance, Method1 in MyFirstController calls Method1.cshtml in Views/MyFirst. These views merge C# and HTML to format data from controller methods. The DRY principle emphasizes component reuse, KISS promotes simplicity, and YAGNI discourages unnecessary features, aligning with agile development.

3.6 Review Questions

Question 3.1

In Chapter One, you learned one of the benefits of MVC is "Convention over configuration". Explain the benefit with the materials you learned in this chapter.

Question 3.2

In Chapter Two, you learned that you can add an html file to the project. In this chapter, you learned you can add a cshtml file to the project. Explain the differences by giving an example of each and how to make them work.

Question 3.3

What is ASP.NET tag helper? What are the differences between HTML element and ASP.NET tag helper? How do you make the tag helper work?

Question 3.4

In ASP.NET Core MVC Razor View, if you have several pages sharing same parts such as the navigation menu, what could you do to minimize the duplication of code? Be specific.

Question 3.5

Do you agree with the DRY, KISS, and YAGNI principles in software design and development? Why or why not?

3.7 References

Abrahamsson, P., Salo, O., Ronkainen, J., & Warsta, J. (2017). Agile software development methods: Review and analysis. *arXiv preprint arXiv:1709.08439*.

Hunt A, Thomas D (1999) The pragmatic programmer: from journeyman to master. Boston: Addison-Wesley.

Kelly, S., & Pohjonen, R. (2009). Worst practices for domain-specific modeling. *IEEE software, 26*(4).

Rich, B. R. (1995). Clarence leonard (kelly) johnson. *National Academy of sciences*.

Sarkar, S., Ramachandran, S., Kumar, G. S., Iyengar, M. K., Rangarajan, K., & Sivagnanam, S. (2009). Modularization of a large-scale business application: A case study. *IEEE software, 26*(2), 28-35.

Sedano, T., Ralph, P., & Péraire, C. (2017, May). Software development waste. In *Proceedings of the 39th International Conference on Software Engineering* (pp. 130-140). IEEE Press.

Shmueli, O., Pliskin, N., & Fink, L. (2015). Explaining over-requirement in software development projects: an experimental investigation of behavioral effects. *International Journal of Project Management, 33*(2), 380-394.

Turk, D., France, R., & Rumpe, B. (2014). Assumptions underlying agile software development processes. *arXiv preprint arXiv:1409.6610*.

Walker, B. (2017). Software Architect as an Agent for Product Success.

Wäyrynen, J., Bodén, M., & Boström, G. (2004, August). Security engineering and eXtreme programming: An impossible marriage?. In *Conference on Extreme Programming and Agile Methods* (pp. 117-128). Springer, Berlin, Heidelberg.

Wilson, G., Aruliah, D. A., Brown, C. T., Hong, N. P. C., Davis, M., Guy, R. T., ... & Waugh, B. (2014). Best practices for scientific computing. *PLoS biology, 12*(1), e1001745.

3.8 Answers to Test Your Understanding

3.1 A; 3.2 B; 3.3 C; 3.4 B; 3.5 C; 3.6 A; 3.7 A; 3.8 D; 3.9 C; 3.10 C; 3.11 D; 3.12 B; 3.13 B; 3.14 A; 3.15 A;

3.16 B; 3.17 C; 3.18 B; 3.19 C; 3.20 B; 3.21 D; 3.22 B; 3.23 A; 3.24 B; 3.25 C; 3.26 C; 3.27 A; 3.28 A; 3.29 B;

3.30 B; 3.31 C; 3.32 C; 3.33 C; 3.34 A; 3.35 D; 3.36 A; 3.37 B; 3.38 A; 3.39 A; 3.40 B; 3.41 C; 3.42 C; 3.43 C;

3.44 B; 3.45 B; 3.46 D; 3.47 A; 3.48 B; 3.49 C; 3.50 C; 3.51 C; 3.52 C; 3.53 C; 3.54 D; 3.55 B; 3.56 B; 3.57 B;

3.58 C; 3.59 C; 3.60 C;

Chapter 4: Models

Chapter Learning Objectives

4.1 Demonstrating the ability to construct functional and effective models within the MVC framework.
4.2 Apply the knowledge gained to effectively integrate models into both controllers and views.
4.3 Demonstrate creativity and proficiency by crafting MVC view models.
4.4 Exhibit a deep understanding of the Single Responsibility Principle within the SOLID design principles.

4.1 Model Binding and Data Structure

In Chapter Two, we discussed how controllers handle browser requests, which can be initiated either through a URL or an HTML form submission. These controllers then return simple data.

Chapter Three introduced the concept of views. These are responsible for formatting the data received from a controller and returning the formatted result back to the controller. The controller then sends this result back to the browser.

In all the examples we've covered so far, the data passed from browsers to controllers, or between controllers and views, has been relatively simple. For instance, in Chapter3Example1, a course is represented solely by its title. However, what happens when a course comprises multiple elements, such as a course number, departmental prefix, and seat capacity? Passing several values between a Razor View and a controller method can become quite cumbersome.

This is where models come into play. Models in ASP.NET MVC serve as a crucial component in the architecture. They are responsible for handling the logic for the application's data domain. In other words, models are used for retrieving and storing model state in a database. A Model is essentially a C# class, where each class represents a data table in the database. The properties of these classes represent the columns in the table.

Models can also contain logic to validate data and behavior that can transform it to and from an invalid state. They ensure that the rules of the application are enforced consistently, even when the data source changes.

In the context of our course example, instead of passing individual elements like course number, departmental prefix, and seat capacity separately, we can encapsulate all these elements within a single 'Course' model. This approach simplifies data management and enhances the maintainability and scalability of the application.

Once a model is in place, there is no distinction between passing a string or an object. The object encapsulates all the data to be passed, simplifying the process significantly. Remember, the primary goal of using models is to handle the data logic of your application, ensuring a clean separation of concerns and easier maintainability. Models are a fundamental part of any ASP.NET MVC application, and understanding them is key to mastering the framework.

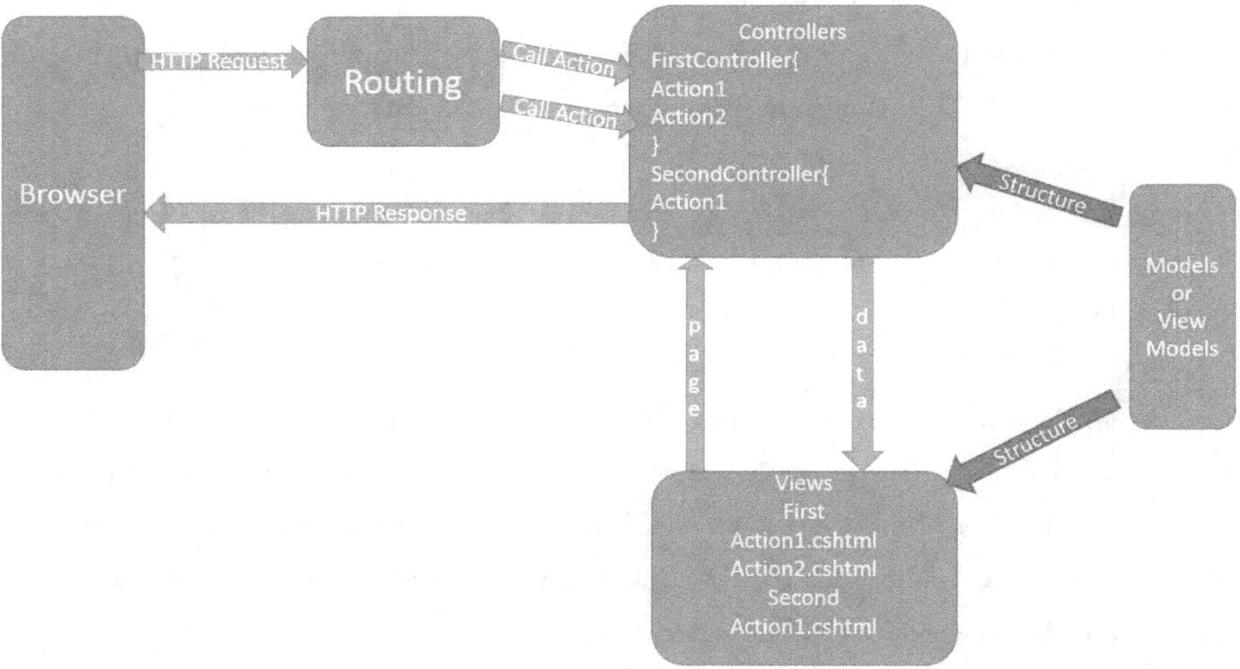

Figure 4.1 Models provide data structure for both controllers and views.

Test Your Understanding 4.1
What initiates browser requests in ASP.NET MVC controllers?
a. CSS files
b. URL or HTML form submission
c. JavaScript functions
d. Database queries

Test Your Understanding 4.2
What is the primary responsibility of views in ASP.NET MVC?

a. Handling data logic
b. Formatting data from controllers
c. Retrieving data from the database
d. Enforcing application rules

Test Your Understanding 4.3
What problem arises when dealing with complex data passing between a Razor View and a controller method?
a. Data corruption
b. Code duplication
c. Cumbersome data passing
d. Inconsistent data validation

Test Your Understanding 4.4
What role do models play in ASP.NET MVC?
a. Formatting views
b. Handling data logic
c. Executing controller actions
d. Managing URL submissions

Test Your Understanding 4.5
In ASP.NET MVC, what does a Model represent?
a. A database table
b. A view template
c. A controller method
d. An HTML form

Test Your Understanding 4.6
What is the primary goal of using models in ASP.NET MVC?
a. Enhancing UI design
b. Simplifying data management
c. Reducing controller actions
d. Minimizing URL length

Test Your Understanding 4.7
How do models ASP.NET MVC ensure in consistency in enforcing application rules?
a. By formatting views
b. Through handling data logic
c. By executing controller actions
d. Managing URL submissions

Test Your Understanding 4.8
What benefits does encapsulating complex data within a single model bring?
a. Enhanced UI design
b. Cumbersome data passing
c. Simplified data management
d. Increased URL length

Test Your Understanding 4.9
Which of the following statement best describe models in ASP.NET MVC?

a. Models handle UI design
b. Models facilitate URL management
c. Models provide data structure for controllers and views
d. Models execute controller actions

Test Your Understanding 4.10
Which of the following statements is true about models in any ASP.NET MVC application?
a. Models are identical to data.
b. Models facilitate data transfer between HTML forms and controllers.
c. Models facilitate data transfer between controllers and views.
d. Models define the structure of the data transferred between application components.

Chapter 4 Example 1

Problem:

Develop an ASP.NET MVC application, Chapter4Example1, using an empty template. The goal is to showcase all students on a page along with a link to add new students. Each student is identified by a student ID, name, and GPA. The URL for this page should be localhost/Student/AllStudent, with an initial display in the browser as follows:

<u>Add a new student</u>

All Students List

No student yet.

Clicking the "Add a new student" hyperlink will reveal an HTML form featuring three text fields and a button, as shown in Figure 4.2:

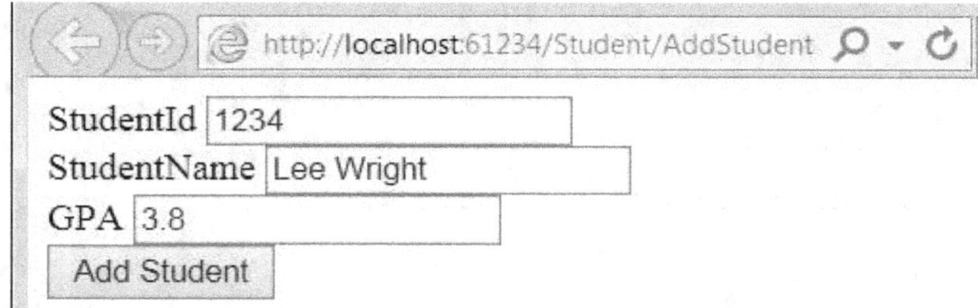

Figure 4.2 Browser display of "add student form".

Upon clicking the "Add Student" button in Figure 4.2, the new student's data will be added. The page will redirect to localhost/Student/AllStudent, showcasing all students added:

<u>Add a new student</u>

All Students List

Student ID	Student Name	GPA
1234	Lee Wright	3.8

Solution:

Step 1: Setting Up the Project

Commence by creating a new Empty ASP.NET MVC Project (.NET 8.0) named Chapter4Example1.

Ensure you update the program.cs file to integrate Routing Middleware (refer to Step 5 of Chapter 2 Example 1) and register Mvc services into the project (refer to Step 6 of Chapter 2 Example 1).

Step 2: Adding the Student Model

Start by adding a new folder named "Models" to the project. Right-click on the project, select "Add," then "New Folder," and name it "Models."

Inside the Models folder, create a new class file. In the Solution Explorer window, right-click on the Models folder, select "Add," and then "Class."

In the "Add New Item" window, opt for "Class" and name the new class "Student.cs." Click on "Add" to open the code window.

Within Student.cs, include three properties to define the Student class: StudentId, StudentName, and GPA, as illustrated below:

```
namespace Chapter4Example1.Models
{
    public class Student
    {
        public int StudentId { get; set; }
        public string? StudentName { get; set; }
        public decimal GPA { get; set; }
    }
}
```

Note: The question mark ("?") after string denotes a nullable reference type. It allows the StudentName property to accept null values, if needed, indicating that it can be null or contain a string value.

Step 3: Configuring URL localhost/Student/AllStudent

This involves three tasks: 1) Adding a controller with an action method, 2) including a corresponding Razor View file, and 3) enabling tag helpers.

Step 3a: Controller and Action Method

Create a folder named "Controllers" and add a new Controller Class named StudentController.cs.

Incorporate a List of Student within the StudentController:

```
static List<Student> allStudents = new List<Student>();
```

Ensure the correct namespace is applied by following the suggested "using" directive.

Implement an action method named AllStudent in the Student controller:

```
public IActionResult AllStudent()
{
    return View(allStudents);
}
```

This method directs to the respective view, passing all data in the allStudents List.

Step 3b: Adding the View

Create a Razor View named AllStudent.cshtml to format the allStudents data.

Within the project's Views folder, include a subfolder named "Student" and add the AllStudent.cshtml file.

Clear the default code in AllStudent.cshtml and insert the following code:

```
@model List<Chapter4Example1.Models.Student>
<p>
    <a asp-controller="Student" asp-action="AddStudent">
        Add a new student
    </a>
</p>
<h3>All Students List</h3>
@{
    if (Model.Count < 1)
    {
        <p>No student yet.</p>
    }
    else
    {
        <table border="1">
            <tr>
                <th>Student ID</th>
                <th>Student Name</th>
                <th>GPA</th>
            </tr>
            @{
                foreach (var student in Model)
                {
                    <tr>
                        <td>@student.StudentId</td>
                        <td>@student.StudentName</td>
                        <td>@student.GPA</td>
                    </tr>

                }
            }
        </table>
```

```
    }
}
```

The "@model List<Chapter4Example1.Models.Student>" line designates a list of Students as the View's model, making the passed data available in the "Model" keyword.

Step 3c: Adding Essential Files

As in Chapter Three, include necessary files for ASP.NET MVC tag helper functionality and for using a layout page across multiple views.

Right-click the "Views" folder in the Solution Explorer, add a Razor View named _ViewImports.cshtml. Add the following lines of code:

```
@using Chapter4Example1
@addTagHelper *, Microsoft.AspNetCore.Mvc.TagHelpers
```

Add a new "Razor View Start" in the "Views" folder with the default file name and content.

Create a folder named "Shared" within the "Views" folder. Inside the "Shared" folder, include a "Razor Layout" View named _Layout.cshtml with the default content.

Step 4: Testing the Current Code

Save your progress and start without debugging.

Enter localhost/Student/AllStudent in the URL. The browser display should show:

<u>Add a new student</u>

All Students List

No student yet.

Step 5: Implementing the "Add a new student" Hyperlink

To enable the functionality defined in AllStudent.cshtml, create an action method named "AddStudent" in the StudentController.cs file:

```
public IActionResult AddStudent()
{
    return View();
}
```

For this method to work, add a corresponding view named "AddStudent.cshtml" to the Student folder. Remove the default code and insert the following code:

```cshtml
@model Chapter4Example1.Models.Student
<form asp-controller="Student"
    asp-action="AddStudent" method="post">
    <label asp-for="StudentId"></label>
    <input asp-for="StudentId" />
    <br />
    <label asp-for="StudentName"></label>
    <input asp-for="StudentName" />
    <br />
    <label asp-for="GPA"></label>
    <input asp-for="GPA" />
    <br />
    <button type="submit">Add Student</button>
</form>
```

Explanation:

The `@model Chapter4Example1.Models.Student` line indicates the Student model for this view, recognizing the Student class properties: StudentId, StudentName, and GPA.

Each `<input asp-for="PropertyName" />` line generates an <input> HTML element where the PropertyName is directly tied to the respective Student class property. This construct represents a Student object and submits it to the server when the form is submitted.

During coding "AddStudent.cshtml," Visual Studio IntelliSense assists with each asp-for tag helper because of the inclusion of the Student model in the first line of the file.

Step 6: Testing the Current Code

Save your work and start without debugging.

Enter the URL: localhost/Student/AllStudent. Click the "Add a new student" link. You'll see a webpage displaying an HTML form with three text fields and a button. You can fill out the form, but at this point, clicking the submit button won't trigger any action.

Step 7: Enabling the "Add Student" Button

As per the requirements in "AddStudent.cshtml," add an action method named "AddStudent" in the StudentController.cs file. Since a method with this name already exists, change its signature and add the [HttpPost] action verb above the method using the following code:

```csharp
[HttpPost]
public IActionResult AddStudent(Student student)
{
    allStudents.Add(student);
    return RedirectToAction("AllStudent");
}
```

This method will receive a student object containing the entered form properties. It adds the student to the allStudents list and redirects to the AllStudent action method.

Step 8: Testing the Application

Save your changes and start without debugging.

Enter the URL: localhost/Student/AllStudent.

Click the "Add a new student" link. Fill in the form with some data, and click the "Add Student" button.

You should now see all students displayed in a table.

Test Your Understanding 4.11
_______ define the structure of data passed between controllers and views.
a. Controllers
b. Views
c. Models
d. ViewData

Test Your Understanding 4.12
A model in ASP.NET Core MVC is just a C# _________.
a. model
b. controller
c. view
d. class

Test Your Understanding 4.13
In an ASP.NET Razor View, the keyword ________ represents the model used in the view.
a. static
b. Model
c. View
d. Controller

Test Your Understanding 4.14
If the following line appears on an ASP.NET Razor View file,
@model Chapter4Example1.Models.Student
The page can receive or return _______.
a. a Student class
b. an instance of Student
c. a list of student objects
d. a list of Student classes

Test Your Understanding 4.15
If the following line appears on an ASP.NET Razor View file,
@model List<Chapter4Example1.Models.Student>
The page can receive or return ________.
a. a Student class
b. an instance of Student
c. a list of student objects

d. a list of Student classes

Test Your Understanding 4.16
The following code in a form of a Razor View file:
    <input asp-for="StudentId" **/>**
Will become an <input> element with __________ when the file is sent to the browser.
a. id attribute value of "StudentId"
b. asp-for attribute value of "StudentId"
c. type attribute value of "StudentId"
d. student attribute value of "StudentId"

Test Your Understanding 4.17
When adding a new Razor view to a project, you may want to search the term "View" in the "add new item" window. Which of the following view types will NOT show?
a. Razor Layout
b. Razor View Layout
c. Razor View Start
d. Razor View Imports

Test Your Understanding 4.18
What does the following action method do?
```
public IActionResult AddStudent()
{
    return View();
}
```
a. Add a student to the Razor view for browser display.
b. Add a student to the list and return the Razor view for browser display.
c. Find a Razor view called AddStudent and return it to the browser for display.
d. Find a Razor view called AddStudent, add a student to the list, and return the Razor view.

Test Your Understanding 4.19
What does the following action method do? Assuming allStudents is a C# List of Student.
```
public IActionResult AllStudent()
{
    return View(allStudents);
}
```
a. Return the list of students to the browser for display.
b. Return the list of allStudents from the Razor view for browser display.
c. Find a Razor view called AllStudents and return it to the browser for display.
d. Find a Razor view called AllStudent, pass the list of allStudents, and return the Razor view.

Test Your Understanding 4.20
In addition to add a student to allStudent List, what does the following action method do?
```
[HttpPost]
public IActionResult AddStudent(Student student)
{
    allStudents.Add(student);
    return RedirectToAction("AllStudent");
}
```
a. Call the AllStudent action method in the same controller.
b. Return the list of allStudents from the Razor view for browser display.
c. Find a Razor view called AllStudents and return it to the browser for display.
d. Find a Razor view called AllStudent, pass the list of allStudents, and return the Razor view.

Programming Challenge 4.1

Set up an ASP.NET MVC application using the empty template to exhibit a list of employees and enable adding new ones. Each employee includes an ID, name, and hourly wage, managed through a model class named Employee. Access the employee list via the URL: localhost/Employee/AllEmployee, will display:.

Figure 4.3 Employee List Display

Clicking the "Add a new employee" link in Figure 4.3 reveals an HTML form, allowing users to input details for a new employee, as illustrated in Figure 4.4.

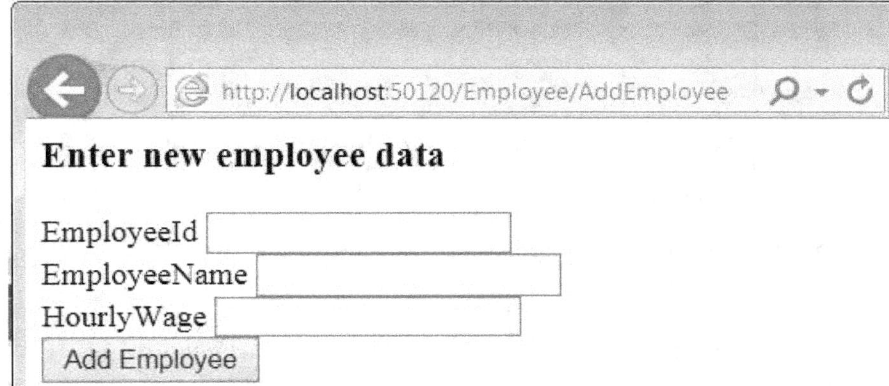

Figure 4.4 Add Employee Form

Once the data is entered and the "Add Employee" button is clicked, the new employee is included. Subsequently, the page displays all employees, including the newly added one, in a tabulated format, as presented in Figure 4.5:

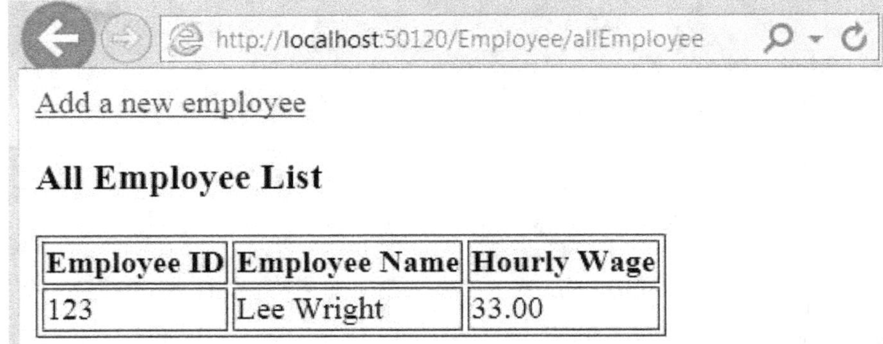

Employee ID	Employee Name	Hourly Wage
123	Lee Wright	33.00

Figure 4.5 List of Employees

4.2 ViewModels: Bridging Multiple Models in Razor Views

In MVC architecture, views are empowered by a "strongly typed" model, signifying direct access to a class within the view itself. Consider a scenario where the AddStudent.cshtml Razor View uses the Student class as its model. This setup grants the view intrinsic knowledge of the Student class, facilitating an intuitive relationship between form fields and class properties. For instance, the StudentId input field in the form aligns precisely with the StudentId property of the Student class. Upon form submission, the view effortlessly compiles an instance of the class and dispatches it to the appropriate action method.

However, what if a single view necessitates the interaction of two distinct classes? MVC doesn't inherently support adding multiple models to a singular view. Enter the ViewModel – a strategic solution. The ViewModel acts as a container, amalgamating the required models into a cohesive structure. By leveraging this ViewModel in a view, akin to how a model is used, you can seamlessly integrate and work with multiple classes simultaneously. Both models and viewmodels serve as fundamental classes within the MVC framework, each with its specific purpose in enhancing flexibility and structuring data flow within views.

ViewModels provide a powerful abstraction layer, allowing complex views to handle disparate data sources and different model structures. This approach fosters a more cohesive and organized presentation layer, streamlining the view's interaction with multiple data entities. It enables comprehensive and structured data management within the view, enhancing its efficiency and maintainability.

By employing ViewModels, developers can transcend the limitations of a single model and build robust, composite views that cater to diverse data requirements, ultimately contributing to a more flexible and scalable application architecture.

Test Your Understanding 4.21
In MVC, what does a "strongly typed" model imply regarding views?
a. The model is weakly linked to views.
b. Views cannot access the model directly.
c. Views have direct access to a specific class.
d. The model is unrelated to view interactions.

Test Your Understanding 4.22
What purpose does a ViewModel serve in MVC?
a. To limit the number of classes used in a view.
b. To create a substitute for models in views.
c. To consolidate and manage multiple models.
d. To eliminate the need for models in a view.

Test Your Understanding 4.23
How does a ViewModel enhance view flexibility?
a. By allowing direct access to multiple views.
b. By restricting data sources within a view.
c. By amalgamating diverse data sources.
d. By isolating data from the view.

Test Your Understanding 4.24
What role do both models and viewmodels play in MVC?
a. They serve identical purposes.
b. Models handle views while viewmodels manage data.
c. Models focus on data flow while viewmodels manage views.
d. Each serves a specific purpose in structuring data flow within views.

Test Your Understanding 4.25
What advantage do ViewModels offer in complex views?
a. They obviate the need for multiple models.
b. They simplify views by isolating data.
c. They complicate view interactions with data.
d. They allow handling of diverse data structures.

Test Your Understanding 4.26
How do ViewModels contribute to application scalability?
a. By limiting data sources in a view.
b. By constraining interactions between views and models.
c. By allowing for flexible and composite views.
d. By removing the need for models in views.

Chapter 4 Example 2

Problem:

Create an ASP.NET MVC application using an empty template to showcase a student management system. The objective is to display a comprehensive list of students and facilitate the addition of new students. Each student profile includes details such as student ID, name, GPA, and major. A major is characterized by a major ID and major name. The URL for accessing this page should be localhost/Student/AllStudent. The initial browser display appears as follows:

<u>Add a Student</u>

No students yet

Upon clicking the "Add a Student" link, a user-friendly HTML form is presented, allowing users to input new student details including Student ID, name, and GPA. Notably, the Major name is presented as a dropdown menu within the form. The form also encompasses an "Add Student" button for submission.

Post-submission of the "Add Student" button on the HTML form, the newly entered student information is added to the existing student list. Subsequently, the page refreshes to display the updated and comprehensive list of all students currently enrolled.

Solution:

Step 1: Set Up the Project

Initiate a new ASP.NET MVC Project with an Empty template using .NET 8.0, naming it Chapter4Example2. Remember to update the program.cs file to include routing and MVC services, similar to previous configurations.

Step 2: Add Student and Major Models

For better organization and the advantages of "strongly typed" classes, incorporate models early in the project setup. Follow these steps:

Create a folder named Models within the project.

Inside the Models folder, add a class named Student. Implement it as follows:

```csharp
namespace Chapter4Example2.Models
{
    public class Student
    {
        public int StudentId { get; set; }
        public string StudentName { get; set; }
        public decimal GPA { get; set; }
        public Major Major { get; set; }
    }
}
```

Add another class named Major within the same Models folder. Define it with the following structure:

```csharp
namespace Chapter4Example2.Models
{
    public class Major
    {
        public int MajorId { get; set; }
        public string MajorName { get; set;}
    }
}
```

Step 3: Enable URL Routing for All Students View

Step 3a: Create the Controller and Action Method

Add Controller:

Create a "Controllers" folder within the project.

Inside "Controllers," add a new MVC Controller named StudentController.cs.

Define a List within the Controller:

Add a field named "allStudents" as a List<Student> to store added students.

```
static List<Student> allStudents = new List<Student>();
```

Include another list, "allMajors," comprising initial majors for user selection when adding a new student.

```
List<Major> allMajors = new List<Major>
{
    new Major(){MajorId = 1, MajorName="Computer Science"},
    new Major(){MajorId = 2, MajorName="Business Computing"},
    new Major(){MajorId=999, MajorName="Undecided"}
};
```

Add Action Method:

Implement an action method named AllStudent within the controller:

```
public IActionResult AllStudent()
{
    return View(allStudents);
}
```

This method passes the "allStudents" list to a view which formats the data to be displayed in the browser.

Step 3b: Create the View

Add a folder named "Views" to the project.

Inside "Views," create a subfolder "Student."

Within "Student," add a View named AllStudent.cshtml and input the following code:

```
@model List<Chapter4Example2.Models.Student>
<p>
    <a asp-controller="Student" asp-action="AddStudent">
        Add a new student
    </a>
</p>
<h3>All Students List</h3>
@{
    if (Model.Count < 1)
    {
        <p>No student yet.</p>
    }
    else
```

```
{
    <table border="1">
        <tr>
            <th>Student ID</th>
            <th>Student Name</th>
            <th>GPA</th>
            <th>Major</th>
        </tr>
        @{
            foreach (var student in Model)
            {
                <tr>
                    <td>@student.StudentId</td>
                    <td>@student.StudentName</td>
                    <td>@student.GPA</td>
                    <td>@student.Major.MajorName</td>
                </tr>
            }
        }
    </table>
    }
}
```

Step 3c: Implement Necessary View Files

Include the following files as done in Step3c of Chapter 4 Example 1: _ViewImports.cshtml, _Layout.cshtml, and _ViewStart.cshtml.

Step 4: Validate the Current Code

Save the progress. Start the application without debugging. Enter the URL: localhost/Student/AllStudent. The browser display should appear as follows:

<u>Add a student</u>

Not students yet.

Step 5: Integrate a ViewModel

Generate a ViewModel encompassing both the Student and Major classes for use in a single view.

In the project, add a folder named "ViewModels."

Inside "ViewModels," add a class called StudentAddStudentViewModel.cs, with the provided code snippet:

```
using Chapter4Example2.Models;
using Microsoft.AspNetCore.Mvc.Rendering;

namespace Chapter4Example2.ViewModels
```

```
{
    public class StudentAddStudentViewModel
    {
        public Student Student { get; set; }
        public Major Major { get; set; }
        public SelectList MajorList { get; set; }
    }
}
```

Explanation:

The SelectList is a class from the Microsoft.AspNetCore.Mvc.Rendering namespace, allowing the creation

of a collection that represents selectable items for a dropdown list in the view. The MajorList is a property

in the StudentAddStudentViewModel that holds a list of Majors. This property is usually populated in the

controller action and passed to the view. It's commonly used to provide a list of instructors to populate a

dropdown or list within a form, allowing users to select an instructor when adding a course, for example.

Step 6: Implement "Add a student" Hyperlink Functionality

The hyperlink points to an action method named "AddStudent" in the StudentController.cs.

Implement the "AddStudent" action method within the controller. Use the provided code snippet. This

method creates a SelectList for major selection and populates the ViewModel.

```
public IActionResult AddStudent()
{
    var majorDisplay = allMajors.Select
        (x => new { Id = x.MajorId, Value = x.MajorName });
    StudentAddStudentViewModel vm = new StudentAddStudentViewModel();
    vm.MajorList = new SelectList(majorDisplay, "Id", "Value");
    return View(vm);
}
```

Create the AddStudent.cshtml view in the Views/Student folder and input the provided code. This view

employs the StudentAddStudentViewModel to display form elements and a dropdown list for major

selection.

```
@model Chapter4Example2.ViewModels.StudentAddStudentViewModel
<h3>Add a new student</h3>
<form asp-controller="Student"
    asp-action="AddStudent" method="post">
  <label asp-for="Student.StudentId"></label>
  <input asp-for="Student.StudentId" /><br />
  <label asp-for="Student.StudentName"></label>
  <input asp-for="Student.StudentName" /><br />
  <label asp-for="Student.GPA"></label>
  <input asp-for="Student.GPA" /><br />
  <label asp-for="Major.MajorName"></label>
```

```html
    <select asp-for="Major.MajorId"
    asp-items="@Model.MajorList"></select><br />
    <button type="submit">Add Student</button>
</form>
```

Step 7: Validate the Implemented Code

Save your changes. Start the application without debugging. Enter the URL: localhost/Student/AllStudent.

Click on the "Add a student" link. The page should display an HTML form with the implemented features.

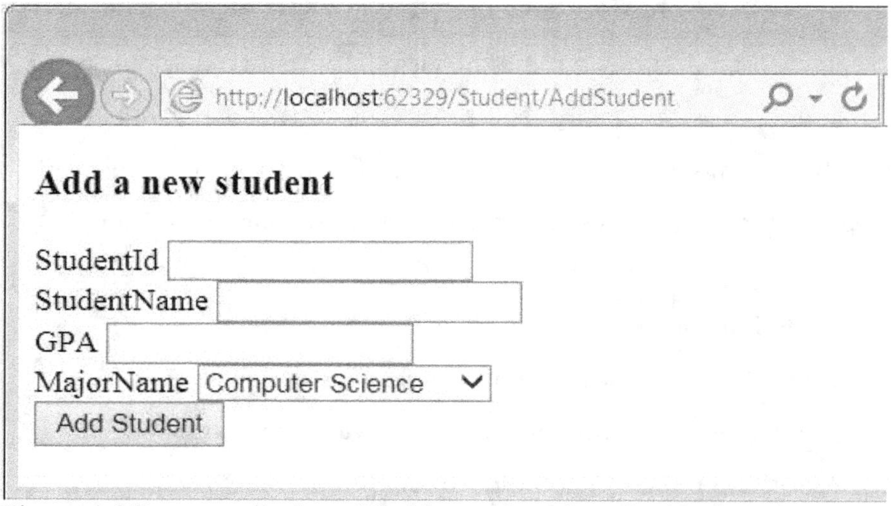

http://localhost:62329/Student/AddStudent

Add a new student

StudentId

StudentName

GPA

MajorName   Computer Science

Add Student

Figure 4.6 Browser display of "add a student form" with the major name dropdown.

Step 8: Activate the "Add Student" Button Functionality

The "Add a new student" form has the following code snippet:

```html
<form asp-controller="Student" asp-action="AddStudent" method="post">
```

To activate this functionality, an action method named "AddStudent" needs to be implemented in the Student controller. However, as a method with that name already exists in the Student controller, the new method should have a different signature and utilize the action verb of "[HttpPost]."

Insert the provided code snippet into the Student controller. This method processes the data from the form and updates the student records accordingly.

```csharp
[HttpPost]
public IActionResult AddStudent(StudentAddStudentViewModel vm)
{
    var major = allMajors.FirstOrDefault(m => m.MajorId==vm.Major.MajorId);
    vm.Student.Major= major;
    allStudents.Add(vm.Student);
    return RedirectToAction("AllStudent");
}
```

The FirstOrDefault() is a method in LINQ that returns the first element of a sequence, or a default value if no element is found. It's not a method of the List class. HTML forms often correspond to two action methods in ASP.NET MVC architecture. The default HttpGet method displays a blank form, while the HttpPost method processes data from the form.

Step 9: Validate the Implemented Code

Save your project. Initiate the application without debugging. Enter the URL: localhost/Student/AllStudent. Click on the "Add a student" link. Complete the fields on the "add new student" form. Click the "Add Student" button. The subsequent page should exhibit a table displaying all students.

Test Your Understanding 4.27
When there are more than one models needed on a Razor View, __________ is often used.
a. MultipleModel
b. DoubleModel
c. ControllerModel
d. ViewModel

Test Your Understanding 4.28
Suppose a viewmodel is called MyViewModel which has two classes: Student and Major as its properties. The Student class has a property called StudentId. How do you access the StudentId property in the Razor View that has MyViewModel as the model?
a. StudentId
b. Student.StudentId
c. Major.Student.StudentId
d. Student.Major.StudentId

Test Your Understanding 4.29
You often use two action methods with the same name for one HTML form. One is _______ and the other is _______.
a. HTTP, FTP
b. HttpGet, HttpPost
c. an error, correct
d. Send, Receive

Test Your Understanding 4.30
Usually, an action method will call a corresponding Razor View with the same name. Sometimes, an action method can call another action method by using _________.
a. RedirectToAction("NameOfAnotherActionMethod")
b. NameOfAnotherActionMethod
c. GoTo("NameOfAnotherActionMethod")
d. This is impossible in ASP.NET Core MVC

Test Your Understanding 4.31
C# List class has a method called ________ that can be used to find the first element in the List with given condition.
a. FindFirst()
b. FindFirstOrDefault()

c. FirstOrDefault()
d. SearchFirst()

Test Your Understanding 4.32
The _______ is a method in LINQ that returns the first element of a sequence.
a. FindFirst()
b. FindFirstOrDefault()
c. FirstOrDefault()
d. SearchFirst()

Test Your Understanding 4.33
The `using Microsoft.AspNetCore.Mvc.Rendering;` directive is needed for _______ type.
a. Microsoft
b. AspNetCore
c. MajorList
d. SelectList

Test Your Understanding 4.34
The SelectList type can be used for the _______ element of an HTML form.
a. <select>
b. <selectlist>
c. <list>
d. <dropdown>

Programming Challenge 4.2

Develop an ASP.NET Core MVC application designed to showcase a comprehensive list of employees, accompanied by a link facilitating the addition of a new employee. Each employee entry comprises an employee ID, name, hourly wage, and department affiliation. The department, a distinct entity, encompasses a department ID and name.

The presentation of employees is organized in a tabular format, with each employee represented as a row within the table. Both the employee and department are encapsulated within classes. Accessing this feature requires navigating to the URL: localhost/Employee/AllEmployee, following the structure depicted below:

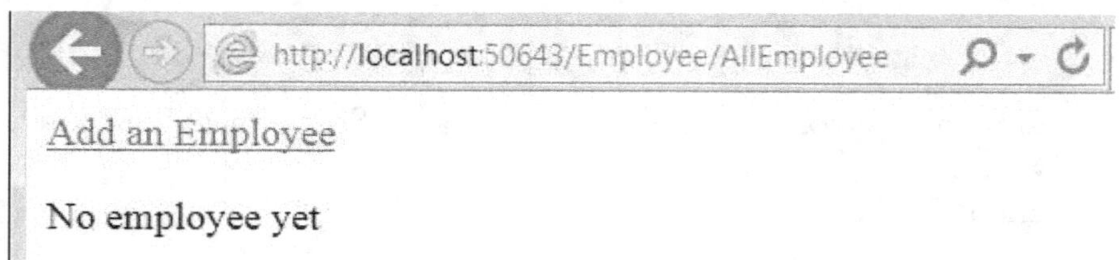

Figure 4.7: Browser view of localhost/Employee/AllEmployee

Clicking on the "Add an employee" link within Figure 4.7 triggers the display of an HTML form (Figure 4.8) enabling users to input details for a new employee. Notably, the department selection is facilitated through a dropdown list comprising dynamically fetched department names, ensuring they are not hardcoded in the MVC Razor View. The application utilizes the following department dataset:

Department ID	Department Name
1	Accounting
2	Information Technology
3	Marketing

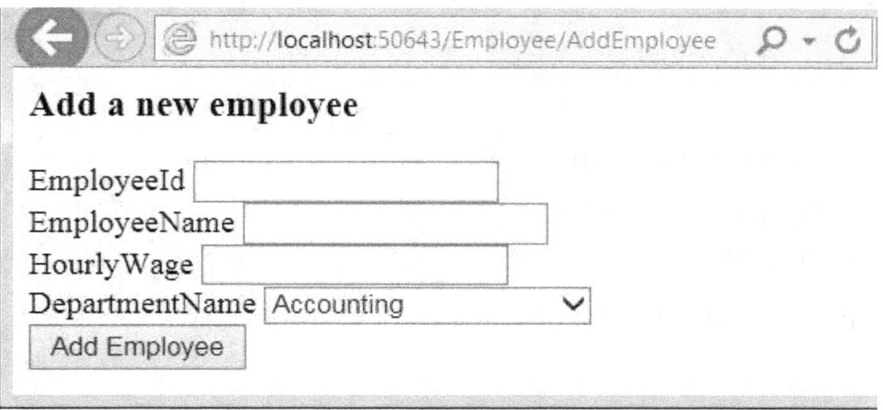

Figure 4.8: Browser view for localhost/Employee/AddEmployee

Users interact with the form displayed in Figure 4.9 to input data for a new employee.

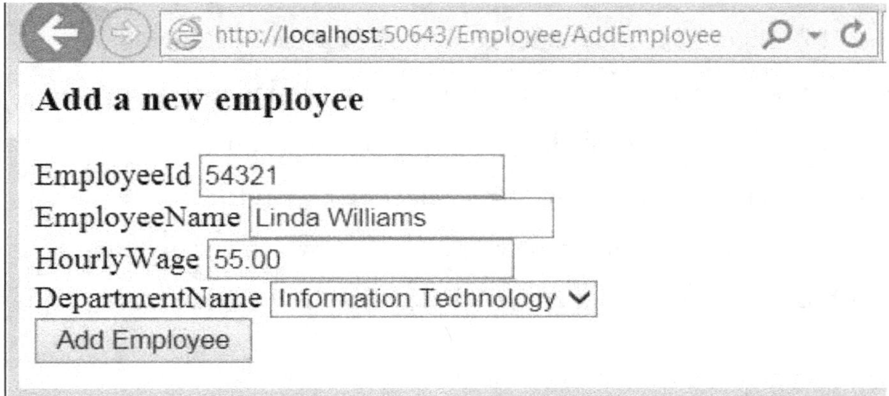

Figure 4.9: Form for adding a new employee with sample data

Upon clicking the "Add Employee" button within Figure 4.9, the application seamlessly incorporates the new employee. Subsequently, the succeeding page showcases all recently added employees (Figure 4.10).

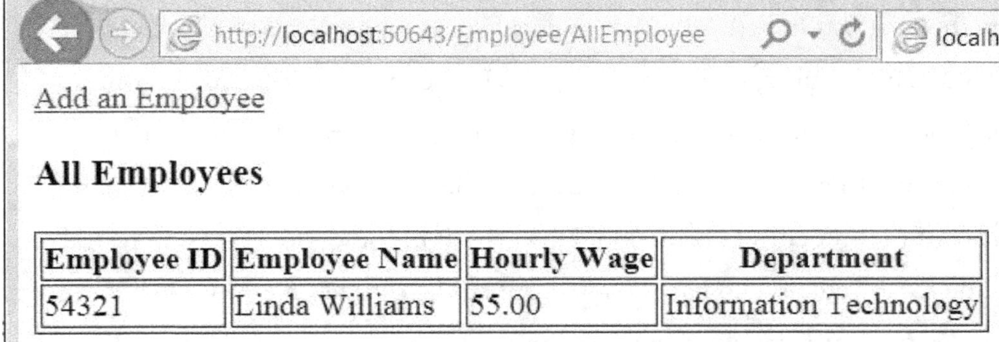

Employee ID	Employee Name	Hourly Wage	Department
54321	Linda Williams	55.00	Information Technology

Figure 4.10: Browser view for localhost/Employee/AllEmployee after adding one employee

4.3 Introduction to SOLID Principles

As you delve deeper into ASP.NET MVC, a framework rooted in the object-oriented programming language C#, the need for robust organizational principles becomes evident. While initially grouping statements into methods and methods into classes may suffice, the increasing complexity of applications demands a more sophisticated approach to software design.

In the preceding chapter, you gained insights into three foundational software design principles. Now, we embark on a journey to explore the five principles encapsulated by SOLID, a set of principles introduced and promoted by Michael Feathers and Robert Martin (Martin, 2017). In this section, our focus is on the first principle represented by the letter S in SOLID—the Single Responsibility Principle (SRP).

4.3.1 Understanding the Single Responsibility Principle (SRP)

The Single Responsibility Principle builds upon the MVC framework's initial benefit of "separation of concerns," emphasizing the importance of each class having a singular responsibility, entirely encapsulated by that class (Joshi, 2016; Nebro et al., 2015). It goes beyond the separation of concerns within the MVC components—Controllers, Views, and Models—and advocates for high cohesion within individual classes, fostering higher-quality software (Krishna, 2017). A "responsibility" in this context is defined as "a reason for change" (Martin, 2002). The SRP asserts that each class should have only one reason for change. Consider the StudentController class, illustrated in Step 2 of Chapter 4 Example 1, which encapsulates a single reason for change—modifications related to the student entity. All three methods within this class are intricately tied to the Student entity.

4.3.2 Challenges of Multiple Responsibilities

To grasp the essence of SRP, let's explore the potential issues arising when a class takes on multiple responsibilities. Suppose, for instance, that the StudentController class, responsible for displaying all students, introduces a new method—PostGrade(). While seemingly logical, a problem emerges when changes are required. The AllStudent() method, designed to display all students, inadvertently becomes entwined with the PostGrade() method. Now, if a student drops a course, the display functionality is impacted by the grading functionality. In other words, if a student decides to drop a course, the system should still allow for the display of the student's information. However, it becomes imperative to restrict instructors from posting a grade for a student who has already dropped the course. In essence, while we aim to maintain visibility of the student's record, certain actions, such as posting grades, should be appropriately controlled to align with the student's enrollment status.

4.3.3 Unveiling Hidden Complexities

In small projects, the presence of multiple responsibilities within a controller may not be immediately apparent. For instance, consider the HomeController.cs in Chapter 1 Example 1, housing two action methods for seemingly unrelated responsibilities. However, as a project evolves, maintaining clarity in the face of changing requirements becomes increasingly challenging.

4.3.4 The Long-Term Benefits of SOLID Principles

While the benefits of sound architectural principles may not be immediately evident in small projects, the SOLID principles provide a guiding compass as your project expands and undergoes maintenance. The Single Responsibility Principle, as the foundational element of SOLID, sets the stage for clean, maintainable, and scalable software architecture. As you navigate through the subsequent chapters, the SOLID principles will continue to illuminate the path toward effective software design and development.

Test Your Understanding 4.35
The "S" in the SOLID principle stands for __________.
a. separation of concerns
b. single responsibility principle
c. StudentController
d. step by step principle

Test Your Understanding 4.36
The __________ suggests that each class should have only one responsibility and this responsibility should be entirely encapsulated by the class
a. separation of concerns
b. single responsibility principle
c. StudentController
d. step by step principle

Test Your Understanding 4.37
A responsibility in SRP is defined as __________.
a. a reason for change
b. duty of a team member
c. accountability of a manager
d. having control over an application

Test Your Understanding 4.38
What is the focus of the Single Responsibility Principle (SRP) in ASP.NET MVC?
a. Separation of files
b. Separation of concerns
c. Separation of methods
d. Separation of data

Test Your Understanding 4.39
What does a "responsibility" mean in the context of the SRP?
a. A class feature
b. A code snippet
c. A reason for change
d. A data type

Test Your Understanding 4.40
Which of the following is NOT a benefit for high cohesion within individual classes, according to SRP?
a. It reduces class complexity
b. It fosters higher-quality software
c. It simplifies MVC components
d. It enhances program security

Test Your Understanding 4.41
What issue might arise when a class takes on multiple responsibilities, as per SRP?
a. Slow down program performance
b. Reduced code responsibilities
c. Potential entanglement of functionalities
d. Increased number of modules necessary for a simple project

Test Your Understanding 4.42
In the context of SRP, what does the term "unveiling hidden complexities" refer to?
a. Revealing concealed features in a class
b. Identifying potential software bugs
c. Recognizing challenges in small projects
d. Exposing intricacies as a project evolves

Test Your Understanding 4.43
What is the focus of the SOLID principles in software architecture?
a. Code efficiency
b. Robust organizational principles
c. User interface design
d. Database optimization

Test Your Understanding 4.44
What is the primary reason for introducing the Single Responsibility Principle (SRP) in ASP.NET MVC?
a. To minimize the number of classes
b. To ensure every class has a reason for change
c. To separate MVC components entirely
d. To increase code duplication

Test Your Understanding 4.45
Which of the following is NOT a reason that the presence of multiple responsibilities within a controller be less apparent in small projects?
a. Small projects have fewer responsibilities
b. Controllers in small projects are more organized
c. Limited interactions in small projects
d. The scale of the project hides complexities

Test Your Understanding 4.46
What potential issue does the scenario of a StudentController with both display and grading functionalities illustrate?
a. Improved code modularity
b. Clear separation of concerns
c. Potential entanglement of responsibilities
d. Efficient data encapsulation

Test Your Understanding 4.47
In what way does SRP contribute to clean, maintainable, and scalable software architecture?
a. By reducing the number of classes
b. By enforcing a singular reason for change in each class
c. By minimizing code duplication
d. By emphasizing MVC components

Test Your Understanding 4.48
Which of the following is NOT a significance of understanding SRP in small projects?
a. Immediate project benefits
b. Enhanced code readability
c. Early detection of hidden complexities
d. Less code for MVC structure

Test Your Understanding 4.49
According to SRP, what defines a responsibility within a class?
a. A class feature
b. A reason for change
c. A data structure
d. A method implementation

Test Your Understanding 4.50
What distinguishes SRP from the MVC framework's separation of concerns?
a. MVC focuses on data encapsulation
b. SRP emphasizes code modularity
c. MVC concerns separate methods
d. SRP advocates high cohesion within classes

Test Your Understanding 4.51
What does SRP assert regarding the relationship between a class and reasons for change?
a. A class can have multiple reasons for change
b. A class should have no reason for change
c. A class should have only one reason for change
d. A class is not affected by reasons for change

4.4 Chapter Summary

This chapter delves into the core of MVC models—C# classes defining data structures for controllers and views, fostering seamless communication between them. All models find their place within the project's

Models folder for clarity. You've also encountered view models, tailored C# classes for views requiring data from multiple models. While some advocate a one-to-one relationship between view models and Razor views, this book prioritizes understanding over strict adherence. Finally, the chapter introduces the SOLID principle, notably the single responsibility principle, empowering the creation of more resilient, comprehensible classes, minimizing maintenance efforts.

4.5 Review Questions

Question 4.1
In Chapter Three, you learned how to pass data from a controller to a view without using a model. Explain the role of models in the communication between a controller and a view.
Question 4.2
Both models and view models define data structure. What's the difference?
Question 4.3
Many beginners of ASP.NET MVC are confused between the data and the model. They think the two are the same. Provide a brief explanation for the differences of the two with examples.
Question 4.4
Explain what single responsibility principle is and why it is important.

4.6 References

Joshi, B. (2016). *Beginning SOLID Principles and Design Patterns for ASP. NET Developers*. Apress.
Krishna, J. V. V. (2017). Refactoring for High Cohesiveness in designing Robust Python Modules.
Martin, R. C. (2002). *Agile software development: principles, patterns, and practices*. Prentice Hall.
Martin, R. C. (2017). *Clean architecture: a craftsman's guide to software structure and design*. Prentice Hall Press.
Nebro, A. J., Durillo, J. J., & Vergne, M. (2015, July). Redesigning the jMetal multi-objective optimization framework. In *Proceedings of the Companion Publication of the 2015 Annual Conference on Genetic and Evolutionary Computation* (pp. 1093-1100). ACM.

4.7 Answers to Test Your Understanding

4.1 B; 4.2 B; 4.3 C; 4.4 B; 4.5 A; 4.6 B; 4.7 B; 4.8 C; 4.9 C; 4.10 D; 4.11 C; 4.12 D; 4.13 B; 4.14 B; 4.15 C; 4.16 A; 4.17 B; 4.18 C; 4.19 D; 4.20 A; 4.21 C; 4.22 C; 4.23 C; 4.24 D; 4.25 D; 4.26 C; 4.27 D; 4.28 B; 4.29 B; 4.30 A; 4.31 A; 4.32 C; 4.33 D; 4.34 A; 4.35 B; 4.36 B; 4.37 A; 4.38 B; 4.39 C; 4.40 D; 4.41 C; 4.42 D; 4.43 B; 4.44 B; 4.45 B; 4.46 C; 4.47 B; 4.48 D; 4.49 B; 4.50 D; 4.51 C;

Chapter 5: Entity Framework: Single Table

Chapter Learning Objectives

5.1 Utilize the Entity Framework code-first approach in a practical scenario.
5.2 Apply the steps of Entity Framework migration to create a relational database.
5.3 Implement CRUD operations on a single table within a database.
5.4 Apply the open-closed principle in designing and developing software components.

5.1 Introduction to Entity Framework

Throughout this book, we've been working with data that is ephemeral - it disappears as soon as you exit the program. To persist data beyond a single session, we need to store it in a database. This chapter introduces you to the Entity Framework and its 'code-first' approach for creating databases.

The 'code-first' approach, as the name suggests, involves writing classes (code) before creating the database. If you've ever noticed similarities between an entity in an Entity-Relationship Diagram (ERD) and a class in a Unified Modeling Language (UML) class diagram, you're well-prepared to understand the Entity Framework. Figures 5.1 and 5.2 illustrate a simple ERD and a corresponding UML class diagram, respectively.

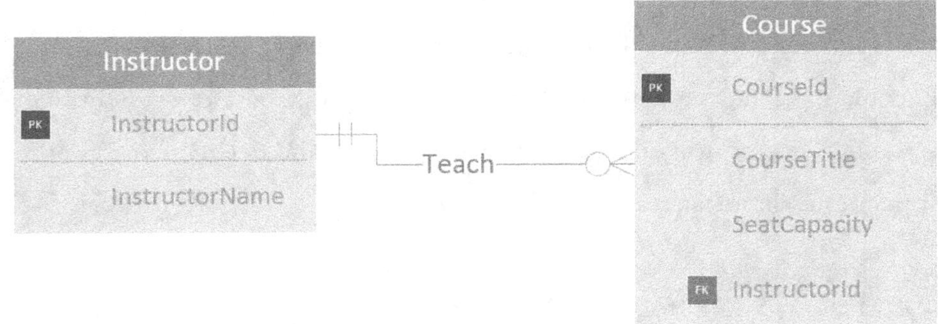

Figure 5.1 A basic ERD.

Figure 5.2 A corresponding UML class diagram.

The Entity Framework (EF) is an Object-Relational Mapping (ORM) framework that simplifies the process of setting up a database from the programming side. It enables programmers to create classes and then allows EF to automatically generate corresponding tables and manage data access in the database. For instance, using the example in Figure 5.2, a programmer simply adds the two classes to a model, and EF takes care of generating the two corresponding tables in the database.

ORM frameworks provide a high-level abstraction upon a relational database, allowing developers to write code in their preferred programming language instead of SQL to create, read, update, and delete data and schemas in their database. This means that developers can work with databases using the same object-oriented principles they use in their programming. In other words, an ORM framework helps map your code objects to your database. For instance, if you have an object in your code, using an ORM framework would allow you to map that object with a database record. This simplifies the process of data persistence in application development.

An ORM framework works by creating a mapping between the objects in an application and the database tables that store the data for those objects1. The ORM framework is responsible for converting the data stored in the database into objects in the application, and vice versa1.

When you save an object to the database using an ORM, it's broken down into smaller parts that the database can store. These parts are then saved in a logical order. When you access the object again, the program can retrieve the parts from the database to reconstruct the object.

For example, if you have a Book class in your code, an ORM would allow you to map that class with a Books table in your database. You could then interact with the Books table in the database directly through instances of the Book class in your code. This means you can create, read, update, and delete records in the Books table by performing these operations on instances of the Book class.

This abstraction provided by the ORM allows you to focus on the object-oriented logic of your application, while the ORM takes care of the details of translating between the object-oriented code and the relational database3.

The relationship of all components in MVC, including the role of EF, is summarized in Figure 5.3.

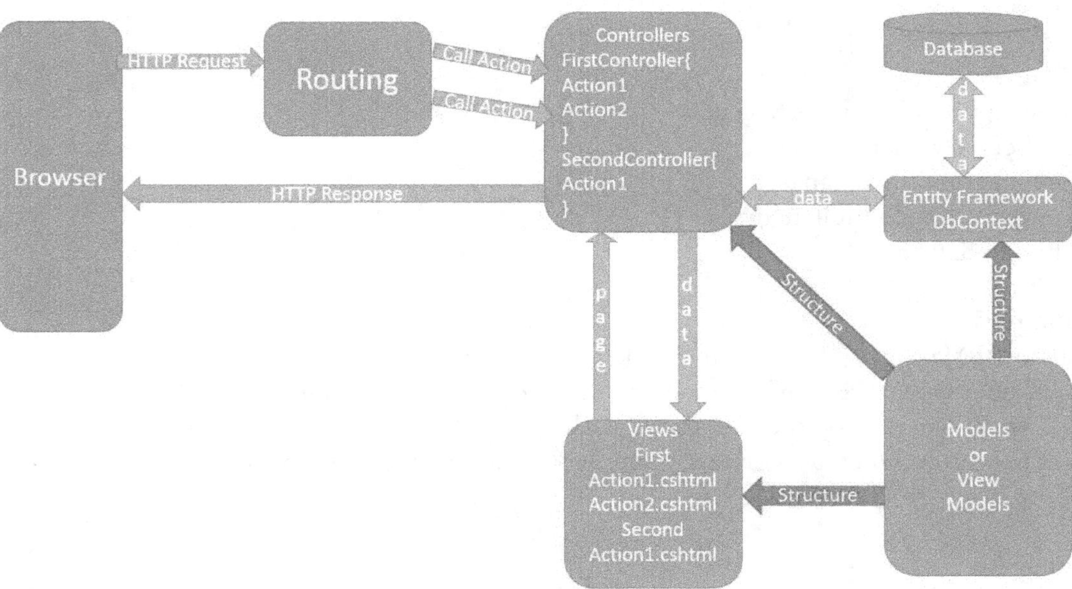

Figure 5.3 The role of the Entity Framework in MVC.

In this chapter, we will focus on working with a single table in a database. You will learn how to retrieve data from a table and display it on a webpage, as well as how to insert a record into a table using data entered by the user via an HTML form. In the following chapter, we will expand on these concepts and explore how to work with multiple tables in a database. This progression will provide you with a solid foundation for managing persistent data in your applications.

Test Your Understanding 5.1
Entity Framework (EF) is a(n) ____________ framework that allows you to work from the programming side to set up the database.
a. Relational database
b. Object-Oriented database
c. Big data
d. Object Relational Mapping

Test Your Understanding 5.2
What happens to the data we've been working with throughout the book before you learned EF once you exit the program?
a. It is stored in a database.
b. It disappears.
c. It is saved in the program's memory.
d. It is transferred to another program.

Test Your Understanding 5.3
What is the primary purpose of the Entity Framework?
a. To create databases using a 'code-first' approach.
b. To store data in a database.
c. To create classes in a database.

d. To exit the program.

Test Your Understanding 5.4
What does the 'code-first' approach in EF involve?
a. Creating the database before writing classes.
b. Writing classes before creating the database.
c. Creating the database and classes simultaneously.
d. Creating classes without a database.

Test Your Understanding 5.5
What is an Object-Relational Mapping (ORM) framework?
a. A framework that simplifies the process of setting up a database from the programming side.
b. A framework that allows programmers to create classes.
c. A framework that automatically generates corresponding tables and manages data access in the database.
d. All of the other options are correct.

Test Your Understanding 5.6
What does an ORM framework provide?
a. A high-level abstraction upon a relational database.
b. A way for developers to write code in SQL to create, read, update, and delete data and schemas in their database.
c. A way for developers to write concise SQL statements.
d. A way for developers to use artificial intelligence automatically generate databases.

Test Your Understanding 5.7
What does an ORM framework provide?
a. A way for developers to use advanced SQL statements.
b. A way for developers to write code in SQL to create, read, update, and delete data and schemas in their database.
c. A way for developers to work with databases using the same object-oriented principles they use in their programming.
d. A way for developers to use artificial intelligence automatically generate databases.

Test Your Understanding 5.8
How does an ORM framework work?
a. It creates a mapping between the objects in an application and the database tables that store the data for those objects.
b. It converts the data stored in the database into objects in the application, and vice versa.
c. It saves an object to the database by breaking it down into smaller parts that the database can store.
d. All of the other options are correct.

Test Your Understanding 5.9
What does the abstraction provided by the ORM allow you to focus on?
a. The object-oriented logic of your application.
b. The details of translating between the object-oriented code and the relational database.
c. The process of setting up a database from the programming side.
d. The process of creating classes.

Test Your Understanding 5.10
What is the role of the Entity Framework in MVC?

a. It is responsible for the view component of MVC.
b. It is responsible for the model component of MVC.
c. It is responsible for the controller component of MVC.
d. It is not involved in MVC.

Test Your Understanding 5.11
What is the purpose of the Entity Framework's 'code-first' approach?
a. To generate databases from the application's model classes.
b. To store data in a database.
c. To create classes in a database.
d. To exit the program.

Test Your Understanding 5.12
What does an ORM framework allow developers to do?
a. Write code in SQL to create, read, update, and delete data and schemas in their database.
b. Work with databases using the same object-oriented principles they use in their programming.
c. Map their code objects to SQL stored procedures in the database.
d. Write concise SQL statement.

Test Your Understanding 5.13
What happens when you save an object to the database using an ORM?
a. It is broken down into smaller parts that the database can store.
b. These parts are then saved in a logical order.
c. When you access the object again, the program can retrieve the parts from the database to reconstruct the object.
d. All the other options are correct.

Test Your Understanding 5.14
What is the purpose of using a database in a program?
a. To persist data beyond a single session.
b. To make the program run faster.
c. To make the program look more complex.
d. To use up less memory.

Test Your Understanding 5.15
What is the 'code-first' approach in the Entity Framework?
a. Writing the database before creating the classes.
b. Writing classes before creating the database.
c. Writing code and database simultaneously.
d. Writing code without a database.

Test Your Understanding 5.16
What does an ORM framework do?
a. It maps code objects to the database.
b. It maps the database to the code objects.
c. It eliminates the need for code objects.
d. It eliminates the need for a database.

Test Your Understanding 5.17
How does an ORM framework work?

a. It creates a mapping between the objects in an application and the database tables.
b. It creates a mapping between the database objects and the objects in an application.
c. It creates a mapping between the objects in an application and the objects in another application.
d. It creates a mapping between the database tables and the database tables in another database.

Test Your Understanding 5.18
What happens when you save an object to the database using an ORM?
a. The object is broken down into smaller parts that the database can store.
b. The object is enlarged to fit the database.
c. The object is converted into a database.
d. The object is deleted from the database.

Chapter 5 Example 1

Develop an ASP.NET MVC application using an empty template and EF to showcase a student database table. The page, accessible via localhost/Student/AllStudent, will exhibit a list of students in a table format, each represented as a row comprising student ID, name, and GPA. The initial browser display:

Add a student

No student in the database yet.

Clicking the "Add a student" link redirects to localhost/Student/AddStudent, presenting an HTML form with text fields for student name and GPA, alongside a submission button.

Input a student's details—e.g., "Lee Wright" with a GPA of 3.8—then click "Add Student" button. This action adds the student data to the database, redirecting the URL to localhost/Student/AllStudent, where all student records are retrieved and displayed in an HTML table:

Add a student

All Students

Student ID	Student Name	GPA
1	Lee Wright	3.8

Solution:

Step 1: Begin by creating a new Empty ASP.NET MVC Project (.NET 8.0) named Chapter5Example1. Update the program.cs file to include routing and MVC services.

Step 2: Adding Entity Framework

Integrate Entity Framework by adding the following two packages:

```
Microsoft.EntityFrameworkCore.SqlServer
```

```
Microsoft.EntityFrameworkCore.Tools
```

To add these packages, follow these steps:

In the "Solution Explorer" window, right-click on "Solution 'Chapter5Example1'" and choose "Manage NuGet Packages for Solution".

In the "NuGet - Solution" window, navigate to the "Browse" tab (indicated with a blue underline). Search for "Microsoft.EntityFrameworkCore.SqlServer" and install the appropriate version (typically 8.0.0).

Still in the "NuGet – Solution" window, search for "Microsoft.EntityFrameworkCore.Tools" and install it.

Step 3: Adding Models

Create a new folder named "Models" within the project.

Inside the Models folder, create a class named Student.cs with the following content:

```csharp
namespace Chapter5Example1.Models
{
    public class Student
    {
        public int StudentId { get; set; }
        public string StudentName { get; set; }
        public decimal GPA { get; set; }
    }
}
```

Create another class inside the Models folder named StudentDbContext.cs. This class should inherit from DbContext and contain the following content:

```csharp
using Microsoft.EntityFrameworkCore;

namespace Chapter5Example1.Models
{
    public class StudentDbContext : DbContext
    {
        public DbSet<Student> Students { get; set; }
        public StudentDbContext(DbContextOptions
            <StudentDbContext> options)
            : base(options)
        { }
    }
}.
```

You may notice red squiggly underlines indicating missing directives. Simply right-click and select the appropriate package to resolve these errors. For instance, adding 'using Microsoft.EntityFrameworkCore' will resolve the DbContext-related error.

Step 4: Add Migration to Create the Database

Open Program.cs in the Solution Explorer window. Update it to include the connection to the database.

The completed file should look like this:

```
using Chapter5Example1.Models;
using Microsoft.EntityFrameworkCore;

var builder = WebApplication.CreateBuilder(args);

var connection =
$"Server=(localdb)\\mssqllocaldb;Database=Chapter5Example;" +
    $"Trusted_Connection=True;MultipleActiveResultSets=true";
builder.Services.AddDbContext<StudentDbContext>(options =>
                options.UseSqlServer(connection));

builder.Services.AddControllersWithViews();

var app = builder.Build();

app.MapControllerRoute(
    name: "default",
    pattern: "{controller=Home}/{action=Index}/{id?}");

app.Run();
```

Open the NuGet Package Manager Console. Click on "Tools" on the menu bar, then "NuGet Package Manager", and finally, "Package Manager Console". The "Package Manager Console" will be displayed, usually at the bottom part of Visual Studio.

At the prompt (PM>), type in "Add-Migration M1" and press "Enter". Note that M1 is the name we give to the migration. You can give it any other name you can remember.

Next, still in the Package Manager Console, enter "Update-Database" and press Enter. You may receive a warning about the GPA column because the database server will pick two decimal places for the GPA column which may not fit your purpose. You can ignore this warning for this example.

The database and the table inside the database are now created. To see where the database is on your computer, click on "View" on the menu bar, then "SQL Server Object Explorer".In the "SQL Server

Object Explorer", you can see a database called "Chapter5Example" and a table called "dbo.Students".

Step 5: Add _ViewImports.cshtml, _Layout.cshtml, and _ViewStart.cshtml

The process for this step is identical to Step 3c from Chapter 4, Example 1. Remember to update the first line of _ViewImports.cshtml with the new project name..

Step 6: Display All Students from the Database

In the Problem, the URL for displaying all students is localhost/Student/AllStudent. You need a StudentController.cs controller and an AllStudent action method in that controller.

Add a folder called "Controllers" to the project.

Add an empty controller called StudentController.cs to the "Controllers" folder.

Add a method called AllStudent() in the StudentController.cs.

Add a field and a constructor in the StudentController. The completed code for the field, constructor, and AllStudent() action method follows:

```csharp
StudentDbContext db;
public StudentController(StudentDbContext db)
{
    this.db = db;
}
public IActionResult AllStudent()
{
    return View(db.Students);
}
```

Explanation:

In the constructor, this.db refers to the field db, while the db on the right side of the assignment refers to the parameter variable db. The this keyword is used to distinguish between the class field and the parameter when they have the same name. In this context, this.db = db; assigns the value of the parameter db to the class field db.

Next, add a subfolder called Student inside the Views folder.

Add a Razor View file called AllStudent.cshtml in the Student folder. Type in the code from below:

```cshtml
@model IEnumerable<Chapter5Example1.Models.Student>
<p>
    <a asp-controller="Student" asp-action="AddStudent">
        Add a student
    </a>
</p>
```

```
@{
    if (Model.Count() < 1)
    {
        <p>No student in database yet.</p>
    }
    else
    {
        <h3>All Students</h3>
        <table border="1">
            <tr>
                <th>Student ID</th>
                <th>Student Name</th>
                <th>GPA</th>
            </tr>
            @{
                foreach (var student in Model)
                {
                    <tr>
                        <td>@student.StudentId</td>
                        <td>@student.StudentName</td>
                        <td>@student.GPA</td>
                    </tr>
                }
            }
        </table>
    }
}
```

Explanation

The first line uses IEnumerable which is an interface that a List implemented. For ease of understanding, you can think of IEnumerable as a list with more flexibility.

Save. Start without Debugging.

Enter URL localhost/Student/AllStudent. You should see a browser display similar to the following:

Add a student

No student in database yet.

Step 7: Display an HTML Form for Adding a New Student

To display an HTML form for adding a new student at the URL localhost/Student/AddStudent, you need to create an AddStudent action method in the StudentController.cs. Here's how you can do it:

Open StudentController.cs and add the AddStudent action method as shown below:

```
public IActionResult AddStudent()
{
```

```
    return View();
}
```

In the Solution Explorer window, right-click the Student subfolder of the Views folder.

Add a Razor View called AddStudent.cshtml. Type in the following code:

```
@model Chapter5Example1.Models.Student
<form asp-controller="Student" asp-action="AddStudent"
     method="post">
   <label asp-for="StudentName"></label>
   <input asp-for="StudentName"/>
   <br />
   <label asp-for="GPA"></label>
   <input asp-for="GPA"/>
   <br />
   <button type="submit">Add Student</button>
</form>
```

Save your changes and start the application without debugging.

Enter the URL: localhost/Student/AddStudent. The browser should display an HTML form with two text fields and a button.

Step 8: Activating the "Add Student" Button

When you click the "Add Student" button in the form we created earlier, the form data will be submitted to the Student controller's AddStudent action method. This method uses an [HttpPost] action verb. Add the following action method to StudentController.cs:

```
[HttpPost]
public IActionResult AddStudent(Student student)
{
    db.Add(student);
    db.SaveChanges();
    return RedirectToAction("AllStudent");
}
```

After saving your changes, start the application without debugging.

Next, enter the URL: localhost/Student/AddStudent. Once the form appears, input some data. For example, enter the name "Lee Wright" with a GPA of 3.8, and then click the "Add Student" button on the form.

The student data will be saved to the database. The URL will change to localhost/Student/AllStudent, and the page will display all student data in the database.

Test Your Understanding 5.19
Which of the following packages is(are) needed to make entity framework work?
a. Microsoft.EntityFrameworkCore.SqlServer
b. Microsoft.EntityFrameworkCore.Tools
c. Microsoft.AspNetCore.All
d. Microsoft.EntityFrameworkCore.SqlServer and Microsoft.EntityFrameworkCore.Tools

Test Your Understanding 5.20
In order to map classes to database tables, a class that inherits from __________ is needed.
a. DbContext
b. Controller
c. View
d. Model

Test Your Understanding 5.21
Which of the following is the prompt for Package Manager Console?
a. $
b. :
c. PM>
d. >

Test Your Understanding 5.22
Which of the following commands creates a migration?
a. Migration M1
b. Add-Migration M1
c. Create-Migration M1
d. Generate-Migration M1

Test Your Understanding 5.23
Which of the following commands creates a database based on a migration?
a. Create-Database
b. Database
c. Update-Database
d. Add-Database

Test Your Understanding 5.24
Which window can you find the database created with migration?
a. Solution Explorer window
b. SQL Server Object Explorer
c. Database Explorer
d. Toolbox

Test Your Understanding 5.25
In order to create a database with entity framework migration, _______ method of the Services must be added to the Program.cs.
a. AddMigration
b. AddDbContext
c. AddDatabase
d. AddClass

Test Your Understanding 5.26
Suppose you want to name a database StudentDb. How do you accomplish this with EF?
a. Create a class called StudentDb.
b. Create a controller called StudentDb.
c. Add the name to the connection string in the Program.cs.
d. Add the name to the class that inherits from the DbContext.

Test Your Understanding 5.27
Based on the MVC architecture you learned, how does the data flow from database to the browser?
a. database -> controller -> view -> browser
b. database -> view -> controller -> browser
c. database -> model -> controller -> browser
d. database -> model -> view -> browser

Test Your Understanding 5.28
Suppose a StudentDbContext variable is db. How do you retrieve all records from a table called Students?
a. db.Student
b. db.Students
c. StudentDbContext.Student
d. StudentDbContext.Students

Test Your Understanding 5.29
Suppose a StudentDbContext variable is db, and a Student instance is student. How do you insert the student into a table called Students?
a. db.add(student); db.SaveChanges();
b. db.Insert(student); db.SaveChanges();
c. db.Students.add(student); db.UpdateChanges();
d. db.Students.Insert(student); db.UpdateChanges();

Programming Challenge 5.1

Create an ASP.NET 8 MVC application using an empty template to showcase employee data from a database table. This application should display all employee information in a table format and provide an option to add new employees. The application should present all employee data retrieved from a designated database table. Each employee's details (Employee ID, Employee Name, Hourly Wage) should be listed as rows within a table. Access this display page via the URL: localhost/Employee/AllEmployee.

Provide a link labeled "Add an employee" on the localhost/Employee/AllEmployee page. Clicking this link should direct users to a new URL: localhost/Employee/AddEmployee. The page at this URL should display a form for adding new employee data (name and hourly wage only, ID should be auto generated by the database). Upon entering the details, click the "Add Employee" button. When the "Add Employee" button is clicked, store the entered employee data in the database. Subsequently, the URL should change to localhost/Employee/AllEmployee. Upon redirection, the updated page should display all employee information (ID Name, and Hourly Wage), including the newly added employee from the database.

5.2 Update and Delete Records in a Table

In last section you learned how to display all records from a database table. You also learned how to insert a new record into a database table. This section, you will learn how to update an existing record in the table and how to delete a record from a table.

Chapter 5 Example 2

In this example, we extend the functionality from Chapter 5 Example 1.

Accessing localhost/Student/AllStudent presents a table view of all students. Each row in the table now contains both "Edit" and "Delete" hyperlinks, depicted as shown in the following figure.

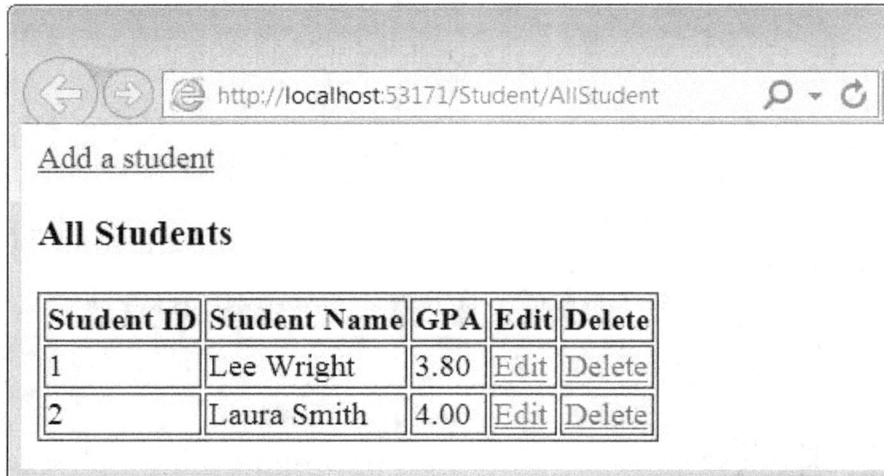

Figure 5.4 Browser display for localhost/Student/AllStudent.

Clicking the "Edit" link for a specific student (e.g., Student ID 2) opens a new window. The window displays the student's data in an editable form, enabling users to modify existing student details. For instance, altering the student's GPA from 4.0 to 3.9, as demonstrated below:

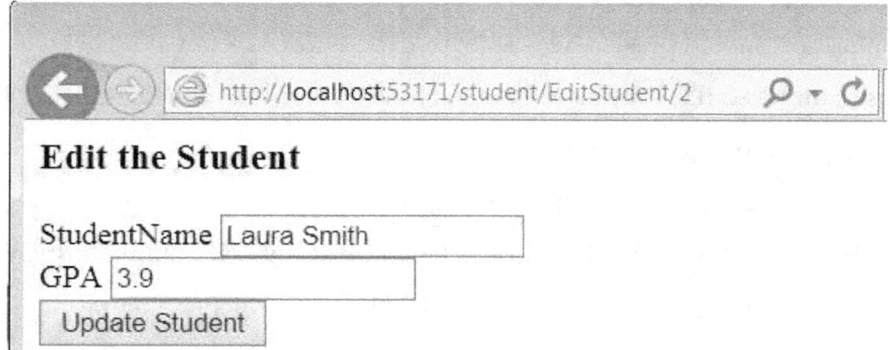

Figure 5.5 Browser display of editing the student GPA from 4.0 to 3.9.

Upon clicking the "Update Student" button, the URL changes to localhost/Student/AllStudent, reflecting the updated data from the database table.

Similarly, selecting the "Delete" link on a student's record (Figure 5.4) triggers a new page. This page prompts users to confirm the deletion with the student's data displayed.

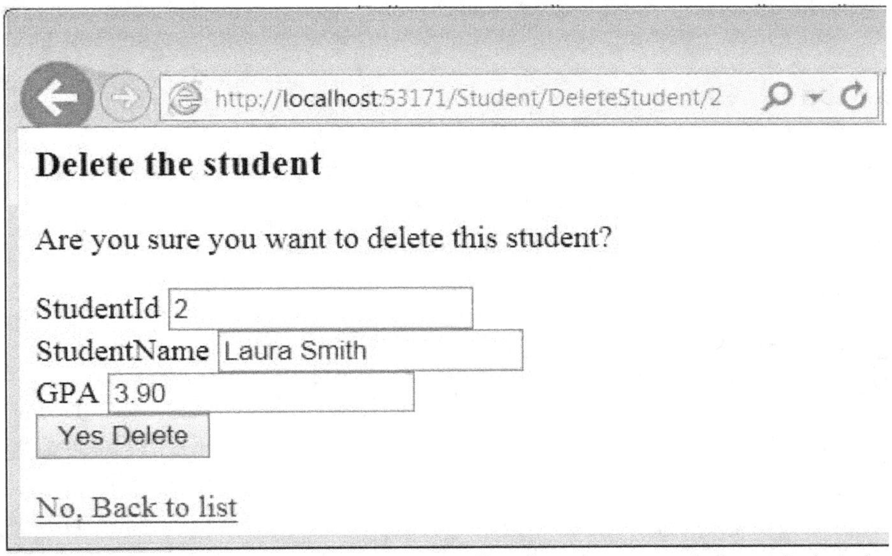

Figure 5.6 Browser display of a page allowing users to change their mind before deleting a record.

It offers a "Yes Delete" button to proceed with the deletion and a "No, Back to list" link to revert to the student list (Figure 5.4). Clicking "Yes Delete" triggers a URL change to localhost/Student/AllStudent, confirming the removal of the specified student (e.g., Laura Smith) from the database.

Solution:

Step 1: Displaying All Students with Edit and Delete Links

To implement the display of all student records with "Edit" and "Delete" links, follow these steps within the Chatper5Example1 project in Visual Studio:

Update AllStudent.cshtml file located inside the Views/Student folder.

Add the following lines to the table header row:

```
<th>Edit</th>
<th>Delete</th>
```

Inside the foreach loop, add these lines for two new cells of each row:

```
<td><a asp-action="EditStudent" asp-route-id="@student.StudentId">Edit</a></td>
<td><a asp-action="DeleteStudent" asp-route-id="@student.StudentId">Delete</a></td>
```

The updated AllStudent.cshtml should resemble the following structure:

```
@model IEnumerable<Chapter5Example1.Models.Student>
<p>
    <a asp-controller="Student" asp-action="AddStudent">
        Add a student
```

```
        </a>
</p>
@{
    if (Model.Count() < 1)
    {
        <p>No student in database yet.</p>
    }
    else
    {
        <h3>All Students</h3>
        <table border="1">
            <tr>
                <th>Student ID</th>
                <th>Student Name</th>
                <th>GPA</th>
                <th>Edit</th>
                <th>Delete</th>
            </tr>
            @{
                foreach (var student in Model)
                {
                    <tr>
                        <td>@student.StudentId</td>
                        <td>@student.StudentName</td>
                        <td>@student.GPA</td>
                        <td>
                            <a asp-action="EditStudent" asp-route-
                            id="@student.StudentId">Edit</a>
                        </td>
                        <td>
                            <a asp-action="DeleteStudent" asp-route-
                            id="@student.StudentId">Delete</a>
                        </td>
                    </tr>
                }
            }
        </table>
    }
}
```

Explanation:

The line:

```
<a asp-action="EditStudent" asp-routeid="@student.StudentId">Edit</a>
```

Generates a hyperlink to the EditStudent action method within the same controller. The student ID is passed as part of the URL for processing.

Save the changes and start the application without debugging. Access the URL localhost/Student/AllStudent in your browser. You should now see a display similar to Figure 5.4 in the problem section.

Step 2: Implementing the Edit Link in AllStudent.cshtml

Add a new action method named "EditStudent" to the StudentController.cs. Here's the code:

```
public IActionResult EditStudent(int id)
{
    Student student;
    student = db.Students.Find(id);
    return View(student);
}
```

Explanation:

This method takes an 'id' parameter. When the "Edit" link in the "All Students" table is clicked, it passes the student's ID to this controller method. The method locates the corresponding student in the Students table by ID and returns that student to the view intended for editing.

As we haven't created the corresponding view yet, add a view called "EditStudent.cshtml" in the Views/Student subfolder. Use the following Razor View code:

```
@model Chapter5Example1.Models.Student
<h3>Edit the Student</h3>
<form asp-controller="Student" asp-action="EditStudent" method="post">
    <input asp-for="StudentId" type="hidden" />
    <label asp-for="StudentName"></label>
    <input asp-for="StudentName"/>
    <br />
    <label asp-for="GPA"></label>
    <input asp-for="GPA"/>
    <br />
    <button type="submit">Update Student</button>
</form>
```

Explanation:

This view is bound to the Student model. It presents a form for editing student information, displaying fields for Student Name and GPA. The form's action points to the "EditStudent" action in the Student controller, allowing updates via HTTP POST.

Add an HTTP POST action method named "EditStudent" to the StudentController:

```
[HttpPost]
public IActionResult EditStudent(Student student)
```

```
{
    db.Update(student);
    db.SaveChanges();
    return RedirectToAction("AllStudent");
}
```

Explanation:

This method receives the updated student information via a POST request. It updates the student data in the database and redirects to the "AllStudent" action to display the updated student list.

Save and start the application without debugging. Access localhost/Student/AllStudent in your browser. Click the "Edit" link for a student). The URL changes to something like localhost/Student/EditStudent/2 (the number may vary in your app). Modify the student's GPA. Click "Update Student" to witness the GPA change.

Step 3: Implementing the Delete Link in AllStudent.cshtml

To initiate the deletion process, add a new action method named "DeleteStudent" to the StudentController.cs:

```
public IActionResult DeleteStudent(int id)
{
    Student student;
    student = db.Students.Find(id);
    return View(student);
}
```

Explanation:

This method takes an 'id' parameter to identify the student to be deleted. It retrieves the specific student from the database by ID and returns it to the corresponding deletion view.

Next, generate a view named "DeleteStudent.cshtml" in the Views/Student subfolder with the following code:

```
@model Chapter5Example1.Models.Student
<h3>Delete the Student</h3>
<p>Are you sure you want to delete this student?</p>
<form asp-controller="Student" asp-action="DeleteStudent"
      method="post">
    <label asp-for="StudentId"></label>
    <input asp-for="StudentId" readonly="readonly" />
    <br />
    <label asp-for="StudentName"></label>
    <input asp-for="StudentName" readonly="readonly"/>
```

```
        <br />
        <label asp-for="GPA"></label>
        <input asp-for="GPA" readonly="readonly"/>
        <br />
        <button type="submit">Yes Delete</button>
</form>
<p><a asp-controller="Student" asp-action="AllStudent">No. Back to list</a></p>
```

Explanation:

This view presents a confirmation page for deleting a student. It displays the student's information and offers options to proceed with deletion or return to the student list.

Finally, add an HTTP POST action method named "DeleteStudent" to the StudentController:

```
[HttpPost]
public IActionResult DeleteStudent(Student student)
{
    db.Remove(student);
    db.SaveChanges();
    return RedirectToAction("AllStudent");
}
```

Explanation:

This method receives the POST request with the student to be deleted. It removes the specified student from the database and redirects to the "AllStudent" action to display the updated student list.

Save the changes and start the application without debugging. Access localhost/Student/AllStudent in your browser. Click the "Delete" link for a student. A confirmation page appears. Click "Yes Delete" to remove the student from the table or click "No, back to list" to return to the list of students.

Test Your Understanding 5.30
In order to update a student record in a student table, the student ID must be passed to the action method. Which of the following ASP tag helpers can pass the student ID from a form to an action method?
a. asp-controller
b. asp-action
c. asp-route-id
d. asp-studentId

Test Your Understanding 5.31
Which method of DbContext can be used to insert a new row into a table?
a. Insert()
b. Add()
c. New()

d. Save()

Test Your Understanding 5.32
Which method of DbContext can be used to edit a row in a table?
a. Edit()
b. Modify()
c. Update()
d. Change()

Test Your Understanding 5.33
Which method of DbContext can be used to delete a row in a table?
a. Delete()
b. Remove()
c. Drop()
d. SaveDelete()

Test Your Understanding 5.34
To commit the insert, update, or delete to the database, _________ method of DbContext should be used.
a. SaveInsert()
b. SaveUpdate()
c. SaveDelete()
d. SaveChanges()

Test Your Understanding 5.35
What does the line <td><a asp-action="EditStudent" asp-route-id="@student.StudentId">Edit</a></td> do?
a. Generates a hyperlink to the EditStudent action method within the same controller.
b. Edits the student's record from the database.
c. Adds a new student record to the database.
d. Redirects to a different controller's method.

Test Your Understanding 5.36
What does the HTTP POST action method "EditStudent" do in the StudentController?

```
[HttpPost]
public IActionResult EditStudent(Student student)
{
    db.Update(student);
    db.SaveChanges();
    return RedirectToAction("AllStudent");
}
```

a. Retrieves student information from the database.
b. Updates student data in the database and redirects to display the updated student list.
c. Adds a new student record to the database.
d. Deletes a student record from the database.

Test Your Understanding 5.37
What does the following action method "EditStudent" do in the StudentController?

```
public IActionResult EditStudent(int id)
{
```

```
    Student student;
    student = db.Students.Find(id);
    return View(student);
}
```

a. Retrieves student information from the database and pass to the corresponding view.
b. Updates student data in the database and redirects to display the updated student list.
c. Adds a new student record to the database.
d. Deletes a student record from the database.

Programming Challenge 5.2

This challenge is an extension of Programming Challenge 5.1.

When accessing localhost/Employee/AllEmployee, the browser should present both "Edit" and "Delete" links for each employee, as illustrated in Figure 5.7.

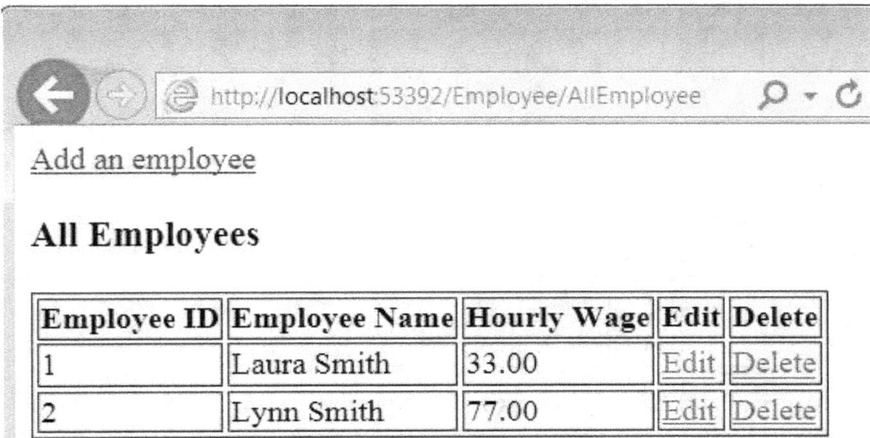

Employee ID	Employee Name	Hourly Wage	Edit	Delete
1	Laura Smith	33.00	Edit	Delete
2	Lynn Smith	77.00	Edit	Delete

Figure 5.7 showcases the browser display for localhost/Employee/AllEmployee.

Upon clicking the "Edit" link for an employee (e.g., Employee ID 2), a new window reveals the employee's existing data within a form for potential modification. Figure 5.8 represents an example of this scenario.

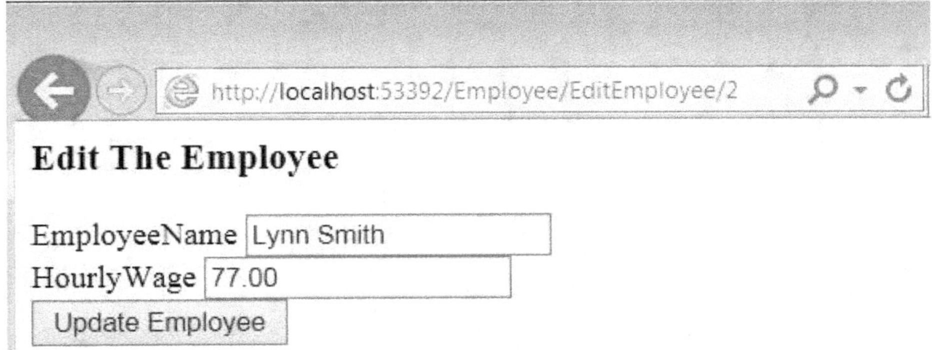

Figure 5.8 illustrates the browser display designed for updating employee details.

For instance, suppose the user alters Lynn Smith's current hourly rate from 77 to 88, and proceeds by clicking the "Update Employee" button, as shown in Figure 5.9.

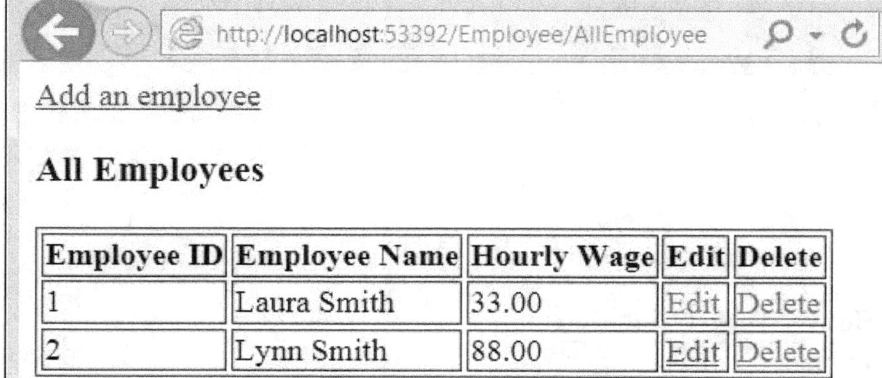

Figure 5.9 demonstrates a browser display with sample data changes.

Upon submission, the URL redirects to localhost/Employee/AllEmployee, displaying the updated data retrieved from the database table. Figure 5.10 visualizes this updated display.

Employee ID	Employee Name	Hourly Wage	Edit	Delete
1	Laura Smith	33.00	Edit	Delete
2	Lynn Smith	88.00	Edit	Delete

Figure 5.10 provides the browser display for localhost/Employee/AllEmployee.

Furthermore, if the user clicks the "Delete" link associated with an employee record from AllStudent.cshtml, a confirmation page appears. This page prompts the user to confirm the deletion action and includes a deletion button, along with a link to cancel the operation and return to the list of all employees. All form fields on this confirmation page are set to read-only. Figure 5.11 depicts the confirmation page layout.

Figure 5.11 showcases the browser display intended for deletion confirmation.

Clicking the "Yes Delete" button executes the removal of the employee record from the database.

5.3 The Open/Close Principle (OCP)

The "O" in SOLID, emphasizes that software components should welcome extensions while resisting modifications (Meyer, 1997). Businesses and software demands evolve, requiring applications to be adaptable for suitable extensions (Larman, 2001).

However, achieving this balance between openness for extension and closure for consistent results demands robust architecture (Chebanyuk & Markov, 2016). Let's illustrate the OCP with a university application example. Consider a component, Prerequisite, within the application—used by Registration (Figure 5.12).

Figure 5.12 Relationship between Prerequisite (Supplier) and Registration (Client).

Everything functions smoothly until the university desires an online four-year planner, named Planner, which also uses Prerequisite (Figure 5.13). However, Prerequisite might lack sufficiency for Planner's needs, as not all courses are available every semester.

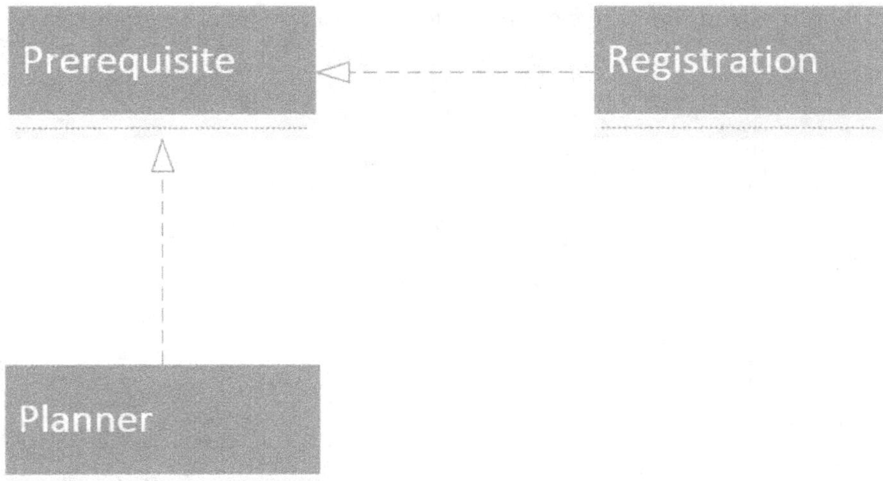

Figure 5.13 Prerequisite (Supplier) is used by both Registration (Client) and Planner (Client).

One solution might involve modifying Prerequisite to incorporate schedule details. Yet, this could impact Registration, which relies on Prerequisite, leading to potential issues.

Another approach might introduce PrerequisiteForPlanner, duplicating code from Prerequisite (Figure 5.14). While this prevents altering the original Prerequisite, it introduces code duplication and inconsistency risks.

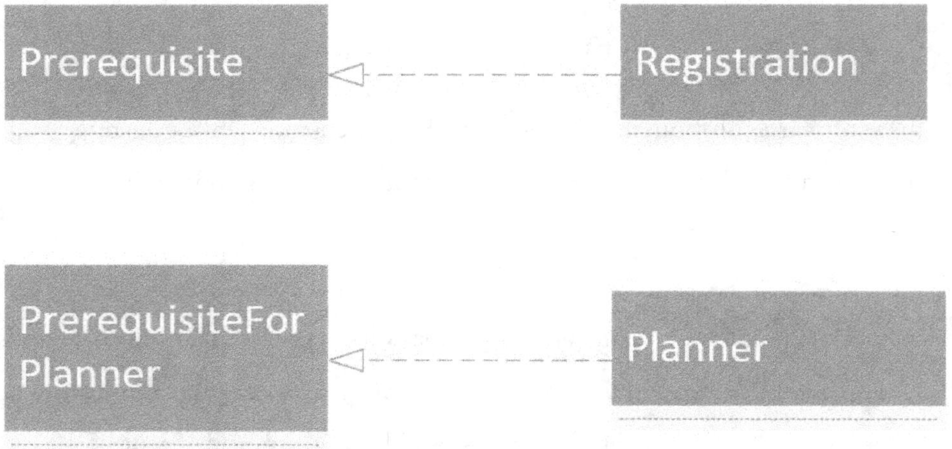

Figure 5.14 Duplication code between Prerequisite and PrerequisiteForPlanner.

To address these challenges, the third solution involves making PrerequisiteForPlanner a child of Prerequisite, enabling additions without altering Prerequisite. This preserves a single update location for the application, enhancing maintainability.

Further, exploring extension points in the base component's derived component reveals three levels of granularity (Hall, 2017), akin to C# language usage.
1. Using a virtual method in the base class (Figure 5.15 below) allows overriding for slightly different business implementations. Using virtual methods in the base class provides a moderate level of granularity.

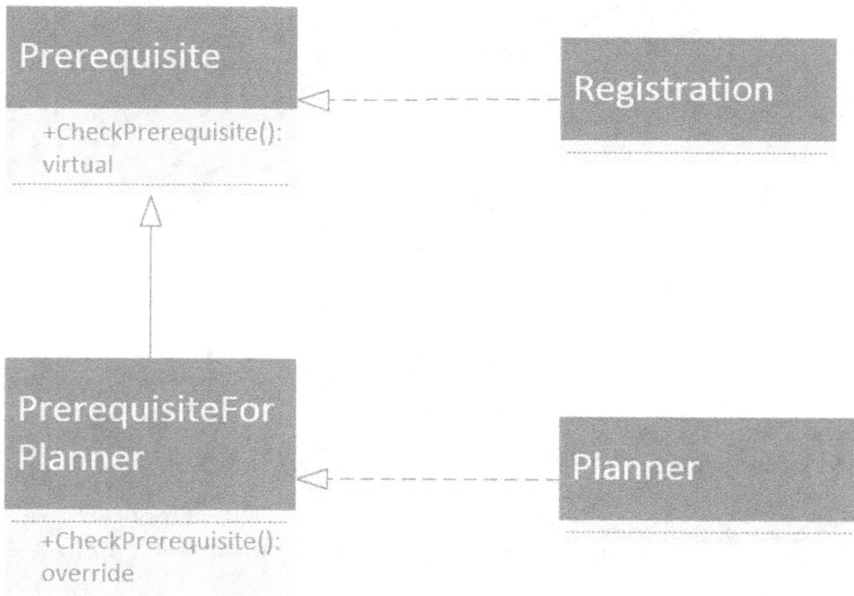

Figure 5.15 Use virtual method as an extension point.

2. Employing an abstract method in the base class (Figure 5.16) permits method definition without implementation, useful for method inclusion in derived classes.

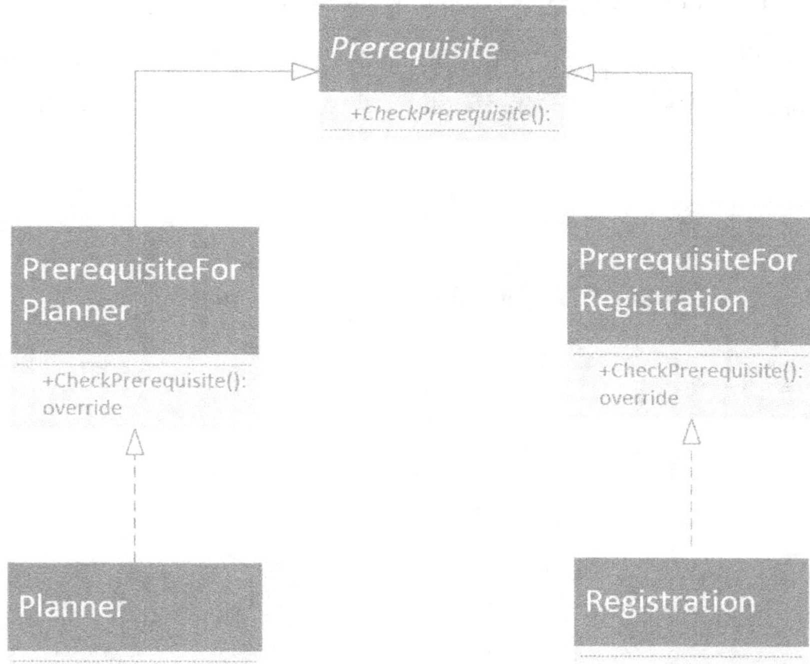

Figure 5.16 Use abstract method as an extension point.

3. Utilizing an interface (Figure 5.17) operates as a contract, ensuring adherence to specified requirements, offering maximal freedom for class designs implementing the interface.

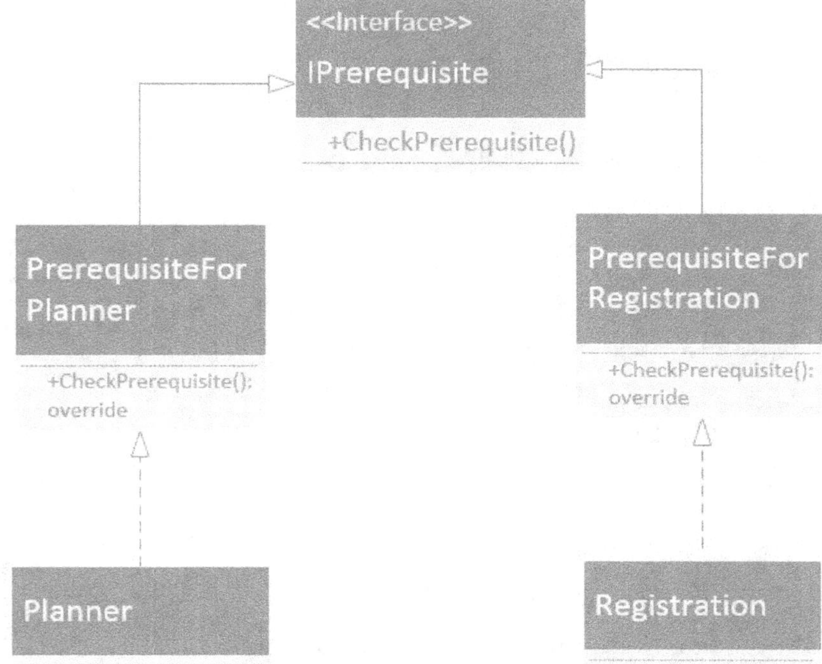

Figure 5.17 Use interface as an extension point.

In software architecture, two significant concepts—tight and loose coupling—illustrate the interdependency between components. If changes in one component of the application requires a corresponding change in another component, these two components are said to be tightly coupled. Otherwise, the two components are loosely coupled. The OCP advocates for a loosely coupled design, favoring scenarios where changes in one component don't necessitate alterations in another. This promotes flexibility and adaptability within software systems.

Test Your Understanding 5.38
The Open/Close principle (OCP) states, "software component should be open _______, but closed _________".
a. to everyone, to hackers
b. to legit users, hackers
c. for open source, for decoration
d. for extension, for modification

Test Your Understanding 5.39
Why should software components be open for extension?
a. less investment in front.
b. keep it simple.
c. there may be new requirements from the business.
d. keep growing.

Test Your Understanding 5.40
Why should software components be closed for modification?
a. better security.
b. other software component may already use it.
c. less investment in front.
d. keep it simple.

Test Your Understanding 5.41
According to OCP, which of the following is NOT an extension point?
a. override the virtual method in the base class.
b. override the simple method in the base class.
c. override the abstract method in the base class.
d. use interface for implementation.

Test Your Understanding 5.42
What does the Open/Close Principle (OCP) in software development emphasize?
a. Allowing modifications for efficient component updates
b. Resistance to extensions for system stability
c. Welcoming extensions while resisting modifications
d. Fixed and rigid component structures

Test Your Understanding 5.43
In the context of software development, why might introducing a new component for specific functionalities pose challenges?
a. It simplifies the overall architecture

b. It introduces code duplication and inconsistencies
c. It minimizes the need for updates
d. It ensures robustness in the system

Test Your Understanding 5.44
What solution preserves a single update location for an application, aiding in its maintainability?
a. Modifying the existing component directly
b. Introducing a new component for additional functionalities
c. Making a new component a child of the existing one
d. Creating a completely separate application

Test Your Understanding 5.45
How do tightly coupled components differ from loosely coupled components in software architecture?
a. Tightly coupled components allow more flexibility in updates
b. Loosely coupled components require fewer alterations
c. Tightly coupled components demand corresponding changes in interconnected components
d. Loosely coupled components restrict changes within a single component

Test Your Understanding 5.46
Which of these extension points allows method definition without implementation in derived classes?
a. Using a virtual method in the base class
b. Employing an abstract method in the base class
c. Utilizing an interface
d. Applying a static method in the derived class

Test Your Understanding 5.47
How does the OCP support adaptability within software systems?
a. By restricting any changes within the components
b. By favoring tightly coupled designs
c. By advocating for a loosely coupled design
d. By mandating constant modifications in interconnected components

Test Your Understanding 5.48
What is the primary advantage of using interfaces as an extension point in software development?
a. Ensuring fixed implementation across all classes
b. Providing maximum freedom in class design
c. Forcing specific method implementations
d. Limiting the flexibility of derived classes

Test Your Understanding 5.49
What does the OCP emphasize about components in a software system?
a. Resistance to change for stability
b. Flexibility through constant modifications
c. Adaptability through interdependent components
d. Balancing openness for extension and closure for modification

Test Your Understanding 5.50
Which concept in software architecture signifies the interdependency between components requiring corresponding changes?
a. Loosely coupled design

b. Open/Close Principle (OCP)
c. Tight coupling
d. Extension points

Test Your Understanding 5.51
What level of granularity is associated with using virtual methods in the base class for extension?
a. Low level
b. Moderate level
c. High level
d. No granularity

5.4 Chapter Summary

In this chapter, we explored the process of establishing a database via the Entity Framework's code-first approach. This began with package installation for Entity Framework, followed by the creation of a class mirroring a database table and another inheriting DbContext. Integration of DbContext into Program.cs ensued, alongside database updates via migration using the Package Manager Console. Utilizing data from the database involved injecting the DbContext-inherited class into a controller's constructor, employing methods like Add(), Update(), Remove(), and SaveChanges(). Furthermore, the chapter delved into the Open/Close Principle (OCP) advocating for extensibility while maintaining stability. Strategies to achieve OCP in Object-Oriented Programming (OOP) included leveraging virtual methods, abstract methods, or interfaces.

5.5 Review Questions

Question 5.1
What is entity framework? If you already know the entity-relationship diagram or class diagram of UML, what do you think can be obstacles for learning entity framework?

Question 5.2
Describe the steps that are necessary to create a database with entity framework code first approach.

Question 5.3
Explain the steps that are necessary to retrieve data from a database and display them on an MVC View page by using entity framework.

Question 5.4
Explain the steps that are necessary to insert data from an MVC View form to a database by using entity framework.

Question 5.5
Explain the steps that are necessary to delete data from a database by using entity framework.

Question 5.6
Explain how to edit data in a database by using entity framework andASP.NET MVC.

Question 5.7
What is the open/close principle? Why is it important?

Question 5.8
What are the three extension points that may help developers follow the open/close principle?

5.6 References

Chebanyuk, E., & Markov, K. (2016, February). An approach to class diagrams verification according to SOLID design principles. In *Model-Driven Engineering and Software Development (MODELSWARD), 2016 4th International Conference on* (pp. 435-441). IEEE.
Hall, G. M. (2017). *Adaptive Code: Agile coding with design patterns and SOLID principles*. Microsoft Press.
Larman, C. (2001). Protected variation: The importance of being closed. *IEEE Software, 18*(3), 89-91.
Meyer, B. (1997). *Object-oriented software construction* 2nd edition. New York: Prentice hall.

5. 7 Answers to Test Your Understanding

5.1 D; 5.2 B; 5.3 A; 5.4 B; 5.5 D; 5.6 A; 5.7 C; 5.8 D; 5.9 A; 5.10 B; 5.11 A; 5.12 B; 5.13 D; 5.14 A; 5.15 B;

5.16 A; 5.17 A; 5.18 A; 5.19 D; 5.20 A; 5.21 C; 5.22 B; 5.23 C; 5.24 B; 5.25 B; 5.26 C; 5.27 A; 5.28 B; 5.29 A;

5.30 C; 5.31 B; 5.32 C; 5.33 B; 5.34 D; 5.35 A; 5.36 B; 5.37 A; 5.38 D; 5.39 C; 5.40 B; 5.41 B; 5.42 C; 5.43 B;

5.44 C; 5.45 C; 5.46 B; 5.47 C; 5.48 B; 5.49 D; 5.50 C; 5.51 B;

Chapter 6: Entity Framework: Multiple Tables

Chapter Learning Objectives

6.1 Apply modifications to an established database table utilizing Entity Framework's code-first approach.
6.2 Expand database structure by incorporating additional tables using Entity Framework's code-first.
6.3 Construct an ASP.NET Core MVC application integrating multiple database tables.
6.4 Interpret the Liskov substitution principle, a key element within the SOLID design principles.

6.1 Entity Framework Handling Multiple Tables

In Chapter Five, you mastered crafting a database featuring a single table via Entity Framework. You delved into inserting, reading, updating, and deleting records in a solitary table (CRUD operations). Now, we explore the extension to multiple tables. The key distinction lies in the relationships interlinking these tables. These relationships manifest through foreign keys and navigation properties.

Chapter 6 Example 1

Develop an ASP.NET 8 MVC application managing two database tables: "courses" and "instructors." Each instructor can teach multiple courses, while each course is linked to a single instructor. A course consists of a course ID, title, seat capacity, and instructor. Meanwhile, an instructor is characterized by an instructor ID and name.

Accessing localhost/Instructor/AllInstructor should exhibit a list of all instructors. In the absence of instructors, the screen should display:

<u>Add an instructor</u>

No instructor in database yet.

Clicking the "Add an instructor" link shifts the URL to localhost/Instructor/AddInstructor. A simple HTML form containing a single text field for the instructor's name enables user input. An automatically generated instructor ID is managed by SQL Server.

Input data for two instructors through the form. Upon clicking "Add Instructor," the URL transitions to localhost/Instructor/AllInstructor, revealing a comprehensive list of all instructors stored in the database.

Similar to the instructor pages, accessing localhost/Course/AllCourse exhibits all courses. When the database lacks courses, the screen shows:

<u>Add a course</u>

No course in database yet.

Clicking "Add a course" reveals a form. Alongside course title and seat capacity inputs, instructor names are populated from the Instructors table as a dropdown menu.

Input data for three courses with different instructors previously added. Upon clicking "Add Course," the URL updates to localhost/Course/AllCourse, presenting a tabulated view of all added courses.

Solution:

Step 1: Initiate a New ASP.NET MVC Project (using .NET 8.0) named Chapter6Example1. Update the Program.cs file to configure routing and integrate MVC services.

Step 2: Integration of Entity Framework

Incorporate Entity Framework by adding the following two packages (refer to Chapter5 Example1):

```
Microsoft.EntityFrameworkCore.SqlServer
Microsoft.EntityFrameworkCore.Tools
```

Step 3: Incorporate Models

Create a folder named "Models" within the project. Within this folder, define three classes: Course, Instructor, and SchoolDbContext. Utilize the subsequent code for the Course.cs file:

```csharp
namespace Chapter6Example1.Models
{
    public class Course
    {
        public int CourseId { get; set; }
        public string CourseTitle { get; set; }
        public int SeatCapacity { get; set; }
        public Instructor Instructor { get; set; }
    }
}
```

Explanation:

The line: public Instructor Instructor { get; set; } represents a navigation property, signifying that a course is associated with an instructor. This property is added to the Course class to establish this link (an FK in the table). Now, proceed with the Instructor.cs file:

```csharp
namespace Chapter6Example1.Models
{
    public class Instructor
    {
        public int InstructorId { get; set; }
        public string InstructorName { get; set; }
        public ICollection<Course> Courses { get; set; }
    }
}
```

Explanation:

The line: public ICollection<Course> Courses { get; set; } also represents navigation property. This signifies that an instructor can teach multiple courses. Hence, this property "Courses" of type ICollection<Course> is added to the Instructor class, similar to a List, to manage multiple courses.

Lastly, include the following code in the SchoolDbContext.cs:

```csharp
namespace Chapter6Example1.Models
{
    public class SchoolDbContext: DbContext
    {
        // Properties
        public DbSet<Instructor> Instructors { get; set; }
        public DbSet<Course> Courses { get; set; }
        // Constructor
        public SchoolDbContext(DbContextOptions
            <SchoolDbContext> options)
            : base(options)
        {
        }
    }
}
```

Explanation:

This class inherits from DbContext. Each property corresponds to a class/table within the database. The constructor accepts and passes DbContextOptions to the base class (DbContext) for configuration.

Step 4: Implement Database Creation via Migration

Follow the instructions in Step 4 of Chapter5Example1, replacing two instances of Chapter5Example1 with

Chapter6Example1, and replace StudentDbContext with SchoolDbContext.

Step 5: Configure _ViewImports.cshtml, _Layout.cshtml, and _ViewStart.cshtml

Refer to Step 3c of Chapter 4 Example 1. Update the first line of _ViewImports accordingly.

Step 6: Displaying All Instructors From the Database

To display all instructors at the URL localhost/Instructor/AllInstructor, create an InstructorController.cs controller and an AllInstructor action method within it.

Create a folder named "Controllers" within the project. Within the "Controllers" folder, add an empty controller named InstructorController.cs. Inside InstructorController.cs, introduce a method named AllInstructor().

```csharp
using Chapter6Example1.Models;
using Microsoft.AspNetCore.Mvc;
using Microsoft.EntityFrameworkCore;

namespace Chapter6Example1.Controllers
{
    public class InstructorController : Controller
    {
        SchoolDbContext db;
        public InstructorController(SchoolDbContext db)
        {
            this.db = db;
        }
        public async Task<IActionResult> AllInstructor()
        {

            var instructor = await db.Instructors.ToListAsync();
            return View(instructor);
        }
    }
}
```

Explanation:

The field db represents the SchoolDbContext instance, initialized through the constructor to access database data.

The AllInstructor() method is asynchronous, enhancing program efficiency. It retrieves instructor data from the database asynchronously using ToListAsync() instead of ToList() due to the await keyword and the method's asynchronous nature.

To render the action method effectively, create a corresponding Razor View file:

Create a "Views" folder within the project and further create a subfolder named "Instructor" within "Views". Generate a Razor View named AllInstructor.cshtml within the "Instructor" folder:

```
@model IEnumerable<Chapter6Example1.Models.Instructor>
<p><a asp-action="AddInstructor">Add an instructor</a></p>
@{
    if (Model.Count() < 1)
    {
        <p>No instructor in database yet.</p>
    }
    else
    {
        <h3>All Instructors</h3>
        <table border="1">
            <tr>
                <th>Instructor ID</th>
                <th>Instructor Name</th>
            </tr>
            @foreach (var instructor in Model)
            {
                <tr>
                    <td>@instructor.InstructorId</td>
                    <td>@instructor.InstructorName</td>
                </tr>
            }
        </table>
    }
}
```

Upon saving these changes, start the application without debugging. Visit the URL localhost/Instructor/AllInstructor. The displayed browser content will resemble the following:

<u>Add an instructor</u>

No instructor in the database yet.

Step 7: Adding a Form to Register a New Instructor

To create a new instructor, navigate to the URL localhost/Instructor/AddInstructor. This involves implementing an "AddInstructor" action method within the InstructorController.cs controller. Access InstructorController.cs and insert the following code to introduce the "AddInstructor" action method:

```
public IActionResult AddInstructor()
{
    return View();
}
```

Next, create a corresponding Razor View file to interact with the "AddInstructor" method.

Navigate to the Views folder in Solution Explorer, then access the Instructor subfolder.

Within the Instructor folder, create a Razor View file named AddInstructor.cshtml and insert the code provided below:

```
@model Chapter6Example1.Models.Instructor
<form asp-controller="Instructor" asp-action="AddInstructor" method="post">
    <label asp-for="InstructorName"></label>
    <input asp-for="InstructorName" />
    <br />
    <button type="submit">Add Instructor</button>
</form>
```

Save your changes. Run the application without debugging.

Visit the URL localhost/Instructor/AddInstructor in your browser. You should see an HTML form for adding a new instructor.

Step 8: Processing the "Add Instructor" Form Submission

Integrate the following code snippet into the InstructorController.cs file to handle the submission from the "Add Instructor" button in the form. Ensure the method includes an HttpPost action verb:

```
[HttpPost]
public async Task<IActionResult> AddInstructor(Instructor instructor)
{
    db.Add(instructor);
    await db.SaveChangesAsync();
    return RedirectToAction("AllInstructor");
}
```

Save your changes and initiate the application without debugging.

Access the URL localhost/Instructor/AddInstructor in your web browser. Once the form displays, input various instructor names and click the "Add Instructor" button. This action will save the instructor names to the database's instructors table. The URL will switch to localhost/Instructor/AllInstructor, showcasing all instructor data retrieved from the Instructors table.

Step 9: Displaying All Courses from the Database

Create a CourseController.cs in the "Controllers" folder, containing an AllCourse() action method. The code below showcases the constructor, field, and action method for CourseController.cs:

```
using Chapter6Example1.Models;
using Chapter6Example1.ViewModels;
using Microsoft.AspNetCore.Mvc;
```

```csharp
using Microsoft.AspNetCore.Mvc.Rendering;
using Microsoft.EntityFrameworkCore;

namespace Chapter6Example1.Controllers
{
    public class CourseController : Controller
    {
        SchoolDbContext db;
        public CourseController(SchoolDbContext db)
        {
            this.db = db;
        }
        public async Task<IActionResult> AllCourse()
        {
            var course = await db.Courses.Include(c => c.Instructor).ToListAsync();
            return View(course);
        }
    }
}
```

Explanation:

The code snippet `db.Courses.Include(c => c.Instructor)` utilizes the Include() method alongside a lambda expression to associate instructors with respective courses. This association is based on the specific course taught by an instructor. Once this line executes, the course object will contain its corresponding instructor information.

Generate a corresponding Razor View file for the action method. Create a subfolder named "Course" inside the Views folder. Within this folder, add a Razor View file called AllCourse.cshtml and use the code below:

```cshtml
@model IEnumerable<Chapter6Example1.Models.Course>
<p><a asp-action="AddCourse">Add a course</a></p>
@{
    if (Model.Count() < 1)
    {
        <p>No course in database yet.</p>
    }
    else
    {
        <h3>All Courses</h3>
        <table border="1">
            <tr>
                <th>Course ID</th>
                <th>Course Title</th>
                <th>Seat Capacity</th>
                <th>Instructor Name</th>
            </tr>
```

```razor
        @foreach (var course in Model)
        {
            <tr>
                <td>@course.CourseId</td>
                <td>@course.CourseTitle</td>
                <td>@course.SeatCapacity</td>
                <td>@course.Instructor.InstructorName</td>
            </tr>
        }
    </table>
    }
}
```

Save your changes and start the application without debugging.

Access the URL localhost/Course/AllCourse in your browser. This action should display a page similar to the following:

<u>Add a course</u>

No course in the database yet.

Step 10: Display a Form to Add a New Course

First, create a ViewModel. Navigate to the Solution Explorer and add a folder named "ViewModels."

Add a class named CourseAddCourseViewModel.cs with the following code:

```csharp
using Chapter6Example1.Models;
using Microsoft.AspNetCore.Mvc.Rendering;

namespace Chapter6Example1.ViewModels
{
    public class CourseAddCourseViewModel
    {
        public Course Course { get; set; }
        public Instructor Instructor { get; set; }
        public SelectList InstructorList { get; set; }
    }
}
```

Next, update the CourseController. Open CourseController.cs and add the AddCourse action method:

```csharp
public async Task<IActionResult> AddCourse()
{
    var instructorDisplay = await db.Instructors.Select(x => new { Id =
    x.InstructorId, Value=x.InstructorName }).ToListAsync();
    CourseAddCourseViewModel vm = new CourseAddCourseViewModel();
    vm.InstructorList = new SelectList(instructorDisplay, "Id", "Value");
    return View(vm);
}
```

Finally, create the Razor View. Within the Views folder, navigate to the Course subfolder. Add a Razor View file named AddCourse.cshtml with the following code:

```
@model Chapter6Example1.ViewModels.CourseAddCourseViewModel
<form asp-controller="Course" asp-action="AddCourse" method="post">
    <label asp-for="Course.CourseTitle"></label>
    <input asp-for="Course.CourseTitle" />
    <br />
    <label asp-for="Course.SeatCapacity"></label>
    <input asp-for="Course.SeatCapacity" />
    <br />
    <label asp-for="Instructor.InstructorName"></label>
    <select asp-for="Instructor.InstructorId"
    asp-items="@Model.InstructorList"></select>
    <br />
    <button type="submit">Add Instructor</button>
</form>
```

Save and start without debugging. Enter the URL: localhost/Course/AddCourse to view the HTML form.

Step 11: Enable the "Add Course" Button in the AddCourse Form

Add the following AddCourse [HttpPost] action method to the CourseController.cs file:

```
[HttpPost]
public async Task<IActionResult> AddCourse(CourseAddCourseViewModel vm)
{
    var instructor = await db.Instructors.SingleOrDefaultAsync(i =>
    i.InstructorId == vm.Instructor.InstructorId);
    if(instructor == null)
    {
        return RedirectToAction("AddCourse");
    }
    else
    {
        vm.Course.Instructor = instructor;
        db.Add(vm.Course);
        await db.SaveChangesAsync();
        return RedirectToAction("AllCourse");
    }
}
```

Save. Start the application without debugging. Enter the URL: localhost/Course/AddCourse. Enter individual courses into the form and click the "Add Course" button. Upon clicking the button, the form data will be submitted to the AddCourse action method. After submission, the URL will change to localhost/Course/AllCourse, displaying all courses alongside their corresponding instructor names.

Test Your Understanding 6.1
Suppose you have an Instructor class and a Course class in the models. An instructor teaches zero or many courses while a course is taught by exactly one instructor. To demonstrate such relationship, you should add __________ property to the Course class.
a. Instructor
b. ICollection<Instructor>
c. Course
d. ICollection<Course>

Test Your Understanding 6.2
Suppose you have an Instructor class and a Course class in the models. An instructor teaches zero or many courses while a course is taught by exactly one instructor. To demonstrate such relationship, you should add __________ property to the Instructor class.
a. Instructor
b. ICollection<Instructor>
c. Course
d. ICollection<Course>

Test Your Understanding 6.3
Suppose you have two classes A and B in the model. To show their relationship, you may add one class/object as a property to another class. Such property is called _______ property.
a. strong
b. weak
c. 1:M
d. navigation

Test Your Understanding 6.4
To create a database using entity framework code first approach, you should create a class in the Models folder that inherits from __________.
a. DbContext
b. DbSet
c. DbContextOptions
d. SqlConnection

Test Your Understanding 6.5
One table in database corresponds to a ________ property in the class that inherits from DbContext.
a. DbContext
b. DbSet
c. DbContextOptions
d. SqlConnection

Test Your Understanding 6.6
Two action methods with the same name are often used to handle one HTML form. One is used to ________ the form and the other to _________ the form.
a. style, structure
b. display, structure
c. display, process
d. style, interact with

Test Your Understanding 6.7

If you don't want an action method to return the corresponding MVC Razor View, you can call the __________ method.
a. Switch()
b. Change()
c. RedirectToAction()
d. SwitchView()

Test Your Understanding 6.8
If you want to retrieve data from the navigation property, you should use _________ method.
a. Navigation()
b. Include()
c. Retrieve()
d. Read()

Test Your Understanding 6.9
You may use SelectList type to add a dropdown menu to a form. The SelectList type is _______.
a. a custom class you added in the Models folder
b. a custom class you added in the ViewModels folder
c. a custom class you added in the Views folder
d. a built-in class you added in the using directive

Test Your Understanding 6.10
In a controller, with the _______ method, the application can do something else while waiting for the user keyboard input.
a. regular
b. async
c. anonymous
d. delegate

Test Your Understanding 6.11
In a controller, A(n) _______ method allows a program to run more efficiently.
a. action
b. async
c. anonymous
d. delegate

Test Your Understanding 6.12
In a Razor View file, the @model Chapter6Example1.Models.Instructor line allows you to use _______ to represent _______ in the file.
a. model, Instructor
b. @model, Instructor
c. Model, Instructor
d. Model, zero or many Instructors

Test Your Understanding 6.13
In a Razor View file, the @model IEnumerable<Chapter6Example1.Models.Instructor> line allows you to use _______ to represent _______ in the file.
a. model, Instructor
b. @model, Instructor
c. Model, Instructor

d. Model, zero or many Instructors

Test Your Understanding 6.14
In a controller action method, the db.SaveChanges(); or the await db.SaveChangesAsync(); line is similar to the _______ command in SQL Server.
a. Commit
b. Save
c. SaveChanges
d. Rollback

Test Your Understanding 6.15
If the database contains Instructors and Courses tables, by using entity framework, the Models folder contains at least _______ classes
a. one
b. two
c. three
d. four

Test Your Understanding 6.16
Using entity framework, given the following model:
```
public class Course
{
    public int CourseId { get; set; }
    public string CourseTitle { get; set; }
    public int SeatCapacity { get; set; }
    public Instructor Instructor { get; set; }
}
```
How many fields of the courses table would you see in the database?
a. one
b. two
c. three
d. four

Test Your Understanding 6.17
Using entity framework, given the following model:
```
public class Course
{
    public int CourseId { get; set; }
    public string CourseTitle { get; set; }
    public int SeatCapacity { get; set; }
    public Instructor Instructor { get; set; }
}
```
Which of the following is the least likely field names for the corresponding table by default?
a. CourseId
b. CourseTitle
c. SeatCapacity
d. Instructor

Test Your Understanding 6.18
Using entity framework, given the following model:

```
public class Course
{
    public int CourseId { get; set; }
    public string CourseTitle { get; set; }
    public int SeatCapacity { get; set; }
    public Instructor Instructor { get; set; }
}
```
Will there be a foreign key for the corresponding table assuming Instructor class also exists?
a. No, because the [foreign key] notation is missing.
b. No, foreign keys are added by SQL DDL statements.
c. Yes, EF will pick a foreign key, most likely CourseId.
d. Yes, EF will pick a foreign key, most likely InstructorId.

Test Your Understanding 6.19
Using entity framework, given the following model:
```
public class Instructor
{
    public int InstructorId { get; set; }
    public string InstructorName { get; set; }
    public ICollection<Course> Courses { get; set; }
}
```
How many fields of the Instructors table would you see in the database?
a. one
b. two
c. three
d. four

Test Your Understanding 6.20
Using entity framework, given the following model:
```
public class Instructor
{
    public int InstructorId { get; set; }
    public string InstructorName { get; set; }
    public ICollection<Course> Courses { get; set; }
}
```
What are the field names in the corresponding table in the database?
a. Instructor and Course
b. InstructorId and InstructorName
c. ICollection and Courses
d. InstructorId and CourseId

Test Your Understanding 6.21
Using entity framework, given the following model:
```
public class Instructor
{
    public int InstructorId { get; set; }
    public string InstructorName { get; set; }
    public ICollection<Course> Courses { get; set; }
}
```

Will there be a foreign key in the corresponding Instructors table in the database?
a. No, there is no such navigation property
b. No, unless the courseId is added as a property
c. Yes, InstructorId
d. Yes, most likely CourseId

Test Your Understanding 6.22
Using entity framework, given the following model:

```
public class SchoolDbContext: DbContext
{
    // Properties
    public DbSet<Instructor> Instructors { get; set; }
    public DbSet<Course> Courses { get; set; }
    // Constructor
    public SchoolDbContext(DbContextOptions<SchoolDbContext> options)
        : base(options)
    {
    }
}
```

What is the database name by default?
a. School
b. SchoolDb
c. SchoolDbContext
d. Cannot tell

Test Your Understanding 6.23
Using entity framework, given the following model:

```
public class SchoolDbContext: DbContext
{
    // Properties
    public DbSet<Instructor> Instructors { get; set; }
    public DbSet<Course> Courses { get; set; }
    // Constructor
    public SchoolDbContext(DbContextOptions<SchoolDbContext> options)
        : base(options)
    {
    }
}
```

How many tables do you see?
a. One
b. Two
c. Three
d. Four

Test Your Understanding 6.24
Using entity framework, if you have a model class named Instructor, what is the name of the corresponding table in the database?
a. Instructor
b. Instructors

c. InstructorTable
d. Cannot tell

Test Your Understanding 6.25
Using entity framework, if you have a model class named Instructor, how do you name the corresponding table in the database?
a. It will be the same as the model class name.
b. It will be the plural form of the class name.
c. You can name it in the property of your DbContext class.
d. You can name it in the connection string property of the program.cs file.

Programming Challenge 6.1

The School of Business features various departments—Accounting, Marketing, and Management—each hosting multiple student clubs like ASA (Accounting Student Association) and Balance Book Club. Every club is affiliated with a single department.

Department details consist of a department ID and name, while clubs possess a club ID, name, student count, and department affiliation.

For an ASP.NET MVC application using an empty template and database, users should be able to:

Add and view department information.

Add and showcase club details, including their respective department associations.

When adding a new club, provide a dropdown list containing all available departments for selection.

6.2 Update Database with Migration

In the last section, you learned how to create a database with two tables. In this section, you will learn how to alter an existing table of the database. You will also learn how to add more tables to an existing database.

Chapter 6 Example 2

Problem:

There are four tasks in this problem.

First, enhance instructor information. Access localhost/Course/AllCourse to view the table of courses. Update the instructor names in the table to be clickable hyperlinks. Clicking an instructor's name should navigate to a new page displaying additional details like email, phone, and office number. Extend the AddInstructor.cshtml Razor view form to include these additional text fields.

Second, add student management feature. Visit localhost/Student/AllStudent to view all student data. Access localhost/Student/AddStudent to find an HTML form for adding new students.

Third, allow student enroll courses. Enable student enrollment in courses by making the course ID clickable on localhost/Course/AllCourse. Upon clicking, redirect to localhost/Student/EnrollCourse with the selected course ID passed in the URL. The new page should contain a text field for entering a student ID and a registration button. Upon registration, redirect to localhost/Course/AllCourse to display updated seat capacities.

Fourth, view seat capacity insights. Make the numbers in the "Seat Capacity" column clickable, leading to a page displaying all students enrolled in that course. If no students are registered yet, show a message indicating the absence of registrations along with a link back to the course list.

Solution:

OpenChapter6Example1 in Visual Studio.

Step 1: Expand Instructor Class Properties

To integrate additional columns (Email, Phone, and Office) into the Instructors table, add the following three properties to the Instructor class and perform a database migration:

```
public string Email { get; set; }
public string Phone { get; set; }
public string Office { get; set; }
```

Save the changes and access the "Package Manager Console" to execute the commands:

```
Add-Migration M2
```

```
Update-Database
```

Navigate to "SQL Server Object Explorer" to confirm the addition of the Email, Phone, and Office columns in the dbo.Instructors table.

Next, update AddInstructor.cshtml. Modify the AddInstructor.cshtml by including Email, Phone, and Office fields:

```
@model Chapter6Example1.Models.Instructor
<form asp-controller="Instructor" asp-action="AddInstructor"
method="post">
    <label asp-for="InstructorName"></label>
    <input asp-for="InstructorName" />
    <br />
    <label asp-for="Email"></label>
    <input asp-for="Email" />
    <br />
    <label asp-for="Phone"></label>
    <input asp-for="Phone" />
    <br />
    <label asp-for="Office"></label>
    <input asp-for="Office" />
```

```
    <br />
    <button type="submit">Add Instructor</button>
</form>
```

Then, update AllCourse.cshtml. Make each instructor name a hyperlink by replacing

```
<td>@course.Instructor.InstructorName</td>
```

With the following:

```
<td><a asp-controller="Instructor" asp-action="InstructorDetails"
    asp-route-id="@course.Instructor.InstructorId">
    @course.Instructor.InstructorName</a></td>
```

To make the hyperlink work, you need InstructorDetails in Instructor Controller. Add the

"InstructorDetails" action method to the "Instructor" controller:

```
public async Task<IActionResult> InstructorDetails(int? id)
{
    var instructor = await db.Instructors.SingleOrDefaultAsync(i =>
    i.InstructorId == id);
    return View(instructor);
}
```

Finally, you need corresponding InstructorDetails View. Create the "InstructorDetails" view inside the

Views/Instructor folder:

```
@model Chapter6Example1.Models.Instructor
<h2>@Model.InstructorName</h2>
<table border="1">
    <tr>
        <th>Instructor ID</th>
        <td>@Model.InstructorId</td>
    </tr>
    <tr>
        <th>Email</th>
        <td>@Model.Email</td>
    </tr>
    <tr>
        <th>Phone</th>
        <td>@Model.Phone</td>
    </tr>
    <tr>
        <th>Office</th>
        <td>@Model.Office</td>
    </tr>
</table>
<p><a asp-controller="Course" asp-action="AllCourse">Back to course
list</a></p>
```

Save and start without debugging. Access localhost/Instructor/AddInstructor to add an instructor. Then, add a course with the new instructor via localhost/Course/AddCourse. Afterward, navigate to localhost/Course/AllCourse and click a new instructor's name to view their details.

Step 2: Add Student and Enrollment Classes to the Models

Create a new Student class in the Models folder:

```
namespace Chapter6Example1.Models
{
    public class Student
    {
        public int StudentId { get; set; }
        public string? StudentName { get; set; }
        public ICollection<Enrollment>? Enrollments { get; set;}
    }
}
```

Note: You'll notice a red squiggly underline for Enrollment, as the Enrollment class hasn't been added yet.

Now, include the Enrollment class inside the Models folder with the following content:

```
namespace Chapter6Example1.Models
{
    public class Enrollment
    {
        public int EnrollmentId { get; set; }
        public int StudentId { get; set; }
        public Student? Student { get; set; }
        public int CourseId { get; set; }
        public Course? Course { get; set; }
    }
}
```

You also need to update the existing classes for the relationships. Include the following navigation property within the Course class:

```
public ICollection<Enrollment> Enrollments { get; set; }
```

This addition is necessary since a course can have multiple enrollments.

Next, update SchoolDbContext for the two newly added tables. Update the SchoolDbContext by adding two new properties:

```
public DbSet<Student> Students { get; set; }
public DbSet<Enrollment> Enrollments { get; set; }
```

Finally, you can update the database in the SQL Server. Navigate to the "Package Manager Console" and execute the following commands sequentially:

```
Add-Migration M3
Update-Database
```

Check the "SQL Server Object Explorer" to ensure the creation of all tables.

Below is a UML class diagram illustrating the relationships between the four classes.

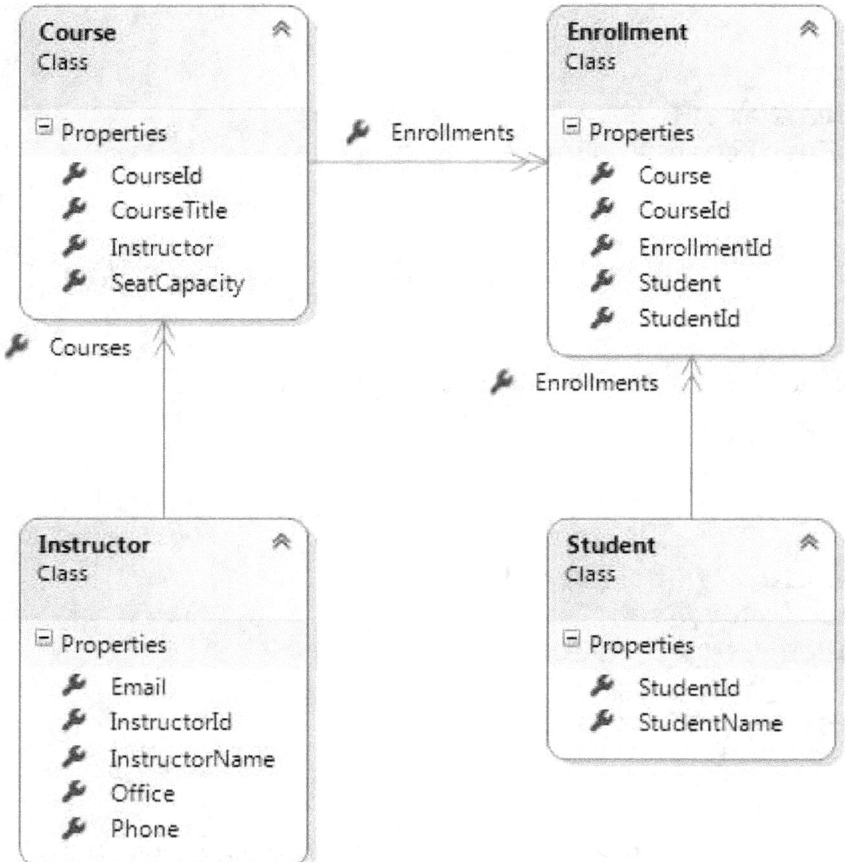

Figure 6.1 UML Class diagram for the project.

Step 3: Make localhost/Student/AllStudent and localhost/Student/AddStudent Work

Add a controller called StudentController.cs and three methods called AllStudent() and AddStudent() (2 of these). Add a new folder called Student to the Views folder. Add two Razor View files called AllStudent.cshtml and AddStudent.cshtml to the Student folder.

This is very similar to add an instructor on Steps 6, 7, and 8 of Chapter 6 Example 1, so I will not show you how to do it again.

Save. Start without Debugging. Add a few students to the database Students table.

Step 4: Allow a Student to Enroll in a Course

Frist, update the AllCourse.cshtml to make the Course ID a hyperlink:

Replace:

```
<td>@course.CourseId</a></td>
```

With:

```
<td><a asp-controller="Student" asp-action="EnrollCourse"
    asp-route-id="@course.CourseId">@course.CourseId</a></td>
```

Next, add EnrollCourse Action Method. Open StudentController.cs and include the EnrollCourse action method:

```
public async Task<IActionResult> EnrollCourse(int? id)
{
    var course = await db.Courses.SingleOrDefaultAsync(c => c.CourseId == id);
    ViewBag.Course = course;
    return View();
}
```

With the above action method, you need the EnrollCourse View. Add EnrollCourse.cshtml to the

Views/Student/ folder:

```
@model Chapter6Example1.Models.Enrollment
<p> Enter a student ID to register this course</p>
<h3>Course Information</h3>
<table border="1">
    <tr>
        <th>Course ID</th>
        <th>Course Title</th>
        <th>Remaining Seats</th>
    </tr>
    <tr>
        <td>@ViewBag.course.CourseId</td>
        <td>@ViewBag.course.CourseTitle</td>
        <td>@ViewBag.course.SeatCapacity</td>
    </tr>
</table>
@{
    if(ViewBag.Course.SeatCapacity < 1)
    {
        <p>THis course is full. Try at a different time.</p>
        <p><a asp-controller="Course" asp-action="AllCourse">
            Back to course list</a></p>
    }
    else
```

```
    {
        <form asp-controller="Student"
            asp-action="EnrollCourse" method="post">
        <label asp-for="StudentId"></label>
        <input asp-for="StudentId" />
        <br />
        <input asp-for="CourseId" type="hidden"
            value=@ViewBag.course.CourseId />
        <button type="submit">Register Course</button>

        </form>
    }
}
```

To actually enroll a student, add EnrollCourse HttpPost Method. Include an HttpPost EnrollCourse action method in the Student controller to save student registration data:

```
[HttpPost]
public async Task<IActionResult> EnrollCourse(Enrollment enrollment)
{
    db.Add(enrollment);
    var course = await db.Courses.FindAsync(enrollment.CourseId);
    course.SeatCapacity--;
    await db.SaveChangesAsync();
    return RedirectToAction("AllCourse", "Course");
}
```

Save and start without debugging and proceed to register students for a course.

Step 5: Display All Students Enrolled in a Course

First, make seat capacity hyperlinks. In the AllCourse.cshtml file, update the Seat Capacity column to hyperlinks by replace:

```
<td>@course.SeatCapacity</td>
```

With:

```
<td><a asp-controller="Student" asp-action="AllClassmate"
asp-route-id="@course.CourseId">@course.SeatCapacity</a></td>
```

To make the links work, add AllClassmate action method. Include an AllClassmate action method in the Student controller:

```
public async Task<IActionResult> AllClassmate(int? id)
{
    var enrollInCourse = await db.Enrollments.Where
    (e => e.CourseId == id).ToListAsync();
```

```csharp
        List<Student> classmate = new List<Student>();
        foreach (var e in enrollInCourse)
        {
            var student = await db.Students.SingleOrDefaultAsync
            (s => s.StudentId == e.StudentId);
            classmate.Add(student);
        }
        ViewData["course"] = db.Courses.Find(id).CourseTitle;
        return View(classmate);
}
```

Finally, you need a corresponding view named AllClassmate View. Add AllClassmate.cshtml to the Views/Student/ folder:

```cshtml
@model IEnumerable<Chapter6Example1.Models.Student>
<h2>@ViewData["Course"]</h2>
@{
    if(Model.Count() < 1)
    {
        <p>No student registerd for this course yet.</p>
    }
    else
    {
        <h3>All Enrolled Students</h3>
        <table border="1">
            <tr>
                <th>Student ID</th>
                <th>Student Name</th>
            </tr>
            @foreach (var student in Model)
            {
                <tr>
                    <td>@student.StudentId</td>
                    <td>@student.StudentName</td>
                </tr>
            }
        </table>
    }
}
<p><a asp-controller="Course" asp-action="AllCourse">
    Back to course list</a></p>
```

Save and start without debugging. Upon visiting localhost/Course/AllCourse, the hyperlinks in the Seat Capacity column should direct to the AllClassmate page, displaying enrolled students for the respective course.

Test Your Understanding 6.26
In ASP.NET MVC, which of the following is NOT a step to alter a table with entity framework?
a. issue alter-table command.
b. update the class corresponding to the table.
c. add migration with a new name.
d. issue update-database command.

Test Your Understanding 6.27
In order to add a new table to an existing database by using entity framework code first approach, you should add a corresponding _________ to the class that inherits from DbContext.
a. DbSet property
b. MVC View page
c. controller
d. option

Test Your Understanding 6.28
Which commands of "Package Manager Console" are required every time you make a change to the database models?
a. Add-Migration & Update-Migration
b. Add-Database & Update-Database
c. Add-Migration & Update-Database
d. Add-Database & Update-Migration

Test Your Understanding 6.29
What is the question mark (?) in the following method header?
```
public async Task<IActionResult> InstructorDetails(int? id)
```
a. id is required
b. id can be null
c. int includes 0
d. int can be negative

Test Your Understanding 6.30
What will the following line of code do?
```
return RedirectToAction(A, B);
```
a. Call the AController's B action method.
b. Call the BController's A action method.
c. Call the AModel's B Razor View.
d. Call the BModel's A Razor View.

Test Your Understanding 6.31
What should you do if you want to add a new field to an existing table in the database?
Statement1: Add a field with that name to the class that generates the table.
Statement2: Update the class that inherits from DbContext.
Statement3: Add a new migration.
Statement4: Issue Update-Database command.
a. Statement1 and Statement2.
b. Statement1 and Statement4.
c. Statement1, Statement2, and Statement4.
d. Statement1, Statement3, and Statement4.

Test Your Understanding 6.32
What should you do if you want to add a new field to an existing table in the database?
Statement1: Update the class that inherits from DbContext.
Statement2: Add a new migration.
Statement3: Add a field with that name to the class that generates the table.
Statement4: Issue Update-Database command.
a. Statement1 and Statement2.
b. Statement1 and Statement4.
c. Statement1, Statement2, and Statement3.
d. Statement2, Statement3, and Statement4.

Test Your Understanding 6.33
Which of the following is necessary if you want to add a new field to an existing table in the database?
a. Update the class that inherits from DbContext.
b. Add a new migration.
c. Drop the class and add a new one with the new field name.
d. Issue a migration command: Add-Field.

Test Your Understanding 6.34
Which of the following is necessary if you want to add a new field to an existing table in the database?
a. Update the class that inherits from DbContext.
b. Issue alter-table command.
c. Add a field with that name to the class that generates the table.
d. Issue a migration command: Add-Field.

Test Your Understanding 6.35
Which of the following is necessary if you want to add a new field to an existing table in the database?
a. Issue Update-Database command.
b. Issue alter-table command.
c. Issue Insert-field command in migration.
d. Issue a migration command: Add-Field.

Test Your Understanding 6.36
Which of the following is the correct sequence of actions if you want to add a new field to an existing table in the database?
Statement1: Add a new migration.
Statement2: Add a field with that name to the class that generates the table.
Statement3: Issue Update-Database command.
a. Statements: 1-2-3
b. Statements: 1-3-2
c. Statements: 2-1-3
d. Statements: 3-2-1

Test Your Understanding 6.37
What should you do if you want to add a new table to an existing table in the database?
Statement1: Add a new class to the Models folder.
Statement2: Update the class that inherits from DbContext.
Statement3: Add a new migration.

Statement4: Issue Update-Database command.
a. Statement1 and Statement2.
b. Statement3 and Statement4.
c. Statement1, Statement3, and Statement4.
d. Statement1, Statement2, Statement3, and Statement4.

Test Your Understanding 6.38
Which of the following actions is NOT necessary if you want to add a new table to an existing table in the database?
a. Add a new class to the Models folder.
b. Update the class that inherits from DbContext.
c. Issue Add-Table command.
d. Issue Update-Database command.

Test Your Understanding 6.39
Which of the following actions is NOT necessary if you want to add a new table to an existing table in the database?
a. Add a new migration.
b. Update the class that inherits from DbContext.
c. Add a new controller class.
d. Issue Update-Database command.

Test Your Understanding 6.40
Which of the following actions is NOT necessary if you want to add a new table to an existing table in the database?
a. Add a new migration.
b. Update the class that inherits from DbContext.
c. Add a new class to the Models folder.
d. Add a new table to the Razor View file.

Programming Challenge 6.2

Continue to work on Programming Challenge 6.1 by adding four features:

First, expand department details to include phone number, email, and office location. On the clubs listing page, make the department name a hyperlink. Clicking it should reveal further department details.

Second, incorporate student data. Students can join multiple clubs or none at all, while each club can have multiple students. Enable users to add and view all student records.

Third, allow students to enroll in a club. Allow students to join a club by clicking the club ID on the "All Clubs" page and entering the student ID.

Lastly, display club's student roster. Provide a link on the "Number of students" of the "All Clubs" page to display all students associated with a particular club.

The All Clubs Page should include the following details: Club ID (hyperlink), Club name, Number of students (hyperlink) in the club, Department name (hyperlink).

6.3 Liskov Substitution Principle

The "L" in the SOLID acronym stands for Liskov Substitution Principle. It states that if S is a subtype of T and an object of T is used in a client, then the object of T in the client can be replaced with an object of S without causing any problems for the client (Liskov 1988; Liskov and Wing 1994).

Let's explore an example. If DomesticStudent is a subtype of the Student class and the Student class is used in a client named Admission class, then replacing the Student object in the Admission class with a DomesticStudent object should not cause any problems. If this holds true, we can say the design adheres to the Liskov Substitution Principle.

Begin by creating a new C# console application (not ASP.NET Core MVC) named Chapter6Liskov. Add a class named Student with the code provided below:

```csharp
namespace Chapter6Liskov
{
    abstract class Student
    {
        // Properties
        public int StudentId { get; set; }
        public string StudentName { get; set; }
        // Constructor
        public Student(int studentId, string studentName)
        {
            StudentId = studentId;
            StudentName = studentName;
        }
        // Methods
        public abstract string AdmissionByScore();
        public override string ToString()
        {
            return $"ID: {StudentId} Name: {StudentName}";
        }
    }
}
```

Next, include a class named DomesticStudent in the project with the following code:

```csharp
namespace Chapter6Liskov
{
    internal class DomesticStudent: Student
    {
        // Property
        public double ACTScore {  get; set; }
```

```csharp
        // Constructor
        public DomesticStudent
            (int studentId, string studentName, double actScore)
            :base(studentId, studentName)
        {
            ACTScore = actScore;
        }
        // Method
        public override string AdmissionByScore()
        {
            if (ACTScore > 30)
                return "Congratulations!";
            else
                return "Try again next time.";
        }
        public override string ToString()
        {
            return base.ToString() + " " + AdmissionByScore();
        }
    }
}
```

Rename the default Program.cs file to Admission.cs and replace its contents with the provided code below:

The application initially appears to comply with LSP as an object of DomesticStudent can replace an object of the Student class. However, drawing conclusions based on a single case isn't conclusive (you can refute a conclusion with just one case).

To illustrate a potential LSP violation, introduce another class named InternationalStudent as shown below:

```csharp
namespace Chapter6Liskov
{
    class Admission
    {
        static void Main(string[] args)
        {
            List<Student> students = new List<Student>();
            DomesticStudent s1 = new DomesticStudent(1, "Albert", 29);
            DomesticStudent s2 = new DomesticStudent(2, "Sam", 34);
            students.Add(s1);
            students.Add(s2);
            foreach(var s in students)
            {
                s.AdmissionByScore();
```

```
                    Console.WriteLine(s);
                }
            }
        }
}
```

Then, add an InternationalStudent object to the student list in the Admission class. Incorporate the following lines inside the Main() method:

```
InternationalStudent s3 = new InternationalStudent(3, "Jeremy");
students.Add(s3);
```

Running the application will result in an exception, indicating a failure to comply with LSP.

To realign the application with LSP, follow these steps:

1. Create a new interface named IStudent to contain common properties.

```
namespace Chapter6Liskov
{
    internal interface IStudent
    {
        int StudentId { get; set; }
        string StudentName {  get; set; }
    }
}
```

Include another interface named IAdmission for unique characteristics.

```
namespace Chapter6Liskov
{
    internal interface IAdmission
    {
        string AdmissionByScore();
    }
}
```

In the Student class, implement both IStudent and IAdmission interfaces:

```
abstract class Student: IStudent, IAdmission
```

For the InternationalStudent class, implement only the IStudent interface:

```
class InternationalStudent: IStudent
```

You will see that the AdmissionByScore method is not allowed and suggest that you remove that method.

Update the InternationalStudent class with the following code:

```csharp
namespace Chapter6Liskov
{
    class InternationalStudent: IStudent
    {
        // Properties
        public int StudentId { get; set; }
        public string StudentName { get; set; }
        // Constructor
        public InternationalStudent
            (int studentId, string studentName)
        {
          StudentId = studentId;
          StudentName = studentName;
        }
    // Method
    public override string ToString()
    {
        return $"ID: {StudentId}, Name: {StudentName}";
    }
    }
}
```

Finally, update the Admission.cs file to use a list of IStudent instead of Student objects:

Replace:
```csharp
List<Student> students = new List<Student>();
```
With:

```csharp
List<IStudent> students = new List<IStudent>();
```

And comment out the following line:

```csharp
s.AdmissionByScore();
```

Save and run the code. It should execute as expected. This redesign strategy segregates common properties under the IStudent interface and unique behaviors under IAdmission, reducing the likelihood of incorrect method inheritance between classes and minimizing the risk of program crashes (Feng et al., 2016).

Test Your Understanding 6.41
The ______________ states that if S is a subtype of T and an object of T is used in a client, then the object of T in the client can be replaced with an object of S without causing any problems for the client.
a. Liskov substitution principle
b. Open/Close principle
c. Single responsibility principle
d. Interface segregation principle

Test Your Understanding 6.42
What does the "L" in the SOLID acronym stand for?
a. Liskov Substitution Principle

b. Logical Programming
c. Lambda Syntax
d. Legacy Systems

Test Your Understanding 6.43
According to the Liskov Substitution Principle, what does it imply if a subtype S of T can replace an object of T in a client?
a. S and T are entirely unrelated.
b. T and S have similar properties.
c. An object of T in the client can be replaced with an object of S without issues.
d. An object of S cannot replace an object of T.

Test Your Understanding 6.44
What solution approach is suggested to realign the application with Liskov Substitution Principle?
a. Separate common properties and behaviors using interfaces
b. Remove common properties
c. Merge classes
d. Eliminate interfaces

Test Your Understanding 6.45
Based on the example of Liskov Substitution Principle in the book, what is the purpose of using interfaces in the described redesign strategy?
a. To enforce strict class hierarchies
b. To reduce the likelihood of incorrect method inheritance
c. To eliminate classes
d. To minimize object instantiation

Test Your Understanding 6.46
How does the redesign strategy contribute to minimizing program crashes?
a. By encouraging complex class hierarchies
b. By removing class properties
c. By reducing method overrides
d. By segregating common properties and unique behaviors

Test Your Understanding 6.47
What does the redesign strategy primarily of Liskov Substitution Principle aim to achieve?
a. To decrease code complexity
b. To increase program efficiency
c. To enhance method inheritance
d. To improve code maintainability and robustness

Test Your Understanding 6.48
Following Liskov Substitution Principle, what is the role of the interfaces IStudent and IAdmission in the redesign strategy?

```
internal interface IStudent
{
    int StudentId { get; set; }
    string StudentName {  get; set; }
}
internal interface IAdmission
```

```
{
    string AdmissionByScore();
}
```
a. To avoid redundant properties
b. To enforce strict inheritance rules
c. To segregate common properties and unique behaviors
d. To simplify class relationships

6.4 Chapter Summary

In this chapter, you've explored altering tables using Entity Framework. To modify a table, you update the respective class. Additionally, you've discovered the process of adding new tables to an established database by incorporating new classes within the models folder and updating the class inheriting from the DbContext class. Whenever alterations are made to the database structure, it's essential to create a migration and update the database accordingly. In the final section of the chapter, you delved into the Liskov Substitution Principle, which enables the creation of classes that are more user-friendly for other programmers.

6.5 Review Questions

Question 6.1
Describe steps that are necessary for altering a table by using entity framework code first approach.
Question 6.2
In an Entity Relationship Diagram (ERD), a foreign key signifies the relationship between two entities. For instance, an instructor may teach multiple courses, whereas a course may only have one instructor. This relationship is established by adding the instructor ID from the instructor entity as a foreign key within the course entity. How is this foreign key relationship represented in Entity Framework models?
Question 6.4
Explain what Liskov substitution principle is and why it is important.

6.6 References

Feng, Q., Kazman, R., Cai, Y., Mo, R., & Xiao, L. (2016, April). Towards an architecture-centric approach to security analysis. In *Software Architecture (WICSA), 2016 13th Working IEEE/IFIP Conference on* (pp. 221-230). IEEE.
Liskov, B. (1988). Keynote address-data abstraction and hierarchy. *ACM Sigplan Notices, 23*(5), 17-34.
Liskov, B. H., & Wing, J. M. (1994). A behavioral notion of subtyping. *ACM Transactions on Programming Languages and Systems (TOPLAS), 16*(6), 1811-1841.

6.7 Answers to Test Your Understanding

6.1 A; 6.2 D; 6.3 D; 6.4 A; 6.5 B; 6.6 C; 6.7 C; 6.8 B; 6.9 D; 6.10 B; 6.11 B; 6.12 C; 6.13 D; 6.14 A; 6.15 C; 6.16 D; 6.17 D; 6.18 D; 6.19 B; 6.20 B; 6.21 A; 6.22 D; 6.23 B; 6.24 D; 6.25 C; 6.26 A; 6.27 A; 6.28 C; 6.29 B; 6.30 B; 6.31 D; 6.32 D; 6.33 B; 6.34 C; 6.35 A; 6.36 C; 6.37 D; 6.38 C; 6.39 C; 6.40 D; 6.41 A; 6.42 A; 6.43 C; 6.44 A; 6.45 B; 6.46 D; 6.47 D; 6.48 C;

Chapter 7: ASP.NET Identity

Chapter Learning Objectives

7.1 Discuss the principles of interface segregation within the SOLID design principles.
7.2 Apply the steps required to implement Identity in an ASP.NET MVC project.
7.3 Implement user and role management functionalities within an ASP.NET MVC application.

7.1 Introduction to ASP.NET Identity

While exploring the creation of dynamic content through databases for web applications, it becomes essential to control user access to various data within the database. This need for a membership system leads us to ASP.NET Identity.

This chapter focuses on understanding the implementation of ASP.NET Identity, including the installation process, the addition of essential tables, managing user credentials like usernames and passwords, and controlling user access to specific action methods or controllers based on the role they were assigned. An illustrative example will showcase the roles within Identity, demonstrating how instructors post grades while students access and review their grades.

Role-based access control (RBAC) in ASP.NET Identity is a mechanism that manages access permissions based on predefined roles assigned to users within an application. It allows administrators to categorize users into different roles, where each role holds specific permissions or access rights.

Roles represent a set of permissions or responsibilities within the application. Examples might include 'Admin', 'Manager', 'User', 'Guest', etc. Users are assigned to one or multiple roles based on their responsibilities or access needs within the application. Access Control: Permissions or access rights are associated with each role. These permissions determine what actions or resources a user in a particular role can access or perform within the application.

This approach streamlines access management by allowing administrators to define and manage permissions at the role level, simplifying security administration and ensuring that users have appropriate access to the application's resources and functionalities based on their roles.

Test Your Understanding 7.1
What is the primary purpose of ASP.NET Identity?
a. To manage user data
b. To control user access
c. To create dynamic content
d. To design web applications

Test Your Understanding 7.2
Which term refers to predefined sets of permissions or responsibilities within ASP.NET Identity?
a. Users
b. Access Control
c. Roles
d. Permissions

Test Your Understanding 7.3
What is Role-based Access Control (RBAC) in ASP.NET Identity?
a. It manages users' access credentials
b. It categorizes users into roles
c. It assigns specific permissions to users
d. It controls user access based on predefined roles

Test Your Understanding 7.4
How are permissions associated with users in ASP.NET Identity?
a. Directly assigned to users
b. Defined through controllers
c. Assigned to roles, and roles are assigned to users
d. Based on the user's actions

Test Your Understanding 7.5
What does ASP.NET Identity allow administrators to do?
a. Define and manage permissions at the user level
b. Define and manage permissions at the role level
c. Assign permissions to specific controllers
d. Limit access to predefined actions

Test Your Understanding 7.6
In ASP.NET Identity, what does RBAC stand for?
a. Role-Based Access Control
b. Role-Based Action Control
c. Role-Based Authorization Control
d. Role-Based Application Control

Test Your Understanding 7.7
What do roles represent in ASP.NET Identity?

a. Specific actions
b. User categories
c. Application functionalities
d. User interface elements

Test Your Understanding 7.8
How does ASP.NET Identity simplify access management?
a. By defining user-specific permissions
b. By assigning permissions directly to users
c. By allowing administrators to manage permissions at the role level
d. By restricting user access to specific controllers

Test Your Understanding 7.9
What aspect of ASP.NET Identity streamlines security administration?
a. User categorization
b. Permission inheritance
c. Role-based access management
d. User-specific permissions

Test Your Understanding 7.10
Which term refers to managing access permissions based on predefined roles assigned to users in ASP.NET Identity?
a. User control
b. Role categorization
c. Permission assignment
d. Role-based access control

Chapter 7 Example 1

Problem:

Develop an ASP.NET MVC application enabling user registration on the site and empowering administrators to create roles such as 'student' and 'instructor.' The goal is to assign the appropriate role(s) to each registered user. Instructors have the capability to add courses to the school catalog and post grades for the courses they teach. Students can enroll in courses that have available slots and check the grades they receive for the courses they are enrolled in.

Solution:

Note: For brevity, the following solution excludes the four required steps:

Initiate an Empty ASP.NET MVC Project named "Chapter7Example1".

Update the Program.cs file by integrating MVC services and incorporating routing middleware.

Integrate Entity Framework (two packages).

Add _ViewImports.cshtml, _Layout.cshtml, and _ViewStart.cshtml files.

Details for these steps are available in Chapter 6 Example 1, steps 1, 2, and 5.

Step 1: Install Identity

Similar to integrating Entity Framework, add the following package via the "NuGet Package Manager":

```
Microsoft.AspNetCore.Identity.EntityFrameworkCore
```

Subsequently, introduce a new folder named Models to the project.

Create a class named ApplicationUser within the Models folder, containing the provided code snippet:

```csharp
using Microsoft.AspNetCore.Identity;

namespace Chapter7Example1.Models
{
    public class ApplicationUser:IdentityUser
    {
    }
}
```

Explanation:

The ApplicationUser.cs file extends IdentityUser as its base class. It doesn't require additional properties.

However, if needed, extra attributes like hobbies or date of birth can be added inside the ApplicationUser class.

Proceed by introducing a class named ApplicationDbContext within the Models folder. The content should match the code snippet below:

```csharp
using Microsoft.AspNetCore.Identity.EntityFrameworkCore;
using Microsoft.EntityFrameworkCore;

namespace Chapter7Example1.Models
{
    public class ApplicationDbContext :
        IdentityDbContext<ApplicationUser>
    {
        public ApplicationDbContext(DbContextOptions
            <ApplicationDbContext> options)
            : base(options)
        {
        }
    }
}
```


Update the Program.cs file with the provided modifications:

```csharp
using Chapter7Example1.Models;
using Microsoft.AspNetCore.Identity;
using Microsoft.EntityFrameworkCore;
```

```
var builder = WebApplication.CreateBuilder(args);

// Add services to the container.
var connection =
    @"Server=(localdb)\mssqllocaldb;Database=Chapter7Db;
                    Trusted_Connection=True;";
builder.Services.AddDbContext<ApplicationDbContext>
    (options => options.UseSqlServer(connection));
builder.Services.AddIdentity<ApplicationUser, IdentityRole>()
    .AddEntityFrameworkStores<ApplicationDbContext>()
    .AddDefaultTokenProviders();

builder.Services.AddControllersWithViews();

var app = builder.Build();

app.UseRouting();
app.UseAuthentication();
app.UseAuthorization();
app.MapControllerRoute(
    name: "default",
    pattern: "{controller=Home}/{action=Index}/{id?}");

app.Run();
```

Finally, in the "Package Manager Console," execute the following commands to generate the database and its associated tables for Identity usage:

```
Add-Migration M1
Update-Database
```

Upon successful execution, the Chapter7Db database is created. To view the database and its respective tables, navigate to the "SQL Server Object Explorer" window and expand the relevant items.

Step 2: Adding a Password Protected Page

Create a folder named Controllers.

Inside the Controllers folder, add a controller called HomeController.cs and retain the Default Index action method.

Create a folder named Views within the project.

Inside the Views folder, create a Home folder.

Inside the Home folder, add a Razor View file named Index.cshtml. Insert the following line of code into Index.cshtml:

```
<p>This is a password protected page.</p>
```

Save and start without debugging. You'll see the displayed sentence in your browser.

Now, let's restrict access to this page for authorized users only.

Open HomeController.cs. Add the [Authorize] attribute directly above the Index method, as demonstrated below:

```
using Microsoft.AspNetCore.Authorization;
using Microsoft.AspNetCore.Mvc;

namespace Chapter7Example1.Controllers
{
    public class HomeController : Controller
    {
        [Authorize]
        public IActionResult Index()
        {
            return View();
        }
    }
}
```

This notation restricts access to the method solely to registered users. Consequently, only registered users can access the default page using the same URL as localhost/Home/Index.

Save and start without debugging.

Upon attempting to access the default page, you'll receive a denial message: "This localhost page can't be found".

Test Your Understanding 7.11
What package is required to integrate Identity in an ASP.NET Core project?
a. Microsoft.AspNetCore.Mvc.Identity
b. Microsoft.AspNetCore.Identity.EntityFrameworkCore
c. Microsoft.EntityFrameworkCore.Identity
d. Microsoft.AspNetCore.Authorization

Test Your Understanding 7.12
The ApplicationUser class in the book example allows you to add additional fields to the asp.netuser table.What does the class ApplicationUser within the Models folder extend?
a. DbContext
b. IdentityUser
c. IdentityRole
d. ApplicationRole

Test Your Understanding 7.13
To restrict access to the Index method for authorized users only. Open HomeController.cs. Add the
_______ attribute directly above the Index method, as demonstrated below:
a. [Authorized]
b. [Authorize]
c. [Restricted]
d. [Restrict]

Test Your Understanding 7.14
What command is used in the Package Manager Console to generate the database and its associated tables
for Identity usage?
a. Generate-DB
b. Add-Migration and Update-Database
c. Update-Identity
d. Update-Database

Test Your Understanding 7.15
What denial message is received upon attempting to access the default page without authorization?
a. "Access Denied"
b. "This page is restricted"
c. "This localhost page can't be found"
d. "Authentication Required"

Test Your Understanding 7.16
In order to generate all necessary tables for Identity usage, two classes must be inside the Models folder.
One inherits from _______ and the other inherits from _______.
a. IdentityUser, IdentityDbContext
b. ApplicationUser, IdentityUser
c. IdentityUser, DbContext
d. ApplicationUser, IdentityDbContext

Step 3: Adding a Page That Allows Users to Register.

Create a controller named AccountController.cs inside the Controllers folder. Include the required fields

and a constructor:

```
private ApplicationDbContext db;
private UserManager<ApplicationUser> userManager;
private SignInManager<ApplicationUser> signInManager;
private RoleManager<IdentityRole> roleManager;
public AccountController(UserManager<ApplicationUser> userManager,
        SignInManager<ApplicationUser> signInManager,
        RoleManager<IdentityRole> roleManager, ApplicationDbContext db)
        {
            this.userManager = userManager;
            this.signInManager = signInManager;
            this.roleManager = roleManager;
            this.db = db;
        }
```

Next, add an action method named Register inside the AccountController:

```csharp
public IActionResult Register()
{
    return View();
}
```

Create a folder named ViewModels in the project's Solution Explorer. Inside this folder, add a class called

AccountRegisterViewModel.cs with the following code:

```csharp
using System.ComponentModel.DataAnnotations;

namespace Chapter7Example1.ViewModels
{
    public class AccountRegisterViewModel
    {
        [Required, MaxLength(256), EmailAddress]
        [Display(Name = "Email Address")]
        public string Email { get; set; }
        [Required, MinLength(6), MaxLength(20)]
        [DataType(DataType.Password)]
        [Display(Name = "Password")]
        public string Password { get; set; }
        [Required, MinLength(6), MaxLength(20)]
        [DataType(DataType.Password)]
        [Display(Name = "Confirm Password")]
        [Compare("Password", ErrorMessage = "Password not match")]
        public string ConfirmPassword { get; set; }
    }
}
```

Explanation:

The annotations within square brackets in this file help control display settings and perform form validation, ensuring specific requirements for input fields.

Add a folder named Account inside the Views folder. Inside the Account folder, create a Razor View file named Register.cshtml with the following code:

```html
@model Chapter7Example1.ViewModels.AccountRegisterViewModel

<h2>User Registration</h2>
<form asp-action="Register" method="post">
    <div asp-validation-summary="All"></div>
    <label asp-for="Email"></label>
    <input asp-for="Email" />
    <span asp-validation-for="Email"></span>
    <br />
```

```html
    <label asp-for="Password"></label>
    <input asp-for="Password" />
    <span asp-validation-for="Password"></span>
    <br />
    <label asp-for="ConfirmPassword"></label>
    <input asp-for="ConfirmPassword" />
    <span asp-validation-for="ConfirmPassword"></span>
    <br />
    <button type="submit">Register</button>
</form>
```

Explanation:

The `<div asp-validation-summary="All"></div>` code displays all error messages. Whereas, `<span asp-validation-for="Email"></span>` will only show the error message for the email field.

Next, add an [HttpPost] action method named Register to the AccountController.cs:

```csharp
[HttpPost]
public async Task<IActionResult> Register(AccountRegisterViewModel vm)
{
    if (ModelState.IsValid)
    {
        var user = new ApplicationUser
        {
        UserName = vm.Email, Email = vm.Email};
        var result = await userManager.CreateAsync(user, vm.Password);
        if (result.Succeeded)
        {
        await signInManager.SignInAsync(user, false);
        return RedirectToAction("Index", "Home");
        }
        else
        {
        foreach (var error in result.Errors)
        {
        ModelState.AddModelError("", error.Description);
        }
    }
}
return View(vm);
}
```

Explanation:

userManager.CreateAsync(user, vm.Password) adds a new user to the database with the provided password.

signInManager.SignInAsync(user, false) signs in the new user without using a persistent cookie.

Save and start without debugging.

Access the URL localhost/Account/Register to view the registration form. Fill in the required details and click on the "Register" button. You'll be redirected to the password-protected page as you now have access after successfully registering an account.

Step 4: Adding a Login Page for Registered Users

Start from implementing a method named Login in the AccountController.cs to display the login page:

```
public IActionResult Login()
{
    return View();
}
```

Next, create a new view model named AccountLoginViewModel.cs inside the ViewModels folder with the following code:

```
using System.ComponentModel.DataAnnotations;

namespace Chapter7Example1.ViewModels
{
    public class AccountLoginViewModel
    {
        [Required, EmailAddress]
        public string Email { get; set; }
        [Required, DataType(DataType.Password)]
        public string Password { get; set; }
    }
}
```

Next, generate a Razor View file named Login.cshtml inside the Views/Account/ folder using the code below:

```
@model Chapter7Example1.ViewModels.AccountLoginViewModel

<h2>User Login</h2>
<form asp-action="Login" method="post">
    <div asp-validation-summary="All"></div>
    <label asp-for="Email"></label>
    <input asp-for="Email" />
    <span asp-validation-for="Email"></span>
    <br />
    <label asp-for="Password"></label>
    <input asp-for="Password" />
```

```
    <span asp-validation-for="Password"></span>
    <br />
    <button type="submit">Log In</button>
</form>
```

Next, add an [HttpPost] action method named Login to the AccountController.cs to handle the login process:

```
[HttpPost]
public async Task<IActionResult> Login(AccountLoginViewModel vm)
{
    if (ModelState.IsValid)
    {
        var result = await signInManager.PasswordSignInAsync
            (vm.Email, vm.Password, false, false);

        if (result.Succeeded)
        {
        return RedirectToAction("Index", "Home");
        }
        ModelState.AddModelError("", "Login Failure.");
    }
    return View(vm);
}
```

Save and start without debugging.

Access the URL localhost/Account/Login to view the login page.

Enter the username and password you used during registration in Step 3 to log in. Upon successful login, you will be directed to the password-protected page.

Test Your Understanding 7.17
A class in the Models can have annotations. The annotations within square brackets in this file ________, ensuring specific requirements for input fields.
a. help control display settings
b. bring flexibility for using the database
c. allow developers to add any control over the database table
d. increase the performance of the application

Test Your Understanding 7.18
A class in the Models can have annotations. The annotations within square brackets in this file ________, ensuring specific requirements for input fields.
a. help perform form validation
b. bring flexibility for using the database
c. allow developers to add any control over the database table
d. increase the performance of the application

Test Your Understanding 7.19
In ASP.NET MVC Razror View, what is necessary to make the <span asp-validation-for="Email"></span> work?
a. Add notations in the model.
b. Add notations in the controller.
c. Add notations in the razor view.
d. Add typos in the razor view code.

Test Your Understanding 7.20
In ASP.NET MVC Razror View, what notation can make the <span asp-validation-for="Email"></span> work?
a. [Required]
b. [Display]
c. Both [Required] and [Display]
d. Neither [Required] nor [Display]

Test Your Understanding 7.21
In ASP.NET MVC Razror View, what notation can make the <span asp-validation-for="Email"></span> work?
a. [Required]
b. [EmailAddress]
c. Both [Required] and [EmailAddress]
d. Neither [Required] nor [EmailAddress]

Test Your Understanding 7.22
What method signs in a new user without using a persistent cookie in the AccountController of the book?
a. signInManager.SignInAsync(user, false)
b. userManager.CreateAsync(user, vm.Password)
c. signInManager.PasswordSignInAsync(vm.Email, vm.Password, false, false)
d. userManager.AddToRoleAsync(user, roleName)

Test Your Understanding 7.23
Which of the following statements in an action method can be used to check the validity of a model from a razor view?
a. Model.Valid
b. ModelState.Valid
c. Model.IsValid
d. ModelState.IsValid

Test Your Understanding 7.24
What method adds a new user to the database with the provided password in the AccountController of the book example?
a. signInManager.SignInAsync(user, false)
b. userManager.CreateAsync(user, vm.Password)
c. signInManager.PasswordSignInAsync(vm.Email, vm.Password, false, false)
d. userManager.AddToRoleAsync(user, roleName)

Test Your Understanding 7.25
In a Razor View, The `<div asp-validation-summary="All"></div>` code displays _______.
Whereas, `<span asp-validation-for="Email"></span>` will only show _______.

a. all error messages of the project, the error message for the email field
b. all error messages, the error message for the email field
c. a summary of the Razor View, a summary of the email message
d. a summary of the Razor View, a validation of the email message

Test Your Understanding 7.26
Which method is used to handle the login process in the AccountController of the book?
a. Login()
b. Register()
c. CreateAsync()
d. PasswordSignInAsync()

Step 5: Adding and Displaying Roles

You need to have roles in the database to implement role-based access control. Create a controller named

RoleController.cs in the Controllers folder and define fields and a constructor as shown below:

```csharp
// Properties
ApplicationDbContext db;
UserManager<ApplicationUser> userManager;
RoleManager<IdentityRole> roleManager;
// Constructor
public RoleController(ApplicationDbContext db,
    UserManager<ApplicationUser> userManager,
    RoleManager<IdentityRole> roleManager)
{
    this.db = db;
    this.userManager = userManager;
    this.roleManager = roleManager;
}
```

Still inside the RoleController, add an action method named AllRole:

```csharp
public IActionResult AllRole()
{
    var roles = roleManager.Roles.ToList();
    return View(roles);
}
```

Create a view named AllRole.cshtml in the Views/Role folder with the code below:

```cshtml
@model IEnumerable<Microsoft.AspNetCore.Identity.IdentityRole>
<p><a asp-action="AddRole">Add a role</a></p>
@{
    if (Model.Count() < 1)
    {
        <p>No role in database yet.</p>
    }
    else
    {
```

```
    <h3>All Roles</h3>
    <table border="1">
        <tr>
            <th>Role Name</th>
        </tr>
        @foreach (var role in Model)
        {
            <tr>
                <td>@role.Name</td>
            </tr>
        }
    </table>
    }
}
```

Access the URL localhost/Role/AllRole to view the "Add a role" hyperlink. To enable the "Add a role"

hyperlink, add an action method called AddRole to the RoleController.cs:

```
public IActionResult AddRole()
{
    return View();
}
```

Create a Razor View file named AddRole.cshtml in the Views/Role folder:

```
@model Microsoft.AspNetCore.Identity.IdentityRole
<form asp-controller="Role"
      asp-action="AddRole" method="post">
    <label asp-for="Name"></label>
    <input asp-for="Name" />
    <br />
    <button type="submit">Add Role</button>
</form>
```

Implement an [HttpPost] action method named AddRole in the RoleController.cs to process role addition:

```
[HttpPost]
public async Task<IActionResult> AddRole(IdentityRole role)
{
    var result = await roleManager.CreateAsync(role);
    if (result.Succeeded)
    {
        return RedirectToAction("AllRole");
    }
    return View();
}
```

Access the URL localhost/Role/AllRole, then click on the "Add a role" link to enter role names like "student," "instructor," and "admin" into the database. This enables the creation and display of roles, allowing differentiation of user access based on assigned roles.

Step 6: Assigning a Role to a User

Create an action method named AllUser() in the Account controller to list all users and their assigned roles:

```
public IActionResult AllUser()
{
    var users = db.Users.ToList();
    var userRoles = new Dictionary<string, List<string>>();
    foreach (var user in users)
    {
        var roles = userManager.GetRolesAsync(user).Result.ToList();
        userRoles[user.Id] = roles;
    }
ViewBag.UserRoles = userRoles;
return View(users);
}
```

Generate a Razor View file named AllUser.cshtml in the Views/Account/ folder:

```
@model IEnumerable<Microsoft.AspNetCore.Identity.IdentityUser>
<p><a asp-action="Register">Add a user</a></p>
@{
    if (Model.Count() < 1)
    {
        <p>No user in database yet.</p>
    }
    else
    {
        <h3>All Users</h3>
        <table border="1">
        <tr>
        <th>User Name</th>
        <th>Assigned Roles</th>
        <th>Add Role</th>
        </tr>
        @foreach (var user in Model)
        {
        <tr>
        <td>@user.UserName</td>
        <td>
        @{
        var userRoles = ViewBag.UserRoles as Dictionary<string, List<string>>;
        if (userRoles.ContainsKey(user.Id))
```

```
            {
                var roles = userRoles[user.Id];
                <text>@string.Join(", ", roles)</text>
            }
            }
        </td>
        <td>
        <a asp-controller="Role" asp-action="AddUserRole"
        asp-route-id="@user.Id">Add a role</a>
        </td>
        </tr>
    }
    </table>
    }
}
```

Implement an action method called AddUserRole in the RoleController.cs:

```
public async Task<IActionResult> AddUserRole(string id)
{
    var roleDisplay = db.Roles.Select(x => new {Id = x.Id, Value = x.Name}).ToList();
    RoleAddUserRoleViewModel vm = new RoleAddUserRoleViewModel();
    var user = await userManager.FindByIdAsync(id);
    vm.User = user;
    vm.RoleList = new SelectList(roleDisplay, "Id", "Value");
    return View(vm);
}
```

Create a ViewModel named RoleAddUserRoleViewModel.cs in the ViewModels folder:

```
using Chapter7Example1.Models;
using Microsoft.AspNetCore.Mvc.Rendering;

namespace Chapter7Example1.ViewModels
{
    public class RoleAddUserRoleViewModel
    {
        public ApplicationUser User { get; set; }
        public string Role { get; set; }
        public SelectList RoleList { get; set; }
    }
}
```

Generate a Razor View file named AddUserRole.cshtml in the Views/Role/ folder:

```
@model Chapter7Example1.ViewModels.RoleAddUserRoleViewModel
<p>Pick a role for @Model.User.UserName</p>
```

```html
<form asp-controller="Role" asp-action="AddUserRole"
    method="post">
  <div asp-validation-summary="All"></div>
  <input asp-for="@Model.User.Id" type="hidden" />
  <label asp-for="Role"></label>
  <select asp-for="Role"
        asp-items="@Model.RoleList">
    <option value="">-- Select a role --</option>
  </select>
  <br />
  <button type="submit">Add Role</button>
</form>
<p>
  <a asp-controller="Account" asp-action="AllUser">
    Back to user list
  </a>
</p>
```

Implement an [HttpPost] action method called AddUserRole in the RoleController.cs:

```csharp
[HttpPost]
public async Task<IActionResult> AddUserRole(RoleAddUserRoleViewModel vm)
{
    var user = await userManager.FindByIdAsync(vm.User.Id);
    var role = await roleManager.FindByIdAsync(vm.Role);
    var result = await userManager.AddToRoleAsync(user, role.Name);
    if (result.Succeeded)
    {
        return RedirectToAction("AllUser", "Account");
    }
    foreach (var error in result.Errors)
    {
        ModelState.AddModelError(error.Code, error.Description);
    }
    var roleDisplay = db.Roles.Select(x => new {Id = x.Id,
    Value = x.Name}).ToList();
    vm.User = user;
    vm.RoleList = new SelectList(roleDisplay, "Id", "Value");
    return View(vm);
}
```

Access the URL localhost/Account/AllUser to view the list of users and their roles. Click on the "Add a role" link to assign roles to registered users. Make sure you assign at least one user to the admin role.

Test Your Understanding 7.27
Which method retrieves all roles from Identity database in ASP.NET using the book examples?

a. `var roles = identity.Roles.ToList();`
b. `var roles = roleManager.Roles.allRoles;`
c. `var roles = roleManager.Roles.ToList();`
d. `var roles = identity.Roles.allRoles;`

Test Your Understanding 7.28
Which model is used on a Razor View when accessing all roles in ASP.NET Identity from the book?
a. `@model Microsoft.AspNetCore.Identity`
b. `@model Microsoft.AspNetCore.Identity.IdentityRole`
c. `@model IEnumerable<Microsoft.AspNetCore.Identity>`
d. `@model IEnumerable<Microsoft.AspNetCore.Identity.IdentityRole>`

Test Your Understanding 7.29
Which statement adds a role to ASP.NET Identity from the book examples?
a. `var result = await roleManager.CreateAsync(role);`
b. `var result = await roleManager.AddAsync(role);`
c. `var result = await roleManager.AddRoleAsync(role);`
d. `var result = await roleManager.CreateRoleAsync(role);`

Test Your Understanding 7.30
Which statement retrieves all roles of a specific user in ASP.NET Identity from the book examples?
a. `var roles = userManager.GetUserRolesAsync(user)ToList();`
b. `var roles = userManager.GetUserRolesAsync(user).Result.ToList();`
c. `var roles = userManager.GetRolesAsync(user).ToList();`
d. `var roles = userManager.GetRolesAsync(user).Result.ToList();`

Test Your Understanding 7.31
What does this line of code do?
`var userRoles = new Dictionary<string, List<string>>();`
a. Creates a dictionary without any keys.
b. Creates a dictionary to store strings and lists of strings.
c. Creates a dictionary with string keys and lists of strings as values.
d. Creates a dictionary using strings for both keys and values.

Step 7: Authorize Admin Role Access to Role Controller

To restrict access to the Role Controller solely to administrators, follow these steps:

Open RoleController.cs.

Add the following line just before the RoleController class declaration (before public class RoleController : Controller):

`[Authorize(Roles ="Admin")]`

Additionally, in AccountController.cs, locate the AllUser() method.

Insert the same line just before the AllUser() method declaration (before public IActionResult AllUser()).

Save. Start without debugging.

Now, accessing the Role Controller or the AllUser() method in the Account Controller will require administrative privileges. Users must have the 'Admin' role assigned to access these functionalities.

Step 8: Adding Additional Tables to the Database

Create four classes - Instructor, Student, Course, and Enrollment - in separate files within the Models folder:

Instructor.cs code below:

```csharp
namespace Chapter7Example1.Models
{
    public class Instructor
    {
        public int InstructorId { get; set; }
        public string InstructorName { get; set; }
        public string OfficeLocation { get; set; }
        public string UserId { get; set; }
        public virtual ApplicationUser User { get; set; }
        public virtual ICollection<Course> Courses { get; set; }
    }
}
```

Student.cs code:

```csharp
namespace Chapter7Example1.Models
{
    public class Student
    {
        public int StudentId { get; set; }
        public string StudentName { get; set;}
        public string UserId { get; set;}
        public virtual ApplicationUser User { get; set; }
        public virtual ICollection<Enrollment> Enrollments { get; set; }
    }
}
```

Course.cs code:

```csharp
namespace Chapter7Example1.Models
{
    public class Course
    {
        public int CourseId { get; set; }
        public string CourseTitle { get; set; }
        public int SeatCapacity { get; set; }
        public int InstructorId { get; set; }
        public virtual Instructor Instructor { get; set; }
```

```csharp
        public virtual ICollection<Enrollment> Enrollments { get; set; }
    }
}
```

Enrollment.cs file code:

```csharp
using System.ComponentModel.DataAnnotations;

namespace Chapter7Example1.Models
{
    public enum LetterGrade
    {
        A, B, C, D, E, F, I, W, P
    }
    public class Enrollment
    {
        public int EnrollmentId { get; set; }
        public int? StudentId { get; set;}
        public int? CourseId { get; set; }
        public virtual Student Student { get; set; }
        public virtual Course Course { get; set; }
        [DisplayFormat(NullDisplayText="No Grade")]
        public LetterGrade? LetterGrade { get; set; }
    }
}
```

Update ApplicationDbContext.cs in the Models folder by adding DbSet properties for the newly created classes:

```csharp
using Microsoft.AspNetCore.Identity.EntityFrameworkCore;
using Microsoft.EntityFrameworkCore;
namespace Chapter7Example1.Models
{
    public class ApplicationDbContext :
        IdentityDbContext<ApplicationUser>
    {
        public DbSet<Instructor> Instructors { get; set; }
        public DbSet<Course> Courses { get; set; }
        public DbSet<Student> Students { get; set; }
        public DbSet<Enrollment> Enrollments { get; set; }
        public ApplicationDbContext(DbContextOptions
            <ApplicationDbContext> options)
            : base(options)
        {
        }
    }
}
```

Open the Package Manager Console and execute commands:

```
Add-Migration M2

Update-Database
```

Confirm the creation of the instructors, students, courses, and enrollments tables in the Chapter7Db database using SQL Server Object Explorer.

Test Your Understanding 7.32
Which attribute is used to restrict access to the Role Controller to administrators only in the book example?
a. [Authorize(AdminAccess = true)]
b. [Authorized(Roles ="Admin")]
c. [Authorize[Roles ="Administrator"]]
d. [Authentic(Role ="Admin")]

Test Your Understanding 7.33
What modification is made in the AccountController.cs file to enforce administrative privileges for the AllUser() method in the book example?
a. Insert [Authorize(AdminAccess = true)] before the method
b. Add [Authorized(Roles ="Admin")] above the method
c. Insert [Authorize(Roles ="Admin")] before the method
d. Include [Authentic(Role ="Admin")] after the method

Test Your Understanding 7.34
Which of the following activities are required if you want to add a table called Instructors to an existing database by using EF?
a. Add a class called Instructor.
b. Add a class called Faculty.
c. Add a class called Student before adding a class called Instructor.
d. Add a class of any name, but Instructor may be more appropriate.

Test Your Understanding 7.35
What does the following code snippet do?
```
public enum LetterGrade
{
    A, B, C, D, E, F, I, W, P
}
```
a. It defines an enumeration type named LetterGrade.
b. It defines a class named enum that implement LetterGrade.
c. It defines a class named enum that inherits from LetterGrade.
d. It assigns the specified letter grade to a student.

Test Your Understanding 7.36
Which of the following activities are required if you want to add a table called Instructors to an existing database by using EF?
a. A Dbset property must be added to the DbContext class.
b. A constructor must be added to the DbContext class.

c. A constructor named Instructor must be added to the DbContext class.
d. A table named Instructor must be added to the DbContext class.

Test Your Understanding 7.37
Which commands are executed in the Package Manager Console to apply database changes after creating
the classes?
a. Add-Migration Update and Update-Database
b. Create-Migration NewTables and Update-Tables
c. Add-Migration M2 and Update-Database
d. Apply-Migration and Update-Tables

Step 9: Redirecting Users to Appropriate Portal Page by Role

To enable the functionality of remembering a user as they navigate from one page to another, we will utilize

"sessions". In order to implement this, the Newtonsoft.Json package is required. Search for and install the

`Microsoft.AspNetCore.Mvc.NewtonsoftJson` 8.0.0 package.

Modifying Login Method in AccountController

```
[HttpPost]
public async Task<IActionResult> Login(AccountLoginViewModel vm)
{
    if (ModelState.IsValid)
    {
        var result = await signInManager.PasswordSignInAsync(vm.Email,
        vm.Password, false, false);

        if (result.Succeeded)
        {
            var user = await userManager.FindByEmailAsync(vm.Email);
            var roles = await userManager.GetRolesAsync(user);

            if (roles.Count > 1)
            {
                HttpContext.Session.SetString("UserRoles",
                JsonConvert.SerializeObject(roles));
                return RedirectToAction("SelectRole");
            }
            else if (roles.Contains("Admin"))
            {
                return RedirectToAction("Index", "Admin");
            }
            else if (roles.Contains("Instructor"))
            {
                return RedirectToAction("Index", "Instructor");
            }
            else if (roles.Contains("Student"))
            {
```

```
            return RedirectToAction("Index", "Student");
        }
        return RedirectToAction("Index", "Home");
    }
    ModelState.AddModelError("", "Login Failure.");
}
return View(vm);
}
```

Adding SelectRole Method in the AccountController and Corresponding Razor View

```
public IActionResult SelectRole()
{
    var roles = HttpContext.Session.GetString("UserRoles");
    var roleList = JsonConvert.DeserializeObject<List<string>>(roles);
    return View(roleList);
}
```

The SelectRole.cshtml inside Views/Account folder:

```
@model List<string>
<form method="post" asp-action="SetRole">
    <select name="SelectedRole">
        @foreach (var role in Model)
        {
            <option value="@role">@role</option>
        }
    </select>
    <input type="submit" value="Select Role" />
</form>
```

Handling Selected Role in AccountController when the above form is submitted.

```
[HttpPost]
public IActionResult SetRole(string SelectedRole)
{
    if (SelectedRole == "Admin")
    {
        return RedirectToAction("Index", "Admin");
    }
    else if (SelectedRole == "Instructor")
    {
        return RedirectToAction("Index", "Instructor");
    }
    else if (SelectedRole == "Student")
    {
        return RedirectToAction("Index", "Student");
    }
}
```

```
    return RedirectToAction("Index", "Home");
}
```

Updating Program.cs by adding the following before `builder.Services.AddControllersWithViews();`

```
builder.Services.AddDistributedMemoryCache();
builder.Services.AddSession(options =>
{
    options.IdleTimeout = TimeSpan.FromMinutes(30);
    options.Cookie.HttpOnly = true;
    options.Cookie.IsEssential = true;
});
```

Additionally, add this line:

```
app.UseSession();
```

right before this line: right before this line: "`app.MapControllerRoute("`

Finally, adding Landing Page for Instructor. Add InstructorController.cs inside Controllers folder:

```
using Chapter7Example1.Models;
using Microsoft.AspNetCore.Authorization;
using Microsoft.AspNetCore.Mvc;
using Microsoft.EntityFrameworkCore;
using System.Security.Claims;

namespace Chapter7Example1.Controllers
{
    [Authorize(Roles="Instructor")]
    public class InstructorController : Controller
    {
        private readonly ApplicationDbContext db;
        public InstructorController(ApplicationDbContext db)
        {
            this.db= db;
        }
        public IActionResult Index()
        {
            var currentUserId =
            this.User.FindFirst(ClaimTypes.NameIdentifier).Value;
            ViewData["Instructor"] = db.Instructors.FirstOrDefault(i =>
            i.UserId == currentUserId);
            return View();
        }
    }
}
```

Add a Razor View (Index.cshtml) inside Views/Instructor folder:

```
<h2>Instructor Home</h2>
@{
    if(ViewData["Instructor"] == null)
    {
        <p><a asp-action="AddProfile">Add profile</a></p>
    }
    else
    {
        <p><a asp-action="AddProfile">Add profile</a></p>
        <p><a asp-action="AddCourse">Add a course</a></p>
        <p><a asp-action="CourseByInstructor">
         Post grade for a course</a></p>
    }
}
```

Save. Start without Debugging.

When you log in as an instructor, the browser will display the instructor portal page. The first time an instructor logs in, the portal page will only show the "Add Profile" link.

Step 10: Implementing "Add Profile" Link on the Instructor Portal Page

Update Instructor Controller by adding a methoded called AddProfile():

```
public IActionResult AddProfile()
{
    var currentUserId =
    this.User.FindFirst(ClaimTypes.NameIdentifier).Value;
    Instructor instructor = new Instructor();
    if (db.Instructors.Any(i => i.UserId == currentUserId))
    {
      instructor =
      db.Instructors.FirstOrDefault(i=>i.UserId==currentUserId);
    }
    else
    {
        instructor.UserId = currentUserId;
    }
    return View(instructor);
}
```

Add Razor View (AddProfile.cshtml) in Views/Instructor Folder

```
@model Chapter7Example1.Models.Instructor
<h2>Add Your Profile</h2>
<form asp-controller="Instructor" asp-action="AddProfile"
method="post">
```

```html
<input asp-for="@Model.UserId" type="hidden" />
<label asp-for="InstructorName"></label>
<input asp-for="InstructorName" />
<br />
    <label asp-for="OfficeLocation"></label>
<input asp-for="OfficeLocation" />
<br />
<button type="submit">Add Profile</button>
</form>
<p><a asp-action="Index">Back to instructor home</a></p>
```

Handle Form Submission in InstructorController by adding an [HttpPost] AddProfile() method:

```csharp
[HttpPost]
public async Task<IActionResult> AddProfile(Instructor instructor)
{
    var currentUserId = this.User.FindFirst(ClaimTypes.NameIdentifier).Value;
    if (db.Instructors.Any(i => i.UserId == currentUserId))
    {
        var instructorToUpdate =
        db.Instructors.FirstOrDefault(i=>i.UserId == currentUserId);
        instructorToUpdate.InstructorName = instructor.InstructorName;
        instructorToUpdate.OfficeLocation = instructor.OfficeLocation;
        db.Update(instructorToUpdate);
    }
    else
    {
        db.Add(instructor);
    }
    await db.SaveChangesAsync();
    return RedirectToAction("Index");
}
```

Save. Start without debugging. Add a few instructor profiles to observe how the functionality operates.

Test Your Understanding 7.38
What package is necessary to implement user session functionality for remembering users as they navigate between pages?

```csharp
HttpContext.Session.SetString("UserRoles",
JsonConvert.SerializeObject(roles));
var roles = HttpContext.Session.GetString("UserRoles");
```
a. Microsoft.AspNetCore.Mvc.CookiesSession
b. Newtonsoft.Json.Session
c. Microsoft.AspNetCore.Session.MemoryCache
d. Microsoft.AspNetCore.Mvc.NewtonsoftJson

Test Your Understanding 7.39

Where is the most likely place for the following code?

```
HttpContext.Session.SetString("UserRoles",
JsonConvert.SerializeObject(roles));
```

a. In a model

b. In a view model

c. In a Razor View

d. In a controller

Test Your Understanding 7.40

Which configuration sets the session timeout to 30 minutes in the Program.cs file?

a. options.IdleTimeout = TimeSpan.FromMinutes(30);

b. options.Timeout = TimeSpan.FromMinutes(30);

c. options.Expiration = TimeSpan.FromMinutes(30);

d. options.SessionTimeout = TimeSpan.FromMinutes(30);

Test Your Understanding 7.41

What does the following code do?

```
this.User.FindFirst(ClaimTypes.NameIdentifier).Value;
```

a. Find the first claim.

b. Find the first user.

c. Find the currently logged in user.

d. Find the first name identifier.

Step 11: Allowing an Instructor to Add a Course

Update Instructor Controller by adding a method called "AddCourse":

```
public async Task<IActionResult> AddCourse()
{
    Course course = new Course();
    var currentUserId=
    this.User.FindFirst(ClaimTypes.NameIdentifier).Value;
    var instructor = await db.Instructors.SingleOrDefaultAsync(i =>
    i.UserId == currentUserId);
    if (instructor != null)
    {
        course.InstructorId = instructor.InstructorId;
    }
    return View(course);
}
```

Add Razor View (AddCourse.cshtml) in Views/Instructor Folder

```
@model Chapter7Example1.Models.Course
<h2>Add A New Course</h2>
<form asp-controller="Instructor" asp-action="AddCourse" method="post">
    <label asp-for="CourseTitle"></label>
    <input asp-for="CourseTitle" />
    <br />
    <label asp-for="SeatCapacity"></label>
```

```html
    <input asp-for="SeatCapacity" />
    <br />
    <input asp-for="InstructorId" type="hidden" />
    <button type="submit">Add Course</button>
</form>
<p><a asp-action="Index">Back to instructor home</a></p>
```

Handle Form Submission in InstructorController by adding an [HttpPost] AddCourse() method:

```csharp
[HttpPost]
public async Task<IActionResult> AddCourse(Course course)
{
    db.Add(course);
    await db.SaveChangesAsync();
    return RedirectToAction("Index", "Instructor");
}
```

Save. Start without debugging. Login as an instructor and add a few courses.

Step 12: Adding Student Portal Page

Create StudentController and Implement Index Action. Use the following code for the StudentController:

```csharp
using Chapter7Example1.Models;
using Microsoft.AspNetCore.Authorization;
using Microsoft.AspNetCore.Mvc;
using Microsoft.EntityFrameworkCore;
using System.Security.Claims;
namespace Chapter7Example1.Controllers
{
    [Authorize(Roles="Student")]
    public class StudentController : Controller
    {
        private readonly ApplicationDbContext db;
        public StudentController(ApplicationDbContext db)
        {
            this.db= db;
        }
        public IActionResult Index()
        {
            var currentUserId =
            this.User.FindFirst(ClaimTypes.NameIdentifier).Value;
            ViewData["Student"] = db.Students.FirstOrDefault(i =>
            i.UserId == currentUserId);
            return View();
        }
    }
}
```

Add Razor View (Index.cshtml) in Views/Student Folder:

```
<h2>Student Home</h2>
@{
    if (ViewData["Student"] == null)
    {
        <p><a asp-action="AddProfile">Add profile</a></p>
    }
    else
    {
        <p><a asp-action="AddProfile">Add profile</a></p>
        <p><a asp-action="AllCourse">Register a course</a></p>
        <p><a asp-action="CheckGrade">Check grade</a></p>
    }
}
```

Save. Start without debugging. Login as a student to access the portal page. On the first login, only the "Add Profile" link will be visible.

Test Your Understanding 7.42
With the following code in an action method, what is passed to the corresponding razor view?

```
public async Task<IActionResult> AddCourse()
{
    Course course = new Course();
    var currentUserId=
    this.User.FindFirst(ClaimTypes.NameIdentifier).Value;
    var instructor = await db.Instructors.SingleOrDefaultAsync(i =>
    i.UserId == currentUserId);
    if (instructor != null)
    {
        course.InstructorId = instructor.InstructorId;
    }
    return View(course);
}
```

a. A course with only CourseId.
b. A course with only InstructorId.
c. A course with both CourseId and InstructorId.
d. A course with CourseId, InstructorId, and currentUserId.

Test Your Understanding 7.43
The razor view for an HTML form allows an instructor to add a new course, why do we need a hidden field?

```
<input asp-for="InstructorId" type="hidden" />
```

a. For privacy purpose.
b. The InstructorId is not required in a course.
c. It will not work if you don't hide it.
d. So that the HTML form can pass the value as part of the model back to the controller.

Test Your Understanding 7.44
What is the purpose of the if statement in the following razor view?

```
if (ViewData["Student"] == null)
{
    <p><a asp-action="AddProfile">Add profile</a></p>
}
else
{
    <p><a asp-action="AddProfile">Add profile</a></p>
    <p><a asp-action="AllCourse">Register a course</a></p>
}
```

a. To avoid displaying null student on the page.
b. To avoid a null student adding a profile..
c. To avoid a user without Student role view the page.
d. To avoid a null student registering a course.

Test Your Understanding 7.45
What is the purpose of the if statement in the following razor view?

```
if (ViewData["Student"] == null)
{
    <p><a asp-action="AddProfile">Add profile</a></p>
}
else
{
    <p><a asp-action="AddProfile">Add profile</a></p>
    <p><a asp-action="AllCourse">Register a course</a></p>
}
```

a. Students must add profiles when they first land on this page.
b. Students can view their profiles when they first land on this page.
c. Users must become students to view profiles.
d. Users must become students to register a course.

Step 13: Implementing "Add profile" Link on Student Portal Page

Add the "AddProfile()" Action Method to StudentController:

```
public IActionResult AddProfile()
{
    var currentUserId =
    this.User.FindFirst(ClaimTypes.NameIdentifier).Value;
    Student student = new Student();
    if (db.Students.Any(i => i.UserId == currentUserId))
    {
        student = db.Students.FirstOrDefault(i=>i.UserId==currentUserId);
    }
    else
    {
        student.UserId = currentUserId;
    }
    return View(student);
}
```

Add Razor View (AddProfile.cshtml) in Views/Student Folder:

```
@model Chapter7Example1.Models.Student
<h2>Add Your Profile</h2>
<form asp-controller="Student" asp-action="AddProfile" method="post">
    <input asp-for="@Model.UserId" type="hidden" />
    <label asp-for="StudentName"></label>
    <input asp-for="StudentName" />
    <br />
    <button type="submit">Add Profile</button>
</form>
<p><a asp-action="Index">Back to student home</a></p>
```

Handle Form Submission in StudentController by adding an [HttpPost] AddProfile() method:

```
[HttpPost]
public async Task<IActionResult> AddProfile(Student student)
{
    var currentUserId =
    this.User.FindFirst(ClaimTypes.NameIdentifier).Value;
    if (db.Students.Any(i => i.UserId == currentUserId))
    {
    var studentToUpdate = db.Students.FirstOrDefault(i=>i.UserId ==
    currentUserId);
    studentToUpdate.StudentName = student.StudentName;
    db.Update(studentToUpdate);
    }
    else
    {
    db.Add(student);
    }
    await db.SaveChangesAsync();
    return RedirectToAction("Index");
}
```

Save. Start without debugging. Login as a student and complete the profile details using the "Add Profile" link.

Step 14: Student Course Enrollment

Update StudentController by adding an action method called "AllCourse()":

```
public async Task<IActionResult> AllCourse()
{
    var courses = await db.Courses.Include(c =>c.Instructor).ToListAsync();
    return View(courses);
}
```

Add Razor View (AllCourse.cshtml) in Views/Student Folder

```razor
@model IEnumerable<Chapter7Example1.Models.Course>

@{
    if (Model.Count() < 1)
    {
        <p>No course in database yet.</p>
    }
    else
    {
        <h3>All Courses</h3>
        <table border="1">
            <tr>
                <th>Course ID</th>
                <th>Course Title</th>
                <th>Seat Capacity</th>
                <th>Instructor Name</th>
                <th>Enroll Course</th>
            </tr>
            @foreach (var course in Model)
            {
                <tr>
                    <td>@course.CourseId</td>
                    <td>@course.CourseTitle</td>
                    <td>@course.SeatCapacity</td>
                    <td>@course.Instructor.InstructorName</td>
                    <td>@{
                        if (course.SeatCapacity < 1)
                        {
                            <p>Full class</p>
                        }
                        else
                        {
                            <a asp-controller="Student"
                            asp-action="EnrollCourse"
                            asp-route-id="@course.CourseId">Register</a>
                        }
                    }
                    </td>
                </tr>
            }
        </table>
    }
}
<p><a asp-action="Index">Back to student home</a></p>
```

Finally, update the StudentController by adding the EnrollCourse() method:

```csharp
public async Task<IActionResult> EnrollCourse(int id)
{
    var currentUserId =
    this.User.FindFirst(ClaimTypes.NameIdentifier).Value;
    var studentId = db.Students.FirstOrDefault
    (s => s.UserId == currentUserId).StudentId;
    Enrollment enrollment = new Enrollment
    {
        CourseId = id,
        StudentId = studentId
    };
    db.Add(enrollment);
    var course = await db.Courses.FindAsync(enrollment.CourseId);
    course.SeatCapacity--;
    await db.SaveChangesAsync();
    return RedirectToAction("Index", "Student");
}
```

Explanation:

You might wonder why there's a line `db.Add(enrollment)` without seeing something akin to `db.Update(course)`. In Entity Framework, the ORM (Object Relational Mapper) used in ASP.NET MVC, when an entity is retrieved from the database (like the `Course` in the code), it becomes 'tracked' by the DbContext (`db` in the code). This means any alterations made to this entity are detected by the DbContext. So, when you adjust the SeatCapacity with `course.SeatCapacity--;`, the DbContext acknowledges this change. Upon calling `await db.SaveChangesAsync();`, the DbContext scans all modifications in the tracked entities and generates necessary SQL commands to update the database.

Save. Start without debugging. Login as a student to register for available courses using the "Register" link in the course list.

Test Your Understanding 7.46
In Entity Framework used in ASP.NET MVC, when is an entity considered 'tracked' by the DbContext?
a. Upon retrieval from the database
b. After modification using SQL commands
c. Only when using db.Update() method
d. When creating a new entity

Test Your Understanding 7.47
What happens when alterations are made to a tracked entity in Entity Framework?
a. Changes are ignored
b. DbContext generates SQL commands immediately
c. Changes are detected by the DbContext
d. Changes are automatically updated in the database.

Test Your Understanding 7.48
What happens when alterations are made to a tracked entity in Entity Framework?
a. Changes are ignored
b. DbContext generates SQL commands immediately
c. Changes are updated in the database
d. Changes require explicit SaveChanges() call

Test Your Understanding 7.49
Why does the code snippet lack a specific db.Update(course) despite modifying the SeatCapacity property?

```
var course = await db.Courses.FindAsync(enrollment.CourseId);
course.SeatCapacity--;
await db.SaveChangesAsync();
```

a. The SeatCapacity property is immutable
b. DbContext doesn't track modifications to properties
c. Modifications to tracked entities are automatically detected
d. db.Update() is deprecated in Entity Framework

Test Your Understanding 7.50
What triggers the generation of necessary SQL commands to update the database in Entity Framework?
a. Calling db.SaveChanges()
b. Using db.Update() method
c. Modifying entities directly in the database
d. Retrieving entities from the database

Test Your Understanding 7.51
When does an entity in Entity Framework cease to be 'tracked' by the DbContext?
a. After modification
b. Upon retrieval from the database
c. When using db.Update() method
d. When calling db.SaveChanges()

Test Your Understanding 7.52
What is the primary role of the DbContext in Entity Framework's workflow?
a. Executing SQL queries directly
b. Tracking changes in entities
c. Generating C# entity classes
d. Optimizing database performance

Step 15: Instructor Course Grade Posting

Update InstructorController by adding an action method called CourseByInstructor():

```
public async Task<IActionResult> CourseByInstructor()
{
    var currentUserId =
    this.User.FindFirst(ClaimTypes.NameIdentifier).Value;
    var InstructorId = db.Instructors.SingleOrDefault
    (i => i.UserId == currentUserId).InstructorId;
    var course = await db.Courses.Include(c => c.Enrollments).Where
    (i => i.InstructorId == InstructorId).ToListAsync();
```

```
        return View(course);
}
```

Add Razor View (CourseByInstructor.cshtml) in Views/Instructor Folder:

```
@model IEnumerable<Chapter7Example1.Models.Course>

@{
    if (Model.Count() < 1)
    {
        <p>You don't have a course yet.
        <a asp-action="AddCourse">Add a course</a></p>
    }
    else
    {
        <h2>@Model.FirstOrDefault().Instructor.InstructorName</h2>
        <h3>All Courses</h3>
        <table border="1">
            <tr>
                <th>Course ID</th>
                <th>Course Title</th>
                <th>Seat Capacity</th>
                <th>Post Grade</th>
                <th>Enrollment count</th>
            </tr>
            @foreach (var course in Model)
            {
                if (course.Enrollments?.Count > 0)
                {
                    <tr>
                    <td>@course.CourseId</td>
                    <td>@course.CourseTitle</td>
                    <td>@course.SeatCapacity</td>
                    <td>@{
                            <a asp-controller="Instructor" asp-
                            action="PostGrade" asp-route-
                            id="@course.CourseId">Post grade</a>
                        }
                    </td>
                    <td>@course.Enrollments.Count</td>
                    </tr>
                }            }
        </table>
    }
}
<p><a asp-action="Index">Back to instructor home</a></p>
```

Explanation:

The code **course.Enrollments?.Count > 0** uses the question mark to first check if course.Enrollments is null before applying the Count property. Without such a check, it will throw an exception even when course.Enrollments is not null. This check makes the code more robust.

Instructors need an action method called "PostGrade()" to Post Grades for a Course. Update the InstructorController by adding the "PostGrade()" method:

```
public async Task<IActionResult> PostGrade(int? id)
{
    if(id== null)
    {
        return NotFound();
    }
    var allStudents = await db.Enrollments.Include(c =>c.Course)
    .Where(c => c.CourseId == id).ToListAsync();
    if(allStudents == null)
    {
        return NotFound();
    }
    return View(allStudents);
}
```

Add Razor View (PostGrade.cshtml) in Views/Instructor Folder:

```
@model List<Chapter7Example1.Models.Enrollment>
<h2>Enter Student Grades</h2>
<h3>Course: @Model[0].Course.CourseTitle</h3>
<form asp-controller="Instructor" asp-action="PostGrade" method="post">
<table border="1">
    <tr>
        <th></th>
        <th>Student ID</th>
        <th>Grade</th>
    </tr>
    @for(int i=0; i<Model.Count(); i++)
        {
         <tr>
            <td><input asp-for="@Model[i].EnrollmentId" type="hidden"
            value="@Model[i].EnrollmentId" /></td>
            <td>@Model[i].StudentId</td>
            <td><input asp-for="@Model[i].LetterGrade" /></td>
         </tr>
        }
    </table>
    <input type="submit" value="Submit" />
```

```
</form>
<p><a asp-action="Index">Back to instructor home</a></p>
```

Finally, an Action Method called PostGrade() to Save Posted Grades should be added to the

InstructorController:

```
[HttpPost]
public IActionResult PostGrade(List<Enrollment> enrollments)
{
    foreach(var enrollment in enrollments)
    {
        var er = db.Enrollments.Find(enrollment.EnrollmentId);
        er.LetterGrade = enrollment.LetterGrade;
    }
    db.SaveChanges();
    return RedirectToAction("CourseByInstructor");
}
```

Save. Start without debugging. Login as an instructor to post grades for courses assigned to you.

Test Your Understanding 7.53
What is the purpose of using the course.Enrollments?.Count > 0 code snippet in the given context?

```
if (course.Enrollments?.Count > 0)
{
    <tr>
    <td>@course.CourseId</td>
    </tr>
}
```

a. To increment the Enrollments count
b. To bypass null Enrollments
c. To throw an exception
d. To check if Enrollments contain specific data

Test Your Understanding 7.54
What consequence could occur if the null-conditional operator (?.) is not used in the given code snippet?

```
if (course.Enrollments?.Count > 0)
{
    <tr>
    <td>@course.CourseId</td>
    </tr>
}
```

a. It will always return true.
b. It will throw an exception even if the course.Enrollments is not null.
c. It will ignore the Count property.
d. It will bypass null Enrollments if the course.Enrollments is not null.

Step 16: Student Grade Checking

Update StudentController by adding Action Method called CheckGrade():

```
public async Task<IActionResult> CheckGrade()
{
    ClaimsPrincipal currentUser = this.User;
    var currentUserId =
    currentUser.FindFirst(ClaimTypes.NameIdentifier).Value;
    if(currentUserId == null)
    {
        return NotFound();
    }
    var student = await db.Students.SingleOrDefaultAsync(s => s.UserId
    == currentUserId);
    var studentId = student.StudentId;
    var allCourses = await db.Enrollments.Include(e => e.Course)
    .Where(c => c.StudentId == studentId).ToListAsync();
    if (allCourses == null)
    {
        return NotFound();
    }
    ViewData["sname"] = student.StudentName;
    return View(allCourses);
}
```

Add Razor View (CheckGrade.cshtml) in Views/Student Folder

```
@model IEnumerable<Chapter7Example1Net8.Models.Enrollment>
<h3>Student Name: @ViewData["sname"]</h3>
<table border="1">
    <tr>
        <th>Course Title</th>
        <th>Grade</th>
    </tr>
    @foreach (var e in Model)
    {
        <tr>
            <td>@e.Course.CourseTitle</td>
            <td>@Html.DisplayFor(m=>e.LetterGrade)</td>
        </tr>
    }
</table>
<p><a asp-action="Index">Back to student home</a></p>
```

Save. Start without debugging. Login as a student to check your grades.

Step 17: Implementing Admin Portal Page (Details Omitted for Brevity)

Simply create an AdminController and a razor view to showcase two hyperlinks. The first hyperlink facilitates the admin in managing roles, directing to the previously created 'AllRole' page. The second link enables the admin to handle user roles, redirecting to the 'AllUser' page.

Step 18. User Logout Implementation

Update _Layout.cshtml in Views/Shared Folder. Add these lines after the <body> line:

```
@if (this.User.Identity.IsAuthenticated)
{
    <div>Hello, @this.User.Identity.Name</div>
    <form method="post" asp-controller="Account" asp-action="Logout">
    <input type="submit" value="Logout" />
    </form>
}
```

Update AccountController by adding Logout() Method:

```
[HttpPost]
public async Task<IActionResult> Logout()
{
    await signInManager.SignOutAsync();
    return RedirectToAction("Login");
}
```

Save. Start without debugging. Navigate through authorized pages and observe the presence of the logout link and the displayed user email when signed in. Test the logout functionality to ensure it works as expected.

Test Your Understanding 7.55
The ASP.NET Core ____________ is a membership system designed to grant various users access to different types of data.
a. Account
b. Identity
c. Privilege
d. Entity Framework

Test Your Understanding 7.56
Which of the following is NOT needed when installing ASP.NET Core Identity?
a. IdentityPassword
b. IdentityUser
c. IdentityDbContext<>
d. AddIdentity

Test Your Understanding 7.57

Which of the following is NOT needed when installing ASP.NET Core Identity?
a. UseAuthentication
b. IdentityUser
c. IdentityDbContext<>
d. UseIdentity

Test Your Understanding 7.58
Which of the following table is NOT automatically created after successfully installing the ASP.NET Core Identity?
a. AspNetUsers
b. AspNetRoles
c. AspNetPassword
d. AspNetUserRoles

Test Your Understanding 7.59
If you have the following controller and action method, who can visit the localhost/Home/Index?

```csharp
using Microsoft.AspNetCore.Authorization;
using Microsoft.AspNetCore.Mvc;

namespace Chapter7Example1Net8.Controllers
{
    public class HomeController : Controller
    {
        [Authorize]
        public IActionResult Index()
        {
            return View();
        }
    }
}
```

a. admin only
b. instructor only
c. student only
d. any registered user

Test Your Understanding 7.60
If you have the following controller and action method, who can visit the localhost/Instructor/Index?

```csharp
[Authorize(Roles="Instructor")]
public class InstructorController : Controller
{
    private readonly ApplicationDbContext db;
    public InstructorController(ApplicationDbContext db)
    {
        this.db= db;
    }
    public IActionResult Index()
    {
        var currentUserId =
    this.User.FindFirst(ClaimTypes.NameIdentifier).Value;
```

```
        ViewData["Instructor"] = db.Instructors.FirstOrDefault(i =>
        i.UserId == currentUserId);
        return View();
    }
}
```

a. admin only
b. instructor only
c. admin or instructor
d. any registered user

Test Your Understanding 7.61

If you have the following controller and action method, who can visit the localhost/Instructor/Index?

```
[Authorize(Roles="Instructor, Admin")]
public class InstructorController : Controller
{
    private readonly ApplicationDbContext db;
    public InstructorController(ApplicationDbContext db)
    {
        this.db= db;
    }
    public IActionResult Index()
    {
        var currentUserId =
    this.User.FindFirst(ClaimTypes.NameIdentifier).Value;
        ViewData["Instructor"] = db.Instructors.FirstOrDefault(i =>
        i.UserId == currentUserId);
        return View();
    }
}
```

a. admin only
b. instructor only
c. admin or instructor
d. any registered user

Test Your Understanding 7.62

What is the objective of the following code block?

```
if (result.Succeeded)
{
    var user = await userManager.FindByEmailAsync(vm.Email);
    var roles = await userManager.GetRolesAsync(user);
    if (roles.Contains("Instructor"))
    {
        return RedirectToAction("Index", "Instructor");
    }
    else if (roles.Contains("Student"))
    {
        return RedirectToAction("Index", "Student");
    }
    return RedirectToAction("Index", "Home");
```

```
}
```
a. Determine instructors and redirect to the instructor page.
b. Identify students and redirect to the student page.
c. Identify instructors or students and redirect accordingly.
d. Determine the current user's role and redirect to an appropriate page.

Programming Challenge 7.1

In Step 10, an instructor can add profile. In Step 14, a student can see a list of courses with an instructor name for each course. Enhance the project by making those instructor names hyperlinks and lead to corresponding instructor profile.

In Step 13, a student can add profile. In Step 15, an instructor can post grades for a list of student IDs. Enhance the project by making those student IDs hyperlinks and lead to corresponding student profile.

In Step 14, a student can enroll in a course. In fact, a student can enroll in the same course several times. Enhance the project by preventing a student from registering for the same course before receiving the grade for a previously registered instance of the same course.

7.2 Interface Segregation Principle

In SOLID, the letter "I" represents the Interface Segregation Principle. This principle advocates that when a class implements an interface, it should only be compelled to implement methods it actually uses. The issue arises when a class implements an interface that mandates implementation of all its methods, regardless of their necessity.

Let's explore an example that violates this principle and delve into a redesign to adhere to it.

Both domestic and international students require admission. Domestic students typically gain admission based on their ACT scores, while international students can be admitted based on either ACT or TOEFL scores. One potential design solution involves an interface named IAdmission, housing two methods – AdmissionByACT and AdmissionByTOEFL. Both domestic and international student classes are expected to implement the IAdmission interface. The following program follows this design.

Creating a C# Console Application - Chapter7ISP

To begin, initiate a new C# console application (not ASP.NET Core MVC) named Chapter7ISP. Start by adding an interface, IAdmission, including the following code:

```
namespace Chapter7ISP
```

```
{
    internal interface IAdmission
    {
        string AdmissionByACT();
        string AdmissionByTOEFL();
    }
}
```

Following this, introduce a class, DomesticStudent, within the Chapter7ISP project, containing the code below:

```
namespace Chapter7ISP
{
    internal class DomesticStudent: IAdmission
    {
        public int ACTScore { get; set; }
        public string AdmissionByACT()
        {
            if (ACTScore > 30)
                return "Congratulations!";
            else
                return "Try again next time.";
        }

        public string AdmissionByTOEFL()
        {
            throw new NotImplementedException();
        }
    }
}
```

This initial design infringes upon the Interface Segregation Principle (ISP) as it obliges the DomesticStudent class to implement the AdmissionByTOEFL method. This violation poses several issues: AdmissionByTOEFL is non-functional (throws an exception), any new method addition to IAdmission demands implementation in DomesticStudent, leading to maintenance and evolution difficulties (Romano, et al., 2014).

To rectify the violation of the Interface Segregation Principle (ISP) and ensure adherence to it, a redesign becomes imperative. The proposed solution involves the creation of two distinct interfaces: IAdmissionByACT and IAdmissionByTOEFL, each containing only the relevant method.

Begin by adding an interface named IAdmissionByACT to the project with the following code:

```
namespace Chapter7ISP
{
    internal interface IAdmissionByACT
    {
        string AdmissionByACT();
    }
}
```

Following this, introduce another interface titled IAdmissionByTOEFL into the project, encompassing the code below:

```
namespace Chapter7ISP
{
    internal interface IAdmissionByTOEFL
    {
        string AdmissionByTOEFL();
    }
}
```

By segregating the interfaces into IAdmissionByACT and IAdmissionByTOEFL, each interface now contains only the methods pertinent to its context. Consequently, the DomesticStudent class needs to implement only the IAdmissionByACT interface. Conversely, the InternationalStudent class will implement both IAdmissionByACT and IAdmissionByTOEFL interfaces. This revised design strictly adheres to the Interface Segregation Principle.

Test Your Understanding 7.63
The _________ states that no client class should be forced to depend on methods it does not use.
a. Liskov substitution principle
b. Open/Close principle
c. Single responsibility principle
d. Interface segregation principle

Test Your Understanding 7.64
To follow the Interface segregation principle, you often end up with __________.
a. many more classes
b. much fewer classes
c. many more specific interfaces
d. many less specific interfaces

7.3 Chapter Summary

This chapter covered adding Identity to ASP.NET Core MVC for precise access control, enabling restriction of user access to specific controllers or actions based on roles. Additionally, the chapter highlighted the Interface Segregation Principle, emphasizing the importance of designs that don't force classes to depend on unused methods for a more efficient system.

7.4 Review Questions

Question 7.1
When the Identity is installed, several tables were automatically created in the local SQL Server. Draw an Entity Relationship Diagram (ERD) for those entities.

Question 7.2
What are the problems if interface segregation principle is violated?

7.5 References

Romano, D., Raemaekers, S., & Pinzger, M. (2014, September). Refactoring fat interfaces using a genetic algorithm. In *Software Maintenance and Evolution (ICSME), 2014 IEEE International Conference on* (pp. 351-360). IEEE.
Martin, R. C. (2002). *Agile software development: principles, patterns, and practices*. Prentice Hall.

7.6 Answers to Test Your Understanding

7.1 B; 7.2 C; 7.3 D; 7.4 C; 7.5 B; 7.6 A; 7.7 B; 7.8 C; 7.9 C; 7.10 D; 7.11 B; 7.12 B; 7.13 B; 7.14 B; 7.15 C; 7.16 A; 7.17 A; 7.18 A; 7.19 A; 7.20 A; 7.21 C; 7.22 A; 7.23 D; 7.24 B; 7.25 B; 7.26 D; 7.27 C; 7.28 D; 7.29 A; 7.30 D; 7.31 C; 7.32 B; 7.33 C; 7.34 D; 7.35 A; 7.36 A; 7.37 C; 7.38 D; 7.39 D; 7.40 A; 7.41 C; 7.42 B; 7.43 D; 7.44 D; 7.45 A; 7.46 A; 7.47 C; 7.48 D; 7.49 C; 7.50 A; 7.51 D; 7.52 B; 7.53 B; 7.54 B; 7.55 B; 7.56 A; 7.57 D; 7.58 C; 7.59 D; 7.60 B; 7.61 C; 7.62 D; 7.63 D; 7.64 C;

Chapter 8: xUnit and Bootstrap

Chapter Learning Objectives

8.1 Demonstrate the execution of unit tests for models within an ASP.NET Core MVC application.
8.2 Implement unit tests to evaluate the functionality of controllers within an ASP.NET Core MVC setup.
8.3 Implement Bootstrap elements and components within MVC to enhance application layout and design.
8.4 Develop HTML forms optimized for uploading image files in an ASP.NET Core MVC context.
8.5 Explain the significance and benefits of the Dependency Inversion Principle in software design.

8.1 Unit Testing in ASP.NET MVC

ASP.NET MVC offers the advantage of isolating and testing specific parts of a program without impacting other sections, known as unit tests. This section focuses on using xUnit to test models within an ASP.NET Core MVC application.

xUnit encompasses frameworks for automated test case execution. In this chapter, the term "xUnit" specifically refers to the C# version. Details on these concepts will be provided as you delve into unit testing models. Let's set up an ASP.NET Core MVC project to initiate the unit testing process.

Chapter8 Example 1

Problem:

Create an ASP.NET Core MVC application named Chapter8Example1. This application facilitates college applicants to submit basic data and check their admission status. To simplify, the system only requires the user to input their name and ACT score.

Upon submission by the user, the page displays the application status determined by the ACT score:

ACT score above 25: Automatic acceptance with a status of "accepted."

ACT score below 20: Automatic denial with a status of "denied."

Other scores: Require manual review by admission officers with a status of "In process."

A valid ACT score falls within the range of 1 to 36.

For instance, inputting the name "Tim Smith" with an ACT score of 22 will yield the following outcome:

Your application status:

Name: Tim Smith

Admission Decision: In process.

Solution:

Step 1: Configuring the Project

Begin by creating a new Empty ASP.NET 8 MVC Project. Update Program.cs File by injecting MVC services and incorporate routing middleware. For detailed steps, refer to Chapter 2 Example 1.

Step 2: Adding Models

Create a folder named Models within the project. Inside Models, introduce a class called "Applicant" with the following code:

```csharp
using System.ComponentModel.DataAnnotations;

namespace Chapter8Example1.Models
{
    public class Applicant
    {
        public int ApplicantId { get; set; }
        [Required, Display(Name ="Your Name")]
        public string ApplicantName { get; set; }
        [Required]
        public int ACTScore { get; set; }
        public string? DecisionNote { get; set; }
    }
}
```

Step 3: Adding Razor Views Configuration

Add the following razor views: Configure _ViewImports.cshtml, _Layout.cshtml, and _ViewStart.cshtml:
For detailed steps, refer to Chapter 6 Example 1, Step 5.

Step 4: Displaying the Application Form

Inside the project, add a folder named Controllers. Within Controllers, introduce a Controller Class named "AdmissionController.cs" with the default Index action method.

Next, create a Razor View associated with the Controller. Add a folder named Views to the project.Inside Views, create a folder called "Admission." Within the Admission folder, add a Razor View file named "Index.cshtml" containing the code below:

```
@model Chapter8Example1.Models.Applicant
<p>Fill out all fields</p>
<form asp-controller="Admission" asp-action="Decision" method="post">
    <fieldset>
        <label asp-for="ApplicantName"></label>
        <input asp-for="ApplicantName" />
    </fieldset>
    <fieldset>
        <label asp-for="ACTScore"></label>
        <input asp-for="ACTScore" />
    </fieldset>
    <button type="submit">Submit</button>
</form>
```

Save and start without debugging.

Access the URL localhost/Admission in your browser to view an HTML form with two text fields and a submit button.

Step 5: Implementing Form Submission and Displaying Application Status

First, create ACTScoreEvaluator.cs in the Models folder. This class will handle the application's business logic, separating it from the controllers. Use the code below for ACTScoreEvaluator.cs:

```
namespace Chapter8Example1.Models
{
    public class ACTScoreEvaluator
    {
        private const int MAX_ACT_SCORE = 36;
        private const int AUTO_ACCEPTED_THRESHOLD = 25;
        private const int AUTO_REJECTED_THRESHOLD = 20;
        private const int MIN_ACT_SCORE = 1;
        public string AdmissionEvaluator (Applicant applicant)
        {
            if(applicant.ACTScore <= MAX_ACT_SCORE &&
                applicant.ACTScore > AUTO_ACCEPTED_THRESHOLD)
            {
```

```
        return "Accepted with high score.";
    }
    else if (applicant.ACTScore >= AUTO_REJECTED_THRESHOLD)
    {
        return "In process.";
    }
    else if (applicant.ACTScore >= MIN_ACT_SCORE)
    {
        return "Rejected with low score.";
    }
    else
    {
        return "Invalid ACT Score.";
    }
        }
    }
}
```

Next, Update AdmissionController.cs: Add a method named Decision to the AdmissionController. Your completed AdmissionController.cs should resemble the code below:

```
using Chapter8Example1.Models;
using Microsoft.AspNetCore.Mvc;

namespace Chapter8Example1.Controllers
{
    public class AdmissionController : Controller
    {
        public IActionResult Index()
        {
            return View();
        }
        public IActionResult Decision(Applicant applicant)
        {
            if (ModelState.IsValid)
            {
                ACTScoreEvaluator evaluator = new ACTScoreEvaluator();
                applicant.DecisionNote = evaluator.AdmissionEvaluator(applicant);
                return View(applicant);
            }
            return View("Index");
        }
    }
}
```

Finally, add Razor View Decision.cshtml to the Views/Admission folder. Add a Razor View file named

Decision.cshtml with the code below:

```
@model Chapter8Example1.Models.Applicant
<h2>Your application status</h2>
<table>
    <tr>
        <th>Name</th>
        <td>@Model.ApplicantName</td>
    </tr>
    <tr>
        <th>Admission Decision</th>
        <td>@Model.DecisionNote</td>
    </tr>
</table>
```

Save. Start without debugging. Access the URL localhost/Admission in your browser, fill in the name and ACT score on the displayed form to see the application's functionality.

Test Your Understanding 8.1
Which term describes the process of testing specific parts of a program without affecting other sections in ASP.NET MVC?
a. Segregated Testing
b. Unit Testing
c. Comprehensive Testing
d. Integrated Testing

Test Your Understanding 8.2
What does xUnit refer to in the context of ASP.NET Core MVC?
a. Testing Frameworks
b. Integration Tools
c. Debugging Utilities
d. Code Editors

Test Your Understanding 8.3
ASP.NET MVC offers the advantage of _______ and testing specific parts of a program without impacting other sections.
a. isolating
b. coding
c. modeling
d. controlling

Test Your Understanding 8.4
What is the primary purpose of configuring the Program.cs file in ASP.NET 8 MVC Project?
a. To initialize the browser
b. To add models to the project
c. To set up routing middleware and inject MVC services
d. To create a Razor View

Test Your Understanding 8.5
The ACTScoreEvaluator.cs is typically located ______. This class will handle the application's business logic.
a. in the Views folder
b. inside the Controllers folder
c. in the Models folder
d. in the Razor Views folder

Test Your Understanding 8.6
Which file should be configured to define common namespaces and libraries for Razor views in ASP.NET 8 MVC?
a. _ViewImports.cshtml
b. _Layout.cshtml
c. _ViewStart.cshtml
d. Index.cshtml

Test Your Understanding 8.7
Where should the HTML form for entering application data be defined within the project structure?
a. In the Controllers folder
b. Inside the Views folder
c. Within the Models folder
d. In the Razor Views folder

Test Your Understanding 8.8
Which URL should be accessed to view the HTML form for entering application data if you have a controller named Admission with the default Indext action?
a. localhost/Home
b. localhost/Admission
c. localhost/Models
d. localhost/Views

Test Your Understanding 8.9
What action method is associated with the HTML form submission in the described ASP.NET 8 MVC setup? Assume the cshtml file is Decision.cshtml.
a. Index
b. Decision
c. Submit
d. Cannot tell

Test Your Understanding 8.10
What is the purpose of the ACTScoreEvaluator.cs class in the described ASP.NET 8 MVC project setup?

```
namespace Chapter8Example1.Models
{
    public class ACTScoreEvaluator
    {
        public string AdmissionEvaluator (Applicant applicant)
        {
            if(applicant.ACTScore <= 36 && applicant.ACTScore > 25)
            {
                return "Accepted with high score.";
            }
```

```
        }
    }
}
```
a. Handling routing middleware
b. Managing application's business logic
c. Defining Razor views
d. Handling HTTP requests

Test Your Understanding 8.11
Where should the Decision.cshtml Razor View file be placed in the ASP.NET 8 MVC project structure?

```
namespace Chapter8Example1.Controllers
{
    public class AdmissionController : Controller
    {
        public IActionResult Decision(Applicant applicant)
        {
            if (ModelState.IsValid)
            {
                ACTScoreEvaluator evaluator = new ACTScoreEvaluator();
                applicant.DecisionNote = evaluator.AdmissionEvaluator(applicant);
                return View(applicant);
            }
            return View("Index");
        }
    }
}
```
a. Inside the Controllers folder
b. In the Models folder
c. Within the Views/Admission folder
d. In the Views folder

Test Your Understanding 8.12
What action does the Decision method in AdmissionController.cs perform?

```
namespace Chapter8Example1.Controllers
{
    public class AdmissionController : Controller
    {
        public IActionResult Decision(Applicant applicant)
        {
            if (ModelState.IsValid)
            {
                ACTScoreEvaluator evaluator = new ACTScoreEvaluator();
                applicant.DecisionNote = evaluator.AdmissionEvaluator(applicant);
                return View(applicant);
            }
            return View("Index");
        }
    }
}
```

a. Processes form submissions and updates the Applicant model
b. Validates the user's credentials
c. Defines routing paths for HTTP requests
d. Manages the layout of Razor views

Test Your Understanding 8.13
What is the purpose of the AdmissionEvaluator method within the ACTScoreEvaluator class?

```
namespace Chapter8Example1.Models
{
    public class ACTScoreEvaluator
    {
        public string AdmissionEvaluator (Applicant applicant)
        {
            if(applicant.ACTScore <= 36 && applicant.ACTScore > 25)
            {
                return "Accepted with high score.";
            }
        }
    }
}
```

a. Displaying application status
b. Validating form inputs
c. Handling HTTP requests
d. Evaluating admission decisions based on ACT scores

Test Your Understanding 8.14
The process of isolating a small part of the program and testing it without affecting other parts of the programming is often called _______.
a. ASP.NET Core MVC test
b. C# test
c. Unit test
d. integration test

8.2 Unit Test the Model

You have a project ready for testing. Open the project created in section 8.1. In the "Solution Explorer" window, right-click on the solution named "Solution 'Chapter8Example1'", then navigate to "Add" and choose "New Project". This action will first create a project for testing.

The "Add a new project" window will appear. Here, search for "xUnit" and select the C# type. Name the new project "Chapter8Example1Test" and click the "Create" button. You should observe the new project added to the solution in the Solution Explorer window.

Within the Solution Explorer window, right-click on the "Dependencies" of the "Chapter8Example1Test" project. Select "Add Project Reference…", prompting a new window called "Reference Manager" to appear.

In the "Reference Manager" window, check the checkbox next to "Chapter8Example1" and click "OK" to add the reference. This step connects the Chapter8Example1Test project to Chapter8Example1.

Now, navigate to the Solution Explorer window and open the default "UnitTest1.cs" inside the "Chapter8Example1Test" project. Remove all default code and add the code provided in the snippet.

```csharp
using Chapter8Example1.Models;

namespace Chapter8Example1.Test
{
    public class ACTScoreEvaluatorTest
    {
        private const int HIGH_SCORE = 36;
        private const int LOW_SCRE = 19;
        private const int MEDIOCRE_SCORE = 22;
        private const int INVALID_SCORE = 37;
        private const string ACCEPTED = "Accepted with high score.";
        private const string DENIED = "Rejected with low score.";
        private const string MEDIOCRE = "In process.";
        private const string INVALID = "Invalid ACT Score.";
        [Theory]
        [InlineData(HIGH_SCORE)]
        public void HighACTSCoreApplicant(int score)
        {
            //Arrange
            var expected = new ACTScoreEvaluator();
            //Act
            var applicant = new Applicant
            {
                ACTScore = score
            };
            //Assert
            Assert.Equal(ACCEPTED, expected.AdmissionEvaluator(applicant));
        }
        [Theory]
        [InlineData(LOW_SCRE)]
        public void LowACTScoreApplicant(int score)
        {
            //Arrange
            var expected = new ACTScoreEvaluator();
            //Act
            var applicant = new Applicant
            {
```

```csharp
            ACTScore = score
        };
        //Aseert
        Assert.Equal(DENIED, expected.AdmissionEvaluator(applicant));
    }
    [Theory]
    [InlineData(MEDIOCRE_SCORE)]
    public void MEDIOCREACTScoreApplicant(int score)
    {
        //Arrange
        var expected = new ACTScoreEvaluator();
        //Act
        var applicant = new Applicant
        {
            ACTScore = score
        };
        //Assert
        Assert.Equal(MEDIOCRE, expected.AdmissionEvaluator(applicant));
    }
    [Theory]
    [InlineData(INVALID_SCORE)]
    public void INVALIDScoreApplicant(int score)
    {
        //Arrange
        var expected = new ACTScoreEvaluator();
        //Act
        var applicant = new Applicant
        {
            ACTScore = score
        };
        //Assert
        Assert.Equal(INVALID, expected.AdmissionEvaluator(applicant));
    }
    }
}
```

Explanation:

The "Theory" notation indicates that this test type verifies if the method functions with a set of data. The InlineData decorator facilitates providing testing data used in the method. For instance, the first test method checks the high score of 36 and examines if inline data functions as expected.

The "Arrange" phase involves setting up the necessary objects for testing, such as creating an ACTScoreEvaluator object named "expected" in this example.

The "Act" part within the method assigns the ACT score to an applicant, constituting the core of the test. This segment typically involves calling a method, creating an object, or triggering an event to observe the result.

The "Assert" portion within the method validates that expectations are met. In this case, it ensures that the AdmissionEvaluator method returns the expected string: "Accepted with high score." In the first method.

To execute the test, go to the Visual Studio menu. Click on "Test", then select "Test Explorer" to open the window. In the "Test Explorer" window, click on "Run All" to execute the tests.

If you've entered the code exactly as in the book, the "ACTScoreEvaluatorTest.InvalidACTScoreApplicant" method will fail the test. However, the other three methods should pass the test with green check marks.

To rectify this, go back to the original ACTScoreEvaluator class inside the Chapter8Example1 project. Locate the specified code block:

```
else if (applicant.ACTScore >= AUTO_REJECTED_THRESHOLD)
{
    return "In process.";
}
else if (applicant.ACTScore >= MIN_ACT_SCORE)
{
    return "Rejected with low score.";
}
```

And replace it with the following:

```
else if (applicant.ACTScore >= AUTO_REJECTED_THRESHOLD
    && applicant.ACTScore <= AUTO_ACCEPTED_THRESHOLD)
{
    return "In process.";
}
else if (applicant.ACTScore >= MIN_ACT_SCORE
    && applicant.ACTScore < AUTO_REJECTED_THRESHOLD)
{
    return "Rejected with low score.";
}
```

Finally, return to the "Test Explorer" window and click on "Run All" again. This action should ensure that all four tests pass.

Test Your Understanding 8.15
You have a class named "ACTScoreEvaluator" in a project named "Chapter8Example1". How do you conduct an xUnit test on the "ACTScoreEvaluator" class according to the book?
a. Execute the project with all possible inputs.
b. Add a class called "ACTScoreEvaluatorTest" to the same project.
c. Add a method called "xUnitTest" to the "ACTScoreEvaluator" class and reference each method of the class.
d. Add a project called "Chapter8Example1Test" to the same solution and reference the "ACTScoreEvaluator" class.

Test Your Understanding 8.16
Using the examples in the book, what type of project should be selected in the "Add a new project" window?
a. xUnit with C#
b. Java with xUnit
c. Python with xUnit
d. HTML with C#

Test Your Understanding 8.17
When you want to test a project, such as ProjectA, you add a new project called ProjectATest to the same solution. How is ProjectATest related to ProjectA?
a. They are related because they are in the same solution.
b. They are related because they have matching names.
c. They are related because You need to add a reference from ProjectATest pointing to ProjectA.
d. They are related because one is a regular project, and the other contains the "UnitTest1.cs" file.

Test Your Understanding 8.18
What does the "Theory" notation indicate in the provided code snippet?

```
[Theory]
[InlineData(HIGH_SCORE)]
public void HighACTSCoreApplicant(int score)
{
    //Arrange
    var expected = new ACTScoreEvaluator();
    //Act
    var applicant = new Applicant
    {
        ACTScore = score
    };
    //Assert
    Assert.Equal(ACCEPTED, expected.AdmissionEvaluator(applicant));
}
```

a. It checks the high score
b. It creates an object for testing
c. It indicates the method tests with different data
d. It validates the expectations

Test Your Understanding 8.19
What does the "Arrange" phase involve in the testing process?
a. Setting up necessary objects for testing

b. Executing the test
c. Validating expectations
d. Creating objects for the main test

Test Your Understanding 8.20
What action occurs in the "Act" part of the testing process?
a. Validating expectations
b. Executing the test
c. Setting up necessary objects for testing
d. Creating objects for the main test

Test Your Understanding 8.21
What does the "Assert" portion of the test ensure?
a. The method functions with different data
b. Validating expectations
c. Setting up necessary objects for testing
d. Creating objects for the main test

Test Your Understanding 8.22
What menu option is selected to execute the uUnit tests in Visual Studio?
a. File
b. Edit
c. Test
d. View

Test Your Understanding 8.23
The _______ decorator facilitates providing testing data used in the method.
a. HighACTSCoreApplicant
b. InputData
c. InlineData
d. ParameterData

Test Your Understanding 8.24
Which of the following steps is necessary to add an xUnit testing project to an existing project?
a. Using the same project name.
b. Using the existing project name with Test suffix.
c. Project name must be UnitTest1.cs
d. A reference must be added to connect the xUit testing project to an existing project.

Test Your Understanding 8.25
In a theory type of test, the preparation for testing is called ____________.
a. Inlinedata
b. arrange
c. act
d. assert

Test Your Understanding 8.26
In a theory type of test, the ___________ provides the testing data.
a. Inlinedata
b. arrange

c. act

d. assert

Test Your Understanding 8.27

In a theory type of test, the main part for testing is called ___________.

a. Inlinedata

b. arrange

c. act

d. assert

Test Your Understanding 8.28

In a theory type of test, the part that compares the actual result with the expected result for testing is called

___________.

a. Inlinedata

b. arrange

c. act

d. assert

8.3 Unit Test the Controller

We are going to unit test the AdmissionController in this section.

Navigate to the Solution Explorer window.

Right-click on "Chapter8Example1Test" and add a class named "AdmissionControllerUnitTest.cs"

containing the following code:

```csharp
using Chapter8Example1.Controllers;
using Chapter8Example1.Models;
using Microsoft.AspNetCore.Mvc;

namespace Chapter8Example1Test
{
    public class AdmissionControllerUnitTest
    {
        [Fact]
        public void ReturnViewForIndex()
        {
            var controller = new AdmissionController();
            var result = controller.Index();
            Assert.IsType<ViewResult>(result);
        }
        [Fact]
        public void ReturnViewForDecision()
        {
            var controller = new AdmissionController();
            var applicant = new Applicant
            {
```

```
            ApplicantName = "Jenny Grant",
            ACTScore = 34
        };
        var result = controller.Decision(applicant);
        var viewResult = Assert.IsType<ViewResult>(result);
        var model = Assert.IsType<Applicant>(viewResult.Model);
        Assert.Equal(applicant.ApplicantName, model.ApplicantName);
        Assert.Equal(applicant.ACTScore, model.ACTScore);
    }
  }
}
```

Explanation:

The [Fact] attribute defines a unit test differently from [Theory]. While [Theory] involves passing a set of test data to the method, [Fact] is used when the method doesn't require parameter input.

The ReturnViewForIndex() method tests if the Index method of AdmissionController returns the correct type.

The ReturnViewForDecision() method checks if the ApplicantName received by the Decision method of AdmissionController matches the parameter's value.

Access the "Test Explorer" and select "Run All". All six tests should pass.

Test Your Understanding 8.29
What attribute is used to define a unit test method in the code snippet?
```
public void ReturnViewForIndex()
{
    var controller = new AdmissionController();
    var result = controller.Index();
    Assert.IsType<ViewResult>(result);
}
```
a. [TestMethod]
b. [Test]
c. [Fact]
d. [Unit]

Test Your Understanding 8.30
What is the function of the following code snippet?
```
[Fact]
public void ReturnViewForIndex()
{
    var controller = new AdmissionController();
```

```
    var result = controller.Index();
    Assert.IsType<ViewResult>(result);
}
```
a. Tests the outcome of the "Index" method within the "AdmissionController"
b. Verifies if the "Index" method of the "AdmissionController" returns the correct type
c. Evaluates the functionality of the AdmissionController.
d. Assesses the functionality of the "Index" method within the "AdmissionController"."

Test Your Understanding 8.31
When is the [Theory] attribute used in unit testing compared to [Fact]?
a. When a method doesn't require parameter input
b. When multiple test data sets are passed to the method
c. When a method requires specific conditions to pass
d. When testing the equality of method outputs

Test Your Understanding 8.32
What is the purpose of the "Assert.Equal" method in the code snippet?
```
Assert.Equal(applicant.ApplicantName, model.ApplicantName);
```
a. To verify the return type of a method
b. To compare the expected and actual values
c. To check if a method exists
d. To ensure the parameter is of a certain type

Test Your Understanding 8.33
The [Theory] attribute is often used when you want to test a method with __________.
a. a parameter list
b. a return type of string
c. more than one returned values
d. no parameter list

Test Your Understanding 8.34
The [Fact] attribute is often used when you want to test a method with __________.
a. a parameter list
b. a return type of string
c. more than one parameter variables
d. no parameter list

Programming Challenge 8.1

Create a new ASP.NET Core MVC application called ProgrammingChallenge81. This application allows a college student to apply for a computer science major.

To qualify for a computer science major, a student must complete at least 60 credit hours of college study with a GPA of 3.0 or higher.

A student with less than 60 credit hours will be automatically rejected. A student with at least 60 credit hours and a GPA of 3.5 will be automatically accepted. A student that is not automatically rejected or accepted will be manually reviewed by a faculty.

After the user enters data (student name, credit hours, and GPA) and clicks on the "Submit" button, the page will display the application status based on credit hours and GPA outlined in the last paragraph.

Add a xUnit test project called ProgrammingChallenge81Test. Then add a class called MajorEvaluatorTest to test the model. Finally, add a class called CSControllerTest to test the controller.

8.4 Bootstrap ASP.NET MVC

This book assumes you possess a basic understanding of Bootstrap. We'll demonstrate how Bootstrap integrates with ASP.NET Core MVC using a content delivery network (CDN). A Bootstrap CDN is a Content Delivery Network that distributes the Bootstrap files. It is a geographically distributed group of servers that work together to provide fast delivery of Internet content. Your familiarity with Bootstrap significantly influences the webpages' visual appearance.

Chapter 8 Example 2

Problem:

Apply Bootstrap formatting to the project in Chapter 8 Example 1. Essentially, stylize the two Razor view pages.

Solution:

Step 1: Access the Chapter8Example1 project and open _Layout.cshtml. Remember, layouts minimize redundancy in views and adhere to the Don't Repeat Yourself (DRY) principle. Add a link line and a script line from getbootstrap.com:

```
<!doctype html>
<html lang="en">
<head>
    <meta charset="utf-8">
    <meta name="viewport" content="width=device-width, initial-scale=1">
    <title>Bootstrap demo</title>
    <link href=https://cdn.jsdelivr.net/npm/bootstrap@5.3.2/dist/css/bootstrap.min.css
    rel="stylesheet" integrity="sha384-
    T3c6CoIi6uLrA9TneNEoa7RxnatzjcDSCmG1MXxSR1GAsXEV/Dwwykc2MPK8M2HN"
    crossorigin="anonymous">
</head>
<body>
    <div class="container body-content">
        @RenderBody()
        <hr />
```

```
        <footer>
            <p>&copy; @DateTime.Now.Year - Lynn Smith</p>
        </footer>
    </div>
    <script
    src="https://cdn.jsdelivr.net/npm/bootstrap@5.3.2/dist/js/bootstrap.bundle.min.js"
    integrity="sha384-C6RzsynM9kWDrMNeT87bh95OGNyZPhcTNXj1NW7RuBCsyN/o0jlpcV8Qyq46cDfL"
    crossorigin="anonymous"></script>
</body>
</html>
```

Step 2: Apply Bootstrap Classes to Each Razor View File

Begin by opening Index.cshtml and integrating Bootstrap classes:

```
@model Chapter8Example1.Models.Applicant
<p class="text-info lead">Fill out all fields</p>
<form asp-controller="Admission"
      asp-action="Decision" method="post"
      class="form-horizontal">
    <fieldset class="form-group">
        <label asp-for="ApplicantName"
               class="control-label col-xs-2"></label>
        <div class="col-xs-10">
            <input asp-for="ApplicantName" class="form-control" />
        </div>
    </fieldset>
    <fieldset class="form-group">
        <label asp-for="ACTScore" class="control-label col-xs-2">
        </label>
        <div class="col-xs-10">
            <input asp-for="ACTScore" class="form-control" />
        </div>
    </fieldset>
    <div class="form-group">
        <div class="col-xs-offset-2 col-xs-10">
            <button class="btn btn-primary" type="submit">Submit
            </button>
        </div>
    </div>
</form>
```

Then, modify the Decision.cshtml by adding Bootstrap classes:

```
@model Chapter8Example1.Models.Applicant
<h2>Your application status</h2>
<div class="table-responsive">
<table class="table table-striped table-hover">
    <tr>
        <th>Name</th>
```

```
        <td>@Model.ApplicantName</td>
    </tr>
    <tr>
        <th>Admission Decision</th>
        <td>@Model.DecisionNote</td>
    </tr>
</table>
</div>
```

Save. Start without debugging debugging. Observe the Bootstrap-styled transformation in both webpages.

Test Your Understanding 8.35
To make Bootstrap work on an ASP.NET Core MVC page, you add the two Bootstrap CDN links to
__________.
a. a controller
b. a model
c. _Layout.cshtml
d. a method of a controller

Test Your Understanding 8.36
To make Bootstrap work on an ASP.NET Core MVC page, you add the two Bootstrap CDN links to the
_Layout.cshtml file. What types of files are these two CDN links.
a. html file and css file
b. css file and js file
c. js file and html file
d. both are bootstrap files

Test Your Understanding 8.37
What is the primary function of a Bootstrap CDN in the context of integrating Bootstrap with ASP.NET
Core MVC?
a. To manage user authentication
b. To distribute Bootstrap files efficiently
c. To optimize database queries
d. To handle server-side logic

Test Your Understanding 8.38
How does familiarity with Bootstrap impact webpages in ASP.NET Core MVC?
a. It affects server performance
b. It influences the webpage's structural layout
c. It enables database connectivity
d. It manages user sessions

Test Your Understanding 8.39
What does the abbreviation CDN stand for in the context of Bootstrap integration?
a. Content Delivery Network
b. Central Data Network
c. Core Database Navigation

d. Communication Distribution Node

Test Your Understanding 8.40
In what way does Bootstrap integration with ASP.NET Core MVC primarily rely on a CDN?
a. To manage user sessions
b. To secure database connections
c. To distribute Bootstrap files for faster content delivery
d. To handle server-side scripting

Programming Challenge 8.2

Format the Programming Challenge 8.1 with Bootstrap.

8.5 Working with Image Files in ASP.NET MVC

Uploading image files to the server differs slightly from posting a message to the server. In this section, you will learn how to upload an image file using an HTML form and display all uploaded images on a Razor View.

Chapter 8 Example 3

Problem:

Create an ASP.NET Core MVC application called Chapter8Example3. This application enables users to upload a picture to the server and displays all uploaded pictures from the server.

Solution:

Step 1: Start an empty ASP.NET Core 8 MVC Project named Chapter8Example3. Update the Program.cs file by injecting MVC services and adding routing middleware.

Step 2: Add Entity Framework. You need a database to store picture file names. Add the necessary packages to make Entity Framework work.

Step 3: Add Models. Add a folder called "Models" to the project. Within the Models folder, add two classes: Picture.cs and PictureDbContext.cs. The code for Picture.cs is as follows:

```
using System.ComponentModel.DataAnnotations;
using System.ComponentModel.DataAnnotations.Schema;
```

```
namespace Chapter8Example3.Models
{
    public class Picture
    {
        public int PictureId { get; set; }
        [Required]
        public required string AltAttribute { get; set; }
        [NotMapped]
        public IFormFile? MyPicture { get; set; }
        [Display(Name = "Enter Description: ")]
        public string? Description { get; set; }
        [DataType(DataType.Url)]
        public required string Url { get; set; }
    }
}
```

Explanation:

The [NotMapped] notation indicates that the property will exist in the model but won't be a column in the

database table. The IFormFile is an interface that represents a file sent with the HttpRequest. It's used for

handling file uploads in ASP.NET Core MVC.

The code for PictureDbContext.cs:

```
using Microsoft.EntityFrameworkCore;

namespace Chapter8Example3.Models
{
    public class PictureDbContext : DbContext
    {
        public DbSet<Picture> Pictures { get; set; }
        public PictureDbContext(
            DbContextOptions<PictureDbContext> options)
            :base(options)
        {
        }
    }
}
```


Step 4: Add Migration to Create the Database. Update Program.cs to create the necessary database, as done

in earlier chapters.

Step 5: Add _ViewImports.cshtml, _Layout.cshtml, and _ViewStart.cshtml.

Step 6: Add a Portal Page for Uploading Pictures and Displaying All Pictures. Add a folder called Controllers to the project. Include an empty controller named PictureController.cs within the Controllers folder. Maintain the default Index action method.

Inside the Views folder, create a folder named Picture. Within the Picture folder, add a Razor View named Index.cshtml with the following content:

```
<h2>Picture Home</h2>
<p><a asp-controller="Picture"
    asp-action="AddPicture">Add a Picture</a></p>
<p><a asp-controller="Picture"
    asp-action="DisplayPictures">Display Pictures</a></p>
```

Save and start without debugging. Enter the URL localhost/Picture to view the page with two hyperlinks.

Step 7: Make the "Add A Picture" Link on the Portal Page Work.

Open PictureController.cs and add an action method called AddPicture to the controller. Include the completed controller code as follows:

```
using Chapter8Example3.Models;
using Microsoft.AspNetCore.Mvc;
using Microsoft.EntityFrameworkCore;

namespace Chapter8Example3.Controllers
{
    public class PictureController : Controller
    {
        private readonly PictureDbContext db;
        public PictureController(PictureDbContext db)
        {
            this.db = db;
        }
        public IActionResult Index()
        {
            return View();
        }
        public IActionResult AddPicture()
        {
            return View();
        }
    }
}
```

Go to the Views/Picture folder and add a corresponding Razor View file named AddPicture.cshtml with the provided code snippet.

```
@model Chapter8Example3.Models.Picture
<h3>Add a picture</h3>
<form asp-controller="Picture" asp-action="AddPicture" method="post"
enctype="multipart/form-data">
    <label asp-for="AltAttribute">alt attribute:</label>
    <input asp-for="AltAttribute" />
    <br />
    <label asp-for="Description">Description:</label>
    <input asp-for="Description" />
    <br />
    <label asp-for="MyPicture" >Select a file to upload:</label>
    <input type="file" name="MyPicture" />
    <br />
    <button type="submit">Add Picture</button>
</form>
```

Next, you need an action method in the PictureController that saves the picture to the server. Open

PictureController.cs, add an HttpPost action method named AddPicture with the provided code snippet.

```
[HttpPost]
public async Task<IActionResult> AddPicture(Picture p)
{
    var path = Path.Combine(Directory.GetCurrentDirectory(),
    "wwwroot\\images", p.MyPicture.FileName);
    using (var stream = new FileStream(path, FileMode.Create))
    {
        await p.MyPicture.CopyToAsync(stream);
    }
    p.Url = p.MyPicture.FileName;
    db.Add(p);
    await db.SaveChangesAsync();
    return RedirectToAction("Index");
}
```

You need a folder to save the images. Navigate to the Solution Explorer window, add a folder called

wwwroot, and then a subfolder named images. Open the Program.cs file and add the following line:

```
app.UseStaticFiles();
```

This line enables the server to access files within the wwwroot folder. CSS or JavaScript files should also be

added to the wwwroot folder if needed.

Save and start without debugging. Enter the URL: localhost/Picture. Click on the link "Add a picture" and follow the instructions to upload an image file.

After returning to the "Picture Home" page, go to the Solution Explorer window and expand the wwwroot/images folder. You should see the uploaded image file in the folder.

Step 8: Make the "Display Pictures" Link in the Portal Page Work. Open PictureController.cs and add a method named DisplayPictures to the controller with the provided code snippet.

```csharp
public async Task<IActionResult> DisplayPictures()
{
    var pictures = await db.Pictures.ToListAsync();
    return View(pictures);
}
```

You will need a corresponding Razor View file. Navigate to the Views/Picture folder and add a Razor View file named DisplayPictures.cshtml with the provided code snippet.

```cshtml
@model IEnumerable<Chapter8Example3.Models.Picture>
@{
    ViewData["title"] = "Display Pictures";
}
<h3>All Pictures </h3>
@foreach (var p in Model)
{
    <img src="~/images/@p.Url" alt="@p.AltAttribute"
    width="300" class="img-responsive img-circle" />
    <p class="text-info">@p.Description</p>
}
```

Save and start without debugging. Type the URL: localhost/Picture, click on the "Display Pictures" link, and view all the uploaded images.

Test Your Understanding 8.41
In EF, which data annotation is used if you want to have a property in the model, but not a corresponding column in the database table?
a. NotRequired
b. NotMapped
c. ModelOnly
d. NotTable

Test Your Understanding 8.42
What does the [NotMapped] notation indicate in Picture.cs?
a. It specifies required properties
b. It excludes a property from being a database column
c. It marks properties for display

d. It enables data validation

Test Your Understanding 8.43
What is the purpose of the wwwroot folder in the application?
a. To store database files
b. To save C# and JavaScript files
c. To host the application's homepage
d. To store image files uploaded by users

Test Your Understanding 8.44
Given the following code snippet, what is saved to the database?
```
var path = Path.Combine(Directory.GetCurrentDirectory(),
"wwwroot\\images", p.MyPicture.FileName);
using (var stream = new FileStream(path, FileMode.Create))
{
    await p.MyPicture.CopyToAsync(stream);
}
p.Url = p.MyPicture.FileName;
db.Add(p);
await db.SaveChangesAsync();
return RedirectToAction("Index");
```
a. The picture
b. The binary file of the picture uploaded by the user
c. The properties of the picture
d. The methods of the picture

Test Your Understanding 8.45
Given the following code snippet, where is the binary image saved to?
```
var path = Path.Combine(Directory.GetCurrentDirectory(),
"wwwroot\\images", p.MyPicture.FileName);
using (var stream = new FileStream(path, FileMode.Create))
{
    await p.MyPicture.CopyToAsync(stream);
}
p.Url = p.MyPicture.FileName;
db.Add(p);
await db.SaveChangesAsync();
return RedirectToAction("Index");
```
a. The database
b. The images folder
c. The URL specified
d. The MyPicture folder

Test Your Understanding 8.46
What enables the server to access files within the wwwroot folder?
a. A specific URL configuration
b. Adding images to the Views folder
c. The app.UseStaticFiles() line in Program.cs
d. Using a specific file naming convention

Test Your Understanding 8.47
What HTTP method is used to submit the form for adding a picture?
a. GET
b. POST
c. PUT
d. DELETE

Test Your Understanding 8.48
Which folder contains the Razor Views for the Picture-related actions?
a. Controllers
b. wwwroot
c. Models
d. Views

Test Your Understanding 8.49
What is the primary purpose of the IFormFile interface in ASP.NET Core MVC?
a. Representing HTML forms
b. Managing database interactions
c. Handling file uploads
d. Defining routing middleware

Test Your Understanding 8.50
Which attribute of the <form> element is required to upload an image to the server?
a. picture
b. file
c. image
d. enctype

Test Your Understanding 8.51
Which attribute of the <input> element is required to upload an image to the server?
a. picture
b. file
c. image
d. enctype

Programming Challenge 8.3

Enhance Chapter7Example1 to allow student users to upload an avatar within their profiles. Additionally, modify the instructor's grade posting functionality to display not just the student ID but also the student's name and avatar alongside the grades (the current form only exhibits student IDs).

8.6 Dependency Inversion Principle

The letter "D" in SOLID stands for Dependency Inversion Principle (DIP). According to the principle, high-level modules (whether one or many classes) should not depend on low-level modules. Instead, both modules should rely on abstractions. An abstraction should not rely on details, while details should depend on abstractions (Martin 2002).

Consider an example: The SchoolExam class encompasses various methods to compute grades, each tailored to a specific type of exam, such as the EssayExamGrade() method.

Meanwhile, the Student class incorporates a CalculateGrade() method that might utilize the EssayExamGrade() method from the SchoolExam class.

The issue arises from the Student class, which becomes reliant on the SchoolExam class—a situation that leads to tight coupling. Consequently, any alterations in the SchoolExam class might necessitate corresponding changes in the Student class (Chapter 5).

One viable solution involves creating an interface, say Quiz, housing multiple methods for grade calculation. The SchoolExam class then implements this Quiz interface with concrete methods. Consequently, the CalculateGrade(Quiz quiz) method within the Student class receives a Quiz object (e.g., EssayExam) and can accordingly compute the grade based on SchoolExam's definitions. Consequently, modifications to the calculation rules impact student grades but not the structural aspects of the Student class.

Chapter 2 introduced ASP.NET Core MVC's inherent support for dependency injection, aligning with the DIP. In many of our database-related examples, controllers feature a field and constructor structured as:

```
SomeDbContext db;
public SomeController(SomeDbContext db)
{
    this.db = db;
}
```

Henceforth, treating db as the database remains consistent, irrespective of potential alterations to the database structure. For instance, if the database introduces a table named Students and your code requires all students from this table using db.Students, the addition of another table to the database won't impact the code within this controller. This practice is commonly referred to as constructor injection.

The primary advantage of adhering to the DIP is the facilitation of a more adaptable and flexible system (Pati and Hill, 2014).

Test Your Understanding 8.52
The _________ states that high-level modules should not depend on low-level modules and both should depend on abstractions.
a. Dependency inversion principle
b. Open/Close principle
c. Single responsibility principle
d. Interface segregation principle

Test Your Understanding 8.53
The major benefits of following the dependency inversion principle is that you can have a system that __________.
a. contains fewer lines of code
b. is more flexible
c. is easier to understand
d. all other options are correct

Test Your Understanding 8.54
What does the "D" stand for in the SOLID principles?
a. Design
b. Dependency Inversion Principle
c. Development
d. Determination

Test Your Understanding 8.55
According to the Dependency Inversion Principle, how should high-level and low-level modules relate?
a. High-level modules should directly depend on low-level modules
b. Both modules should rely on abstractions
c. Low-level modules should rely on high-level modules
d. Abstractions should rely on details

Test Your Understanding 8.56
What issue arises when the Student class relies directly on the SchoolExam class in the explanation example of Chapter 8?
a. Loose coupling
b. High cohesion
c. Tight coupling
d. Dependency inversion

Test Your Understanding 8.57
How does the Dependency Inversion Principle suggest resolving the issue between Student and SchoolExam classes for the example in Chapter 8?
a. By removing the CalculateGrade() method
b. By adding more methods to the Student class
c. By creating an interface like Quiz and using it in Student class
d. By merging Student and SchoolExam classes

Test Your Understanding 8.58
What advantage does constructor injection in ASP.NET Core MVC provide?
a. Improved performance
b. Reduced code complexity

c. Better database access
d. Consistent database handling despite structural changes

Test Your Understanding 8.59
How does the use of constructor injection support the Dependency Inversion Principle in ASP.NET Core MVC?
a. By reducing the need for controllers
b. By eliminating the need for database access
c. By allowing controllers to directly access the database
d. By facilitating consistent database handling irrespective of structural changes

Test Your Understanding 8.60
What is the primary focus of Dependency Inversion Principle (DIP)?
a. Encouraging direct dependencies between modules
b. Promoting abstraction and reducing dependencies
c. Enhancing class cohesion
d. Reducing the number of methods in a class

Test Your Understanding 8.61
How does the usage of interfaces aid in applying the Dependency Inversion Principle?
a. By creating more dependencies between classes
b. By reducing the need for abstraction
c. By enforcing direct dependencies
d. By enabling classes to rely on abstractions rather than details

Test Your Understanding 8.62
What does the Dependency Inversion Principle seek to achieve in software design?
a. Increased class interdependence
b. Reduced flexibility
c. Tight coupling between modules
d. A more adaptable and flexible system

Test Your Understanding 8.63
Which aspect of software development is emphasized by the Dependency Inversion Principle?
a. Creating rigid structures
b. Encouraging direct module dependencies
c. Building adaptable and flexible systems
d. Increasing class complexity

8.7 Chapter Summary

In this chapter, you delved into unit testing for models and controllers. Testing models helps pinpoint errors within the business logic, while controller testing ensures that the types and values returned from Views align with expectations.

You also explored the incorporation of Bootstrap into projects via content delivery networks (CDNs). Assuming a foundational understanding of Bootstrap, I encourage you to implement Bootstrap across all previous examples and exercises.

The final section introduced the Dependency Inversion Principle. You discovered that the dependency injection employed in ASP.NET Core MVC inherently aligns with this principle, concluding our exploration of SOLID principles.

8.8 Review Questions

Question 8.1
What are the benefits of unit testing a model? Explain with an example.
Question 8.2
What are the benefits of unit testing a controller? Explain with an example.
Question 8.3
Explain the steps that are necessary to apply Bootstrap to an existing ASP.NET Core MVC project.
Question 8.4
What is dependency inversion principle? Why use it?

8.9 References

Martin, R. C. (2002). *Agile software development: principles, patterns, and practices*. Prentice Hall.

Pati, T., & Hill, J. H. (2014). A survey report of enhancements to the visitor software design pattern.

Software: Practice and Experience, 44(6), 699-733.

8.10 Answers to Test Your Understanding

8.1 B; 8.2 A; 8.3 A; 8.4 C; 8.5 C; 8.6 A; 8.7 B; 8.8 B; 8.9 B; 8.10 B; 8.11 C; 8.12 A; 8.13 D; 8.14 C; 8.15 D; 8.16 A; 8.17 C; 8.18 C; 8.19 A; 8.20 B; 8.21 B; 8.22 C; 8.23 C; 8.24 D; 8.25 B; 8.26 A; 8.27 C; 8.28 D; 8.29 C; 8.30 B; 8.31 B; 8.32 B; 8.33 A; 8.34 D; 8.35 C; 8.36 B; 8.37 B; 8.38 B; 8.39 A; 8.40 C; 8.41 B; 8.42 B; 8.43 D; 8.44 C; 8.45 B; 8.46 C; 8.47 B; 8.48 D; 8.49 C; 8.50 D; 8.51 B; 8.52 A; 8.53 B; 8.54 B; 8.55 B; 8.56 C; 8.57 C; 8.58 D; 8.59 D; 8.60 B; 8.61 D; 8.62 D; 8.63 C;

Chapter 9: Projects

Chapter Learning Objectives

9.1 Apply ASP.NET Core MVC to solve business problems.

9.1 Introduction

This chapter introduces three projects where you can apply the knowledge gained from the previous eight chapters. The Smith Swimming School project functions as a platform for managing lessons and enrollments. Meanwhile, the Smith Sweet Shop project is designed to sustain their traditional business model established over the past fifty years. Lastly, the Smith Souvenir Store project resembles a contemporary online retailer but stands out by enabling suppliers to directly post products.

The swimming school project outlines suggested steps for website development, although there's flexibility in the approach; various methods can achieve project completion.

None of the three projects specify web design aspects like wireframes, allowing room for creativity in crafting exceptional user interfaces. Additionally, payment integration isn't explicitly addressed. You can opt to incorporate a simple link such as "Pay by Paypal" or "Pay by Google," simulating a completed payment process without actual financial transactions involved. Alternatively, for a challenge, explore options like "Paypal sandbox developer account" or "Google Pay API for developers" for more detailed payment system implementations.

9.2 Project One: Smith Swimming School

Business Description:

The Smith Swimming School (3S) is a family-owned small business specializing in teaching swimming to both children and adults. Its origin traces back approximately 30 years when Grandpa Smith, a former swimming coach at Tiny University, sought to continue coaching post-retirement. Presently, all full-time employees are either Smith family members or related by marriage. Their website requirements include:

For Visitors:

1. Registration option for visitors to become users.

For Administrators:

2. Ability to view all roles and add new roles (e.g., coach, swimmer).

3. A comprehensive list of registered users and their assigned role(s), and assignment of role(s) to users.

4. Management of lessons (viewing, editing, deletion, addition). Lessons with sessions cannot be deleted.

For Coaches:

5. Capability to add/update their profiles.

6. Access to view all lessons.

7. Addition of sessions to lessons, thereby becoming the coach for that session.

8. Viewing, editing, and deleting their own sessions. Sessions with swimmers cannot be deleted.

9. Selection of their sessions to view enrolled swimmers.

10. Addition/editing/deletion of progress reports for swimmers in their sessions.

For Swimmers:

11. Viewing all available (future and not full) sessions and personal past sessions.

12. Enrollment in new sessions without time conflicts.

13. Dropping enrolled sessions before progress reports added by coaches.

14. Access to progress reports for enrolled sessions.

Business Data Requirements:

3S aims to maintain data on coaches, swimmers, lessons, and sessions. Each lesson possesses a skill level (e.g., teen advanced or adult beginner) and a corresponding tuition. Lessons can have multiple sessions, each led by a coach. Coaches are associated with one or more sessions and possess name and contact details. Sessions include start and end dates, available seats, and daily start times. Swimmers can sign up for multiple sessions provided there are no scheduling conflicts. Swimmers have personal details like name, phone number, gender, and date of birth. Coaches can generate student progress reports during sessions.

Sessions are scheduled from Monday to Friday, excluding holidays, lasting 30 minutes each, potentially following one another immediately. During holiday weeks, the school remains closed. Payment for lessons is due after the first lesson, collected in person at the school; online payments are not accepted.

Guidelines (These are not strict requirements. Certain details are intentionally omitted):

1. Begin with an empty ASP.NET 8 MVC Project (Chapter 2 Example 1 Steps 1, 2, and 3).

2. Update Program.cs to incorporate MVC service and routing (Chapter 5 Example 1 Step 4).

3. Create a 'Controllers' folder and add AdminController.cs within. Include an Index action method within AdminController.cs.

4. Establish a 'Views' folder, then a 'Admin' subfolder within 'Views.' Introduce a Razor View file named Index.cshtml within the Views/Admin directory.

5. Incorporate _ViewImports.cshtml, _Layout.cshtml, and _ViewStart.cshtml files.

6. Save and start without Debugging. Access the URL: localhost/Admin to view admin activities:

> Display all roles
> Add a role
> Assign users to roles
> Display all lessons
> Add a lesson

7. Integrate Entity Framework (Chapter 5 Example 1 Step 2).

8. Install Identity (Chapter 7 Example 1 Step 1).

9. Create AccountController.cs within the Controllers folder. Add Register and Login methods along with corresponding Razor View files for visitor registration and registered user login (Chapter 7 Example 1 Steps 3 and 4).

10. Ensure the functionality of "Add a role" on the Admin portal page. Incorporate three roles: admin, coach, and swimmer.

11. Activate the "Show all roles" link on the Admin portal page.

12. Establish HomeController.cs within the Controllers folder. Introduce a 'Home' folder within 'Views,' adding an Index.cshtml Razor View file. Successful user registrations will redirect to this page: "Thank you for registering at 3S. Your role will be assigned shortly."

13. Enable the "Assign user to a role" link on the Admin portal page. Register at least five users. Assign one to the admin role, two to the coach role, and two to the swimmer role. Ensure a page displays all users before role assignment.

14. Include CoachController.cs within the Controllers folder. Create a portal page for coaches. Upon coach login, they'll be redirected to this page:

> Add profile

Add a session
Write a progress report for a session

15. Implement SwimmerController.cs within the Controllers folder. Establish a portal page for swimmers.

Upon swimmer login, they'll be directed to this page:

Add profile
Sign up for a session
Check progress report

16. Introduce models: coach, swimmer, lesson, session, and enrollment into the models folder (Chapter 7 Example 1 Step 8).

Coach: CoachId, CoachName, phone number
Swimmer: SwimmerId, SwimmerName, gender, phone, date of birth
Lesson: LessonID, SkillLevel, tuition
Session: SessionId, StartDate, EndDate, SeatCapacity, DailyStartTime
Enrollment: An associative class. Remember to add navigation properties for each class.

17. Execute Add-Migration and Update-Database commands (Chapter 7 Example 1 Step 8).

18. Enable "Show all lessons" and "Add a lesson" links on the Admin page (Chapter 7 Example 1 Step 11).

19. Activate the "Add profile" link on the Coach Home page (Chapter 7 Example 1 Step 10).

20. Ensure the functionality of "Add a session" link on the Coach Home page. Initially display all lessons with a link to add a session for each lesson type.

21. Implement the "Add profile" link on the Swimmer Home page (Chapter 7 Example 1 Step 13).

22. Enable the "Sign up for a session" link on the Swimmer Home page (Chapter 7 Example 1 Step 14).

23. Activate the "Write a report for a session" link on the Coach Home page. When clicked, display all coach sessions. Each session should be clickable, showcasing enrolled swimmers. Coaches can click on a swimmer to provide feedback (Chapter 7 Example 1 Step 15).

24. Implement the "Check progress report" link on the Swimmer Home page. When clicked, display all sessions the swimmer has signed up for, including completed and ongoing ones, along with coach feedback (Chapter 7 Example 1 Step 16).

25. Enable user sign-out functionality. Display the user's name at the top of the page upon sign-in, including a sign-out button for signed-in users (Chapter 7 Example 1 Step 17).

9.3 Project Two: Smith Sweet Shop

Business Description:

The Smith Sweet Shop (3S) stands as a longstanding bakery specializing in crafting custom cakes and cookies for special occasions. Originating nearly half a century ago, Grandma Smith initiated this family-owned bakery in an era where Internet awareness was limited. Local patrons traditionally place orders by phone, detailing their preferences, budget, and required delivery dates to Grandma Smith directly. She is adamant about preserving the traditional way of operating her business.

Desired Website Functionalities:

For Visitors:

1. Registration for visitors by providing an email and phone number. Upon registration, Grandma Smith personally contacts and confirms the details, thereby converting the user into a customer.

For Customers:

2. Ordering functionality through a simple form, detailing specifications like item, quantity, occasion, preferred delivery date, and budget.
3. Tracking the status of placed orders.
4. Mandatory approval of design and quantity during the order processing phase.
 5. Feedback provision available exclusively for Grandma Smith's review.

For Employees:

6. Access to view all orders categorized by different statuses.
7. Uploading images illustrating designs and approximate quantities within the specified budget, transitioning the order status to "in process."
8. Updating the status when an order is ready for pickup.
9. Updating the status post-order pickup by the customer.

For Grandma Smith:

10. Role assignment capabilities for registered users.
11. Access to read customer feedback for each order.

Business Data Requirements:

Customer details include name, address, email, and phone number. A customer can place multiple orders, each linked to one customer. Orders feature timestamps, current statuses, and customer feedback. An order may consist of multiple items for a specific occasion. Occasions can have several related orders. Employees possess names and can handle multiple orders. Orders can be managed by one or more employees.

Designs comprise one or more images, and an image can be utilized across multiple designs.

Payment Process:

Customers settle payments during order pickup, eliminating the option for refunds or cancellations.

Grandma Smith offers the baked goods for free if customers are dissatisfied or unable to afford them.

9.4 Project Three: Smith Souvenir Store

Business Description:

Smith Souvenir Store (3S) came into existence following Uncle Smith's retirement after a remarkable 40-year tenure as a salesperson in a multinational corporation. His extensive travels—spanning over 50 countries with frequent visits—cultivated friendships worldwide and amassed an impressive collection of souvenirs. His habit of gifting these souvenirs to relatives upon returning home was greatly cherished. This prompted the idea to launch a business retailing souvenirs globally without maintaining physical inventory.

Desired Website Functionalities:

For Customers:

1. Registration enabling the preservation of shipping and payment data for future visits.

2. Order placement functionality.

3. Order cancellation before shipment.

4. Return authorization for orders within 30 days of delivery.

For Uncle Smith:

5. Setting up product categories (e.g., wine, chocolates, herbs).

6. Crafting gift baskets incorporating multiple products for specific occasions like weddings or birthdays.

7. Accessing total sales within specified time frames.

8. Monitoring inventory levels sourced from "Friends."

For Friends (Uncle Smith's Suppliers):

9. Product posting within assigned categories.

10. Viewing units sold and total revenue generated by their products.

11. Monitoring returned product units and total costs.

12. Receiving low inventory notifications (five or fewer units) upon logging in.

Business Data Requirements:

Customers can place multiple orders, with each order tied to one customer. Orders contain one or more products, and products can be included in numerous orders. Gift baskets encompass multiple products. Friends supply multiple products, with each product sourced from a single friend.

Customer details include name, email, phone, shipping and billing addresses. Orders feature timestamps and allow cancellation pre-shipment and returns within 30 days of delivery.

Product specifics consist of name, description, country of origin, quantity in stock, and price. Friends function as suppliers with names, phone numbers, emails, and addresses.

Revenue from product sales is credited to the respective friend's account. Cancellations or returns reduce the friend's account balance accordingly.

Monthly, Uncle Smith disburses 60% of each friend's revenue. Manually verifying friend balances, he clicks a button (which doesn't directly transfer funds) to deduct the amount from their account.

The 3S website streamlines customer interactions, product management, and supplier interactions, facilitating a virtual marketplace for souvenir enthusiasts.

9.5 Chapter Summary

In this chapter, you've encountered three projects tailored to evaluate your grasp of ASP.NET Core MVC. These tasks demand the application of your acquired knowledge from this book. As often happens in professional scenarios, the provided business requirements might not cover every detail, necessitating some assumptions on your part. If this work is part of a school assignment, consulting your instructor for clarity is advisable. Successfully tackling these challenges will offer a taste of real-world web application development experiences.